THE MYTH OF
GENERATIONAL CONFLICT

The ageing of Western societies has provoked extensive sociological debate, surrounding the role of the state and whether it can afford the cost of an ageing population and about the role of the family, especially women, in supporting older people.

This collection brings together a range of leading researchers and theorists from across Europe to advance sociological understanding of generational relations, in terms of both the state and the family and how they are inter-linked. Authors examine how changes, such as cuts in welfare provision, migration, urbanisation and individualisation influence intergenerational rela-tions. This book addresses theoretical and policy issues connecting age and generation with the family and social policy and focuses both on cross-cultural comparison within societies and analysis across a range of societies. *The Myth of Generational Conflict* will be of interest to academics and researchers in sociology, social policy and ageing and to policy-makers work-ing in the field.

Sara Arber is Professor of Sociology at the University of Surrey.
Claudine Attias-Donfut is Director of Research at CNAV (Caisse Nationale d'Assurance Vieillesse), Paris.

ROUTLEDGE/ESA STUDIES IN EUROPEAN
SOCIETIES
Series Editors: Thomas Boje, Max Haller, Martin Kohli
and Alison Woodward

THE MYTH
OF GENERATIONAL
CONFLICT

The family and state in ageing societies

Edited by
Sara Arber and
Claudine Attias-Donfut

London and New York

First published 2000
by Routledge

2 Park Square, Milton Park, Abingdon, Oxon, OX14 4RN

Simultaneously published in the USA and Canada
by Routledge
270 Madison Ave, New York NY 10016

Transferred to Digital Printing 2007

© 2000 edited by Sara Arber and Claudine Attias-Donfut

Typeset in Garamond by
Colin Bakké Typesetting, Exeter

British Library Cataloging in Publication Data
A catalogue record for this book is available from the British Library

Library of Congress Cataloguing in Publication Data
The myth of generational conflict : the family and state in ageing
societies / edited by Sara Arber and Claudine Attias-Donfut.
p.   cm. — (Routledge/E.S.A. studies in European society ; 3)
Includes bibliographical references and index.
1. Intergenerational relations—Europe. 2. Conflict of
generations—Europe. I. Arber, Sara, 1949– . II. Attias-Donfut,
Claudine. III. Series.
HN380.Z91585   1999
306.87'094—dc21 99–28669
CIP

ISBN10: 0–415–20770–3 (hbk)
ISBN10: 0–415–46327–0 (pbk)

ISBN13: 978–0–415–20770–6 (hbk)
ISBN13: 978–0–415–46327–0 (pbk)

CONTENTS

v

CONTENTS

FIGURES

TABLES

CONTRIBUTORS

Sara Arber is Professor and Head of the Department of Sociology, University of Surrey. Her research focuses on gender and ageing and on inequalities in health. She is co-author with Jay Ginn of *Gender and Later Life* (Sage, 1991) and *Connecting Gender and Ageing* (Open University Press, 1995), and with Nigel Gilbert of *Women and Working Lives* (Macmillan, 1992). She is currently the President of the British Sociological Association.

Claudine Attias-Donfut is Director of Research at Caisse Nationale d'Assurance Vieillesse (CNAV), Paris. Her research mainly focuses on intergenerational relations and ageing. Her recent books include: *Sociologie des Générations.* (Paris, PUF, 1988), *Les Solidarités entre Générations. Vieillesse, Familles, Etat* (Paris, Nathan, 1995) and with Martine Segalen, *Grands-Parents. La Famille à travers les générations* (Paris, Odile Jacob, 1998).

Henk Becker is Professor of Sociology at the Faculty of Social Science at Utrecht University, The Netherlands. His research focuses on discontinuous macro-change, the emergence of patterns of generations and their effects on behaviour and institutions. He is author of *Risiko Generation: andere Zeiten, andere Chancen* (Deutscher Taschenbuch Verlag, 2000).

Miriam Bernard is Professor of Social Gerontology and Head of the School of Social Relations, Keele University. Her research has been primarily oriented around the development of new/healthy life-styles in old age, and she has a particular interest in the lives of older women. She co-edited with Kathy Meade *Women Come of Age – Perspectives on the Lives of Older Women* (Edward Arnold, 1993) and with Judith Phillips *The Social Policy of Old Age – Moving into the 21st Century* (Centre for Policy on Ageing, 1998).

Catherine Delcroix teaches Sociology as 'Maître de conférence' in Versailles Saint-Quentin en Yvelines University. She specialises in ethnic, urban and family studies. Her books include: *Espoirs et réalités de la femme arabe : Algérie, Egypte*, (Paris, L'Harmattan, 1986); *Double mixte la rencontre de* *deux cultures dans le mariage*, (L'Harmattan, 1992); and *Médiatrices dans les quartiers fragilisés: le lien*, (Paris, La Documentation Française, 1996).

Jay Ginn is a Research Fellow in the Sociology Department, University of Surrey, investigating the gender impact of changes in the British mix of state and private pensions. Publications focus on gender, employment and pensions and have included cross-national comparisons. She co-authored *Gender and Later Life* (Sage, 1991) and *Connecting Gender and Ageing* (Open University Press, 1995) both with Sara Arber.

Angela Grotheer studied Education at the University of Oldenburg, where she was a research assistant from 1993 to 1997. Her research focuses on cross-cultural research methods, migration, gender and ageing. She is co-author with Lydia Potts of 'Arbeitsmigration als Frauenprojekt?', in U. Loeber-Pautsch (ed.) *Quer zu den Disziplinen*, (Offizin, 1997). She is currently working in project evaluation, and completing a PhD at the University of Oldenburg.

Lars Gulbrandsen is Research Director at NOVA – Norwegian Social Research. His research focuses on housing, inheritance and family policy.

Gill Jones is Professor of Sociology at Keele University. She has an interest in all aspects of transitions to adulthood and inequalities in youth, and has published widely, including *Leaving Home* (1995) and with Claire Wallace *Youth, Family and Citizenship* (1992), both Open University Press.

Martin Kohli is Professor at the Institute for Sociology at the Free University of Berlin, where he directs the Research Group on Aging and the Life Course, and chairs the Graduate School on Comparative Research in the Social Sciences. He is currently the President of the European Sociological Association.

Harald Künemund is a Research Scientist at the Research Group on Aging and the Life Course at the Institute for Sociology, Free University of Berlin. His research focuses on dimensions of social and political participation in old age.

Åsmund Langsether is a Research Fellow at NOVA – Norwegian Social Research. He has an MA in Economics. His research focuses on time use, maintenance, intergenerational transfers and family obligations.

Dagmar Lorenz-Meyer studied Psychology at the University of Hamburg. From 1994 to 1997 she held a European Human Capital and Mobility Fellowship at the London School of Economics. Her research focuses on gender and generational contracts and social change. She is co-author with Claudia Born and Helga Krüger of *Der unentdeckte Wandel* (Sigma, 1996) and is currently completing a PhD at the Gender Institute, LSE.

Marjatta Marin is Professor of Social Gerontology at the Department of Social Sciences and Philosophy, University of Jyväskylä, Finland. Her research focuses on age categorisation and age images in Finland, and the role of social networks during the life course. She has written articles on ageing, autonomy, social networks and the family.

Andreas Motel is a Research Scientist at the Research Group on Aging and the Life Course at the Institute for Sociology, Free University of Berlin. His research focuses on social inequality and old age and on public and private intergenerational transfers.

Jim Ogg is a Researcher in Gerontology. His research interests include the older person's position in the family, living alone in later life, and comparative research on British/French perspectives on ageing. He is currently based at the Direction des Recherches sur le Vieillissement, CNAV, Paris.

Judith Phillips is Senior Lecturer in Social Work and Gerontology at Keele University. Her research interests include social work and older people, private residential care, housing and community care. She has written widely on carers who are in paid employment. She chairs the External Relations Committee of the British Society of Gerontology.

Chris Phillipson is Professor of Applied Social Studies and Social Gerontology at the University of Keele, and is Director of the Centre for Social Gerontology at Keele. He has published numerous books and articles on a variety of aspects of ageing. His most recent book is *Reconstructing Old Age* (Sage, 1998).

Marc Szydlik is Assistant Professor at the Institute for Sociology at the Free University of Berlin, and member of the Research Group on Aging and the Life Course. His research interests include social inequalities, labour markets, life courses, and generations.

François-Charles Wolff is a Researcher at the Direction des Recherches sur le Vieillissement, Caisse Nationale d'Assurance Vieillesse (CNAV), Paris, and at the Laboratoire d'Economie de Nantes, Centre d'Economie des Besoins Sociaux, Université de Nantes. His research and publications include the motives for private intergenerational transfers within the family.

1

EQUITY AND SOLIDARITY ACROSS THE GENERATIONS

Claudine Attias-Donfut and Sara Arber

Are European societies facing generational conflicts at the start of the third millennium? Such conflicts would be quite different from those which broke out in the 1960s in most Western countries. The latter conflicts opposed two generations, youth and adults, while the supposed new ones involve three generations, and now include the retired. Unlike in the 1960s, the challenge does not lie in the political and cultural spheres but in the economic sphere. The issues are no longer the refutation of generational and gender hierarchies inside the family or in universities and workplaces, but instead focus upon the sharing of public resources between separate cohorts before, during and after the working life. Therefore the risk of conflict comes from generational inequity in welfare contributions, as well as in the distribution of benefits.

The thesis of generational inequity and its corollary 'generational conflict' first emerged in the USA (Preston 1984) and New Zealand (Thomson 1989) and has now extended to many European countries (i.e. in Italy by Sgritta 1997; in France by Saint-Etienne 1993; in the UK by Laslett and Fishkin 1992). It developed as part of the more general debate on the future of welfare states in societies with ageing populations. The central question is whether the state can afford the cost of pensions and health care for a grow-ing older population. In this debate, public transfers between generations have been the focus of attention, whilst economic and social exchanges between generations in the family have been neglected.

This book broadens the understanding of these questions by examining the interaction between public and private transfers and their consequences for social inequalities. The empirical research, presented here from several European countries, rejects the hypothesis of generational conflicts. On the contrary, it shows a strong bond between family generations which is ex-pressed through a range of types of reciprocal help and gifts. This reciprocal support between generations has been termed the 'generational contract' (Bengtson and Achenbaum 1993; Walker 1996). Moreover, it appears that generational contracts, either formal (through state pensions or other legal

1

measures), or informal (through family relations), are founded on the gender contract which ensures the reproduction of society. Social inequalities should therefore not only be analysed between generations, as is proposed in the debate on generational equity, but also between men and women and within generations. We begin by considering the concept of generation.

The meanings of 'generations'

Despite the relevance of the concept of generation, there is confusion both in popular discourse and in social scientific writing about its meaning. The term 'generation' has at least five meanings, but there is some fuzziness and inter-changeability in these different meanings. First, generation is sometimes used to distinguish cohorts, representing a group of people born at a similar time. Cohort originates as a demographic term, referring to people born in the same year (or group of years) who then age together and experience specific trans-itions or societal changes (such as the Second World War) at approximately the same chronological age. According to some scholars, it is preferable to reserve the term age or birth cohort for this meaning, rather than generation (Ryder 1965; Kertzer 1983; Marshall 1983).

Second, the term 'generation' is derived from kinship studies and relates to the lineage between grandparent, parent and child (Pilcher 1995). To distinguish this meaning we use the term 'family generations'. This can be conceptualised as the genealogical rung of the ladder within a family lineage – being a father/mother or a son/daughter.

A third and popular meaning of generation is as a measure of time, historic-ally representing the number of years between the age of parents and children. This concept of generation is found in most cultures and in biblical writing. It was used in the nineteenth century in order to understand the general history of ideas (Cournot 1872) and the history of human progress (Comte, 1880). However, it is a very imprecise measure, since the length of a genera-tion in this sense may vary from under twenty to over forty years, and the average generational length differs between societies according to the average age of childbearing and average family size.

Karl Mannheim (1952) adopted a sociological stance by linking the process of the formation of generations to social change. His argument was that generations not only relate to being born in the same era, but that those who live through a period of rapid social change develop a separate 'historical-social conscience' or collective identity, which influences their attitudes and behaviour and distinguishes them from preceding generations. Such 'histor-ical or social generations' are distinguished by the historical experiences they have shared, which in turn have shaped their common vision of the world.

Finally, Kohli (1996) has described 'welfare generations', which are the product of the process of institutionalisation of society into distinct ages, defined according to the sequences of education, work and retirement. Here,

2

generations are distinguished by whether or not they participate in paid employment, the contributions they make to systems of social security and the benefits they receive. Today, the ages of entering and leaving such life stages as education, work and family life, are becoming much less clear cut and conform to a trend which Riley and Riley (1996) have described as 'age integration'.

The above definitions of the concept of generation require some comments. First, Mannheim's (1952) theory can be criticised in several ways. Social events, especially if they are of major importance (such as the Second World War) have an impact upon *all* members of society and are by definition multi-generational. The depth of the mark that major social events leave depends upon the extent to which each age cohort is exposed to their influences (Elder 1974). This depends on both the age of individuals and on their position as social actors (for example whether they are either a witness or victim of events) relative to wider political and social structures. Furthermore, it is not only important social events which leave their mark. There are also numerous social and cultural identifiers that are linked to the grouping of people of similar ages, (such as the different life stages of school, leisure and military conscription), which create a common reference point and collective pool of shared experience. These points of reference (where history and experience merge) are internalised during formative years. However, historical experiences continue to make an impression throughout the entire life course, both at collective and individual levels. According to this perspective, and contrary to Mannheim's theory, generations are continually evolving regardless of the particular moment in time through which they move and irrespective of whether they witness major social upheavals or more subtle forms of social change (Attias-Donfut 1988).

Social recognition of an 'historical generation' is made *a posteriori*. It is only through selectively reconstructing the past that a generation becomes associated with a particular social event. Such a process is one both of recollection and commemoration, whereby the social event is kept alive through the generation which witnessed the event, for example the generation of the Second World War. This process delegates to a generation the task of serving as a collective testimony to the history and collective memory of society (in the meaning given by Halbwachs 1950). In other words, what is usually defined as an 'historical generation' is a product of social imagery that contributes to constructing social time (Attias-Donfut 1988). Finally, the feeling of belonging to a generation not only comes about through a horizontal process that links a particular moment in history to a shared experience, but also vertically through family lineages.

While our focus is on 'generations', it is also important to recognise the value of a life-course perspective; the present circumstances of women and men can only be understood by reference to their prior life course. This is most vividly seen in later life, since older women's and men's financial

3

circumstances are intimately tied to their previous role in the labour market and thus their pension acquisition (Ginn and Arber 1996, 1998). A life-course approach 'provides a framework for analysing the various influences which contribute to the life experience of different groups of individuals at particular stages of their lives. A life course perspective emphasises the interlinkage between phases of the life course, rather than seeing each phase in isolation' (Arber and Evandrou 1999: 9). It sees lives as dynamic and responding to changed social circumstances and opportunities but often in gendered ways. Gender is a fundamental distinguishing feature throughout the life course, distinguishing what is considered appropriate behaviour in any cultural context, and this will vary for different birth cohorts or historical/social generations.

Gender inequalities among one generation may themselves influence and be predicated on gender inequalities in another generation. For example, the extent to which women forego paid employment to raise children will lead to financial penalties both during their working life and in retirement because of lower pension contributions (see Chapter 8 by Ginn and Arber), but the extent of these penalties will vary between societies and over time, for example, according to the nature of state welfare systems.

We will clarify in more detail the distinction between a 'welfare generation' and a 'family generation' which is central to this volume. In the former case, the interaction of age with participation in the labour force gives rise to three groups of the population: people who are in the active phase of life, those who have yet to enter it, and those who have left either at retirement age or through early retirement, the so-called 'welfare generations' (Kohli 1996). In the family lineage there are no such predetermined groups of generations, since they are determined by the relative position of individuals to their ascendants and descendants within the family's genealogical axis. There is not necessarily a close identity between family generations and welfare generations. It is common, for example, among parents with adult children, for both generations to be in the labour market, as well as for families to have two generations of retired family members. The latter situation is becoming more common today as the duration of retirement has lengthened due to early exit from the labour market, on the one hand, and increased longevity, on the other.

The concept of 'generations of welfare' represents a coming together of age groups at a given moment in time, but we should remember that each member of these groups is linked to some other individuals through kinship ties. Although the rhythm with which one generation passes into another is different along the welfare and family generation axes, there are important areas of overlap as shown in Figure 1.1.

The status of people within family generations and welfare generations overlaps for the great majority, as for example in the case of being a 'child' and being a 'youth' before entry into the labour market, the family role of being

4

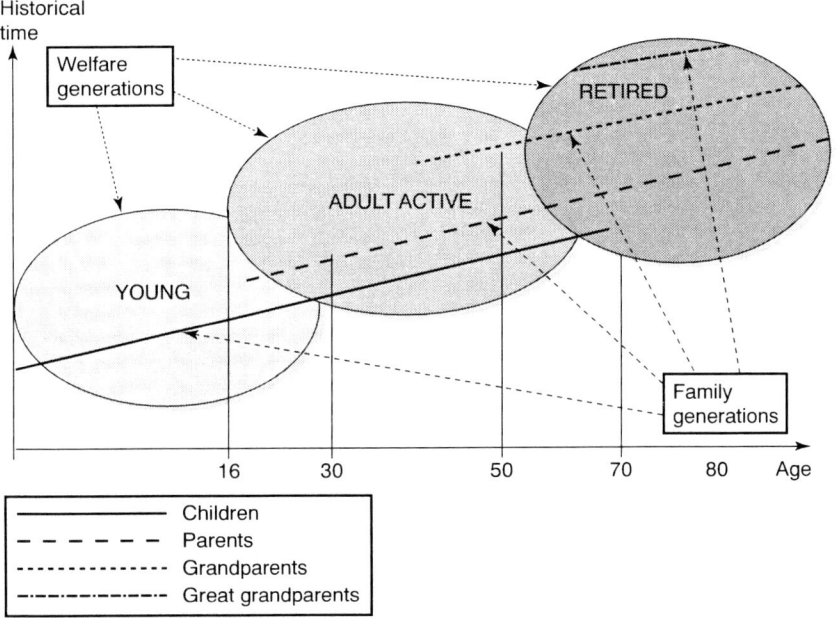

Figure 1.1 Family and welfare generations.

a 'parent' and 'active' in the labour market, and the role of 'grandparent' and being 'retired from employment'. However, the various definitions of 'generation' are usually disassociated in specific research fields, such as political sociology, the sociology of the family and studies on the welfare state, each of them adopting one definition and ignoring others. In reality, a single individual accumulates these different and interacting generational identities. Therefore, the different meanings of the term need to be reunified when examining questions such as equity between generations, since it is always necessary to take economic, social, ethical and philosophical aspects into account.

Equity between generations – an ambiguous debate

The central argument in the debate on intergenerational equity is related to the distribution of public resources. This question was first raised by economists as discussed by Becker in this volume, who refers to Samuelson (1958). Becker reviews the literature on intergenerational equity and shows the influence of Rawl's (1971) theory of social justice between generations. The problem is not restricted to the welfare state but also includes cultural transmissions and the quality of the environment. As far as the welfare state is concerned, public spending on retirement pensions or health care for older people has increased rapidly in all Western countries because of three parallel developments: the increase in longevity, better provision of social protection and health care, and a lowering of the age at which paid employment ceases (thereby increasing the time during which retirement pensions are received). The rise in this expenditure has coincided with a slowing down of economic growth, an increase in unemployment and the reappearance of poverty, particularly for young people. Therefore, some people have expressed the fear (Thomson 1989 and, in the USA, Americans for Generational Equity, AGE 1990) that the consequences for those in paid employment of this high expenditure on the retired generation is both intolerable and inequitable, since older people may become richer to the detriment of the young who, it is argued, will become increasingly poorer. The articulation of this problem is now a central political theme in most Western countries.

The debate has been largely sustained by a 'generational accounting' approach, again developed in the USA (Kotlikoff 1992; Auerbach *et al.* 1994) and more recently applied to Europe (see Becker, Chapter 7, this volume). This approach consists of drawing up for each successive cohort, both in the present and future, a financial balance sheet of contributions paid to the state against allowances and benefits received throughout the life-cycle. From these calculations, estimates are made concerning the contributions which future generations will have to pay whilst taking into account fluctuations in economic growth. The results of these models are indeed alarming; the rights currently being acquired by present generations theoretically will weigh heavily upon future generations. The methodology and interpretation of these results, however, have been the object of numerous criticisms. André Masson (1995) stresses that hypotheses concerning rates of economic growth and upratings are questionable, and he demonstrates that other methods of accounting can arrive at the opposite conclusions. Moreover, these calculations do not include political and financial measures which regularly intervene to bring an equilibrium into 'pay as you go' systems of retirement pensions, and measures which current generations are taking that will in turn lighten the contributions of future generations (Masson 1995).

In addition, the debate on generational equity has confused several different types of norms of equity. In fact, three principal components can be discerned (Attias-Donfut 1995: 21):

1 The allocation of social spending at any given moment between younger and older people.
2 The just treatment of successive cohorts – that is ensuring that the rights of future generations to levels of retirement pensions are the equivalent to those of today's older generation. It is questionable whether it is appropriate to establish a principle of equivalence in the standards of living between different generations of older people who live in different eras

and who are completely separated in terms of consumption patterns, the environment, and acquired customs and habits, etc.

3   The right of just returns, applicable to the same cohort, for the efforts they have made during their lifetime. Drawing up a balance sheet for what has been given in the way of contributions and received in the way of benefits during a lifetime, does not take into account the totality of contributions that an individual makes to the economy, to society and to the family. For example, the generations who took part in post-war reconstruction and who therefore contributed towards creating prosperity, paid relatively small contributions into the welfare state but equally they gave much to society through their participation in the labour force. Finally, and this brings us to our central theme, the collective contribution of successive generations is not limited solely to public transfers, but equally includes private transfers.

Working within a similar perspective, Blanchet *et al.* (1996), in an economic study, have developed three major lines of enquiry that integrate current and temporal aspects of generational transfers; the first compares the economic trajectories of successive generations, the second evaluates the returns from generational transfers for each generation, and the third compares cross-sectionally the different levels of standard of living by age cohort. This study, which widens the scope of generational accounting, shows that it is not possible to simultaneously satisfy all the criteria of intergenerational equity. To assure future retired people the same standards of living as those of present generations means that they would have a relatively lower standard of living than those of the future active generation. In order to establish immediate equity (to guarantee to retired people a standard of living equal to those of the current generation of active people), an unequal distribution of the level of contributions between successive generations would have to be introduced. This approach shows the contradictions that are inherent in a generational equity framework that is limited to a rigid accounting of the payments of contributions made to social security systems compared with the benefits received.

For a broader approach, it is necessary to take into account private transfers between and within family generations. Family transfers, and especially the contributions made by women, participate in the process of social and economic regulation, whilst being at the same time complementary and linked to public forms of transfers. The problem of equity between the generations is part of a more general problem of social inequality within society.

Social and generational inequalities

Generational inequalities are only one type of inequality and, we would contend, are much more modest than other forms within society such as inequalities by class, gender and ethnic group. The transformations that are taking place under the conditions of the 'new industrial revolution' are currently deepening social inequalities (Cohen 1997). In developed countries, such inequalities are measured by the degree of inequality of income and access to employment (Atkinson *et al*. 1995; Piketty 1997). Income inequalities differ between countries. The gap between the richest 10 per cent and the poorest 10 per cent varies between 2.7 in Sweden, 3 in Germany, 3.5 in France, 5 in Canada and 5.9 in the USA (Atkinson *et al*. 1995). These inequalities can also be seen within different age groups of the population.

Among the elderly population, poverty in most European countries has decreased since the Second World War as a consequence of the overall growth in benefits for older people. Among European countries as a whole, 45 per cent of the social security budget comprises benefits to retired people, and these benefits account for 12 per cent of total public expenditure (André 1997). This social expenditure, which is of greater importance in the European Union than in the USA (22 per cent of GDP as opposed to 15 per cent), helps to offset standard of living inequalities between households.

However, current trends represent a reversal of the standard of living attained by households with members, aged over 60, in all European countries, and households that contain people above the age of 70 years are those that on average have the lowest incomes (Montigny and Saunier 1998). The results of the second wave of the European Community Panel Study, undertaken in 1995 by Eurostat in thirteen member countries, show this clearly. Among all these countries, the standard of living in households receiving retirement pensions is approximately 10 per cent lower compared with the average household. There are certainly differences between countries. In Greece, the United Kingdom, Spain and Portugal retired people have the lowest standards of living (approximately 15 per cent below the average of all households). In contrast, in the Netherlands, Ireland and France, retired people on average have a standard of living approaching that of the average household (Montigny and Saunier 1998).

Young people in particular are affected by poverty, as witnessed by data from the USA and from Europe. According to the results of the first wave of the European Community Panel Study (1994), 13.9 per cent of children under 16 years live in a poor household (defined by income per unit of consumption that is less than half of the median income) compared with 11.3 per cent of the entire population (Chambaz 1997). It is in the United Kingdom (20.5 per cent), in Italy (19.5 per cent), in Portugal (18.8 per cent) and in Spain (16.3 per cent) that children in poverty are most likely to be found. Denmark is an exception (3.1 per cent). In France, the proportion is low (7.3 per cent) because of the existence of more generous family allowances. However, young adults have also seen a deterioration in their situation: among the poorest 10 per cent of the population, the proportion who are adults aged under 25 years rose from 32 to 40 per cent between 1987 and 1995

(Roustang *et al.* 1996: 8). The United Kingdom is the country in Europe where the rate of poverty among children is the highest, because of the low level of family allowances, the high proportion of one-parent families, and the lack of employment opportunities particularly for single mothers. It is important to note that in the UK there is both a high proportion of children in poverty and a high proportion of older people in poverty, and therefore no evidence that older people benefit financially from state transfers at the expense of children.

State-provided benefits considerably limit poverty and reduce income inequalities between households: these were the findings of research on the role of state benefits in the income and standard of living among European households using data from the European Community Panel study (Montigny and Saunier 1998). State benefits (excluding pensions) have the greatest impact in the age group 30 to 60 years, and less impact for the two age groups that comprise the highest proportion of households with low incomes (lower than 50 per cent of the median income), that is people aged less than 30 years and those aged more than 60 years. The countries of northern Europe, Denmark and the Netherlands, have the lowest proportion of poor households, and also the most effective social security systems for younger and older age groups. In countries where the system of social protection is based on the principle of insurance, and targeted on households with low incomes (Germany, Austria, Belgium, France, Luxembourg), social benefits substantially reduce poverty, particularly in Belgium (Montigny and Saunier 1998).

It is clear that a well-developed system of social security, together with generous levels of minimum payments, reduces both inequalities between generations and among members of the same generation. Comparative research from several countries shows that these two types of inequality go together, but that European public systems of social security have redistributive effects which reduce such inequalities.

Gender inequalities

Gender inequalities persist throughout society in varying degrees. The report of the co-ordinating body for the fourth international Women's conference in Peking in 1995 (Ephesia 1995) shows that no country in the world has achieved gender equality, whether this is in the political field, in education, in employment, or within the family. Nevertheless, considerable progress has been made throughout the twentieth century, particularly in the participation of women in the labour market. At the beginning of the century there were large differences between countries, with, for example, Austrian women representing two-fifths of the labour force compared with only one-sixth in Spain, and one-third in France, Switzerland and Finland (Kaeble 1988). Today, all Western countries have higher rates of female employment and, as far as younger adults are concerned, in some countries the rate of female participation in the labour force is almost the same as for males. However, women occupy lower status positions than men, and even when they have the same qualifications as men they receive lower wages. According to European data from 1992, female workers receive between 67 per cent and 70 per cent of the salaries of men in the United Kingdom, Luxembourg and Ireland, 82 per cent in Denmark and 80 per cent in France. For professional women, these discrepancies are even higher, at between 55 per cent and 70 per cent (Ephesia 1995). In addition, a higher proportion of women work part-time, especially in Britain and the Netherlands (Rubery *et al.*1998; O'Reilly and Fagan 1998; Drew *et al.* 1998).

This book attempts to shed light on one aspect of gender inequality by showing that generational contracts rely on an implicit gender contract expressed through the gender division of paid and unpaid labour, especially in the home through women as carers (of children and older people). As Ginn and Arber's chapter shows, generational equity should not be achieved at the price of greater inequalities between men and women. In fact there is a new trend of greater gender inequalities taking place in Europe, which represents a sliding back of progress. Increased unemployment has led to reductions in the participation of women in the labour force and an exacerbation of the differences between men and women (Sen 1997). Moreover, young unemployed women are more likely to experience a loss of motivation and dissatisfaction, thereby compromising their subsequent careers (Goldsmith *et al.* 1996). Among retired people, it is also women who form the most disadvantaged groups, especially widows and the oldest age groups of women. Greater reliance on private insurance schemes and personal pensions will worsen the relative situation of older women, as the chapter by Ginn and Arber shows for the UK. In this way, Ginn and Arber provide evidence of the impact of social security systems, and the cultural values that underpin them, in improving the conditions of women. For example, the Swedish social security system, together with those of other Nordic countries with similar types of provision, is the most beneficial to women because of the extent to which it gives women universal rights that in turn diminish gender inequalities. The French system, with its tradition of specific family policies, is also favourable towards women, albeit in a different way from the Swedish model.

Gender equality in the acquisition of social rights presents particular difficulties, such as the 'impossible choice' claim by women to be considered either as part of the labour force or as mothers (Lewis 1995). Public pension systems can contribute towards improving the position of women by guaranteeing a minimum pension which is independent of the amount of time spent in paid employment, by taking into account the years spent child-rearing as a period of employment (as in France), or by making sure that women who remain in the home are covered by the necessary contributions needed to receive a future pension. These social benefits partially compensate for the inequalities of child-bearing. It has been argued that to give specific benefits to women is contrary to the principles of gender equality. But giving identical social benefits to men and women cannot break the vicious circle of female discrimination at work and the impact of women's caring role in the family, and would only serve to exacerbate the existing inequalities between men and women over the life course.

It is at the very least paradoxical that political and policy commentators have called into question social security systems by evoking the notion of equity between the generations, when one considers that countries which have the most developed social protection systems also have the least inequalities both between and within generations, and between women and men.

Family and state

The vitality of intergenerational solidarity within the contemporary family is clearly stated throughout the different chapters of the book and has also been shown in previous studies in European countries (i.e. Rosenmayr and Köckeis 1963; Roussel and Bourguignon 1976; Lye 1996; Coenen-Huther et al. 1994; Bawin-Legros et al. 1997; Attias-Donfut 1997). The trend towards a smaller family size which has taken place under modernity, a trend predicted by Durkheim (1921), has not led to the fragmentation of relationships between the nuclear and extended family as predicted by Parsons and Bales (1956). The nature of kinship relations has been redefined at the same time as the family was being significantly transformed by converging trends. The increase in life expectancy, together with a decrease in the number of children per family and the smaller age gaps between siblings, has transformed the demographic structure of kinship relations, which now span three or four generations. The current structure is one of reduced numbers of kin living together with a concentration at certain points in the life course.

Increased individualism has produced norms of greater autonomy between the generations and social protection schemes have contributed towards residential and financial independence between the generations. The separation between public and private life is a cogent characteristic of individualistic contemporary societies. Faced with increased uncertainty, the hallmark of modernity, individuals tend to retreat to the cocoon of family and friends (Giddens 1992). The modern family has entered into the sphere of intimacy, and has become a central place for the construction of personal identity (Singly 1996). However, these changes have not reduced the ties between the state and the family. On the contrary, the link between them has been redefined with a deeper interdependence emerging. This interdependence is manifest in legal structures and through the welfare state.

The calendar of events that stand out as the landmarks in an individual's life course – education, marriage, employment, retirement – is largely influenced by age-related legislation. Marjatta Marin traces and evaluates these legal measures during the last half century in Finland and shows how they have shaped successive generations. Finland is used as a case study for studying the impact of legislation upon generational relationships. Legislation concerning reciprocal obligations between generations, as Marin shows, deals mainly with economic matters, including asset management, education and all kinds of assistance. The Finnish case analysis exemplifies the value of comparing different types of legislation across Europe relating to generational relationships. However, the gap between legislation and actual behaviour shows that a study of legislation is insufficient for understanding the links between generations. The growing aspiration to protect one's private life from the intrusion of the law conflicts with the trend of the state controlling individuals and families through legislation.

Within welfare states, legal regulations have both a function of social control and a function of redistribution of resources. However, state benefits given to any one member of a family have a direct impact on the family as a whole. The effect of state provision of social benefits on family solidarity has been debated from two opposed political and ideological viewpoints. On the one hand, proponents of social protection maintain that social benefits contribute towards family cohesion. An objective in the creation of these welfare states was the elimination of poverty and the social integration of the working-classes both in employment and within the family domain (Castel 1995). Thus the social control exercised by the state over destitute families has been replaced by the principle of 'well-being' (Segalen 1996).

On the other hand, the liberal (or, in the USA, conservative) position upholds the neutral position of the state. This position foresees many dangers in the development of public aid programmes, arguing that these include the fragmentation of the family and the relinquishing of obligations to the state, the encouragement of idleness and therefore unemployment, and finally, inflated public expenditure which is seen as creating unemployment. Such a view is found in varying degrees of intensity in most welfare states, irrespective of the traditions of solidarity. These fears are, however, not new. From its beginnings in the nineteenth century, the construction of the French social protection system aroused strong reactions from 'defenders of the family'. The fear of a breakdown in family relations also fuelled strong opposition towards retirement pensions. When retirement legislation entered the statutes in France in 1930, it was described in a journal which opposed it as 'a law of domestic corruption' (Dumons and Pollet 1994: 115).

Opposition to the intervention of the state is gaining ground in the current climate of anxiety caused by the difficulties of financing social protection systems and the increase in unemployment. An example of this trend is the new means-tested dependency benefit, recently introduced in France for very disabled older people, which must be reimbursed after their death if they have inheritance wealth (Kessler 1997). The legislators have no doubt been influenced by the concern to place responsibilities back on the family by taking into account legacies. Social policies have always been concerned to both keep the family unit intact and to avoid measures which would put this cohesion at risk. Research on 'family impact' (Glendon 1977), for example, is concerned with the types of intervention that the state can make to reinforce the family and those which would be likely to threaten it. Much research has been undertaken on the effect of family policies on the fertility and activities of women, for instance in France (Tabah and Maugué 1989; Barrere-Maurisson 1992; Commaille 1994; Pitrou 1994).

However, there is little research on exchanges between adult generations within a framework of the interaction between the public and private domains. Künemund and Rein (1997) examined this question using data from a large comparative survey of older people in four Western countries and Japan. They found connections between the frequency of financial and practical support received by older people from their family and the system of social protection in each country. They conclude that the most important forms of solidarity with regard to older people take place in those countries where social policies are generous to the welfare of older people, a finding which confirms the notion that public aid reinforces private aid rather than replacing it.

The complementarity of the public and private spheres between generations has also been attested among three adult generations (see Attias-Donfut and Wolff, Chapter 3). The chapters in this volume examine the complementarity between public and private transfers and also the consequences of their interaction for social inequalities, and in particular gender inequalities, within a number of different European countries.

Public and private transfers in a macro-social perspective

Public financial transfers largely benefit older generations, funded through the 'pay as you go' systems that are financed by the active generations. Conversely, private transfers take place in the opposite direction, from the eldest to the youngest generations. This cycle is clearly demonstrated in several of the studies presented in this volume, by research undertaken in France (by Attias-Donfut and Wolff, Chapters 2 and 3), in Norway (Gulbransen and Langsether, Chapter 4), and in Germany (the former East and West Germany by Kohli et al., Chapter 5). The data from these diverse European countries clearly show the importance of inter vivos transfers that continually flow between the generations. These transfers take place in addition to inheritance wealth, of which the value and frequency has significantly increased as a result of greater household wealth (INSEE 1998).

As the data from the Norwegian research shows (Chapter 4), financial capital increases at regular intervals with increased age, up until the age of 67–79 years. Retired people do not spend their capital, and many continue to save during their retirement. Most retired people express the wish to help both their children and their grandchildren, and to make sure that they will inherit.

Gulbransen and Langsether show that the youngest generations support a system whereby state benefits are directed towards the oldest generations, thereby allowing capital to be preserved and eventually transmitted to younger generations.

Gulbransen and Langsether do not find any evidence of the presence of the risk of generational conflict. This contrasts with Becker's approach in Chapter 7. Whilst critical of the generational accounting approach of Auerbach *et al.* (1994), his own position lies within this framework. Becker therefore emphasises that the generational contract would lead to social inequalities and possibly even social conflict. But although Becker stresses the demand for health and social care needs by the oldest generations (which falls largely upon the shoulders of women), his focus is mainly upon public transfers and his analysis does not take into account economic transfers within the family.

The study of private transfers reveals important elements concerning the mechanisms of exchange between generations. It also reveals the interaction such exchanges have with public transfers and shows the interconnection between the public and private spheres and the adaptations families constantly make in these contexts. The comparison between East and West Germany in Chapter 5 is therefore interesting from several points of view: it reveals the influence of political and economic history on intergenerational ties and shows how the period of transition between the communist and Western models has given rise to varying consequences for different generations. Using data from a representative survey of Germans aged between 40 and 85 years, Kohli *et al.* uncover the existence of intergenerational ties that were stronger in East Germany than in West Germany. Financial help from parents to children was more frequent in East Germany, but the amounts transferred were lower than in West Germany. However, since household incomes were much lower in East Germany, the relative value of intra-familial transfers in reality is more important for those making the transfers in East Germany than in West Germany. Retired people in East Germany were the 'winners' in the process of incorporation into West Germany, since they were included in the latter's pension system. They are therefore now in a better financial position than those in mid-life who have been the 'losers', who have been especially hard-hit by the transformational recession and labour market crisis. From this East/West comparative research, Kohli *et al.* confirm the existence of the complementarity between public and private transfers, showing how retirement pensions also indirectly benefit younger generations.

Research on three generational families in France from a representative sample of multi-generational families also shows that public transfers promote private transfers (Chapters 2 and 3). This finding occurs both for transfers between older parents and their mid-life children (the 'pivot' generation), between 'pivots' and their young adult children, and between the two extreme generations of eldest and youngest. Attias Donfut and Wolff include in their analysis all forms of state benefit, not only retirement pensions, but also benefits directed towards the youngest generation – education grants, housing benefit, family allowances, and unemployment benefit. These public subsidies are often in addition to private transfers, which shows that the hypothesis whereby one form of support crowds out the other can be rejected. Even more important is the fact that the receipt of public transfers influences the shaping of the life course. For example, encouraging children to continue their studies or to live separately from their parents, which, in turn, results in incentives for parents to give additional transfers to their children. Public forms of support, therefore, have consequences for the amount of private transfers that are made, for the quality of intergenerational relations, and for the social status of respective members of the generations.

Attias-Donfut and Wolff also show that family support given to elderly disabled parents does not diminish when these parents receive professional support, but on the contrary, in such cases it has a tendency to increase. Finally, public support which is directed towards the oldest and youngest generations (the two generations that receive the greatest amount of public support) has a knock-on effect for three or four generations within a family. At the macro-social level, the results of the French three-generational study show that these public and private transfers weaken inequalities between the generations and reduce inequalities in incomes within the youngest and oldest generations. Exchanges between family generations have an important function in social and economic regulation, since they operate according to a logic of needs: money circulates in kinship systems from the richest to the poorest, and help is given to those who need it, for example the sick and frail elderly. Grandparents look after their grandchildren to assist the employment of their daughters who are working mothers, which encourages the ascending social mobility of the latter.

The role of women is the essential link in the chain of solidarity between generations, as Ginn and Arber show in Chapter 8. The gender contract is implicit and self-evident: it is women who undertake the largest part of domestic tasks, the education of their children and the care of others. In undertaking this role, often in combination with paid work, they allow men more time to pursue their careers. The unpaid work of women brings a double contribution to welfare systems: on the one hand it increases the availability of men for paid work, and on the other hand it relieves the state of part of its obligation towards children, the elderly and the sick. More fundamentally, the physical reproduction of society depends upon women upholding the gender and generational contracts, since women are the guarantors of procreation. This demonstrates the profound injustice towards women: generational accounting ignores the contributions women make and the wealth they produce. A major problem associated with current trends is that the privatisation of pensions negates the redistributive effects (which operate in

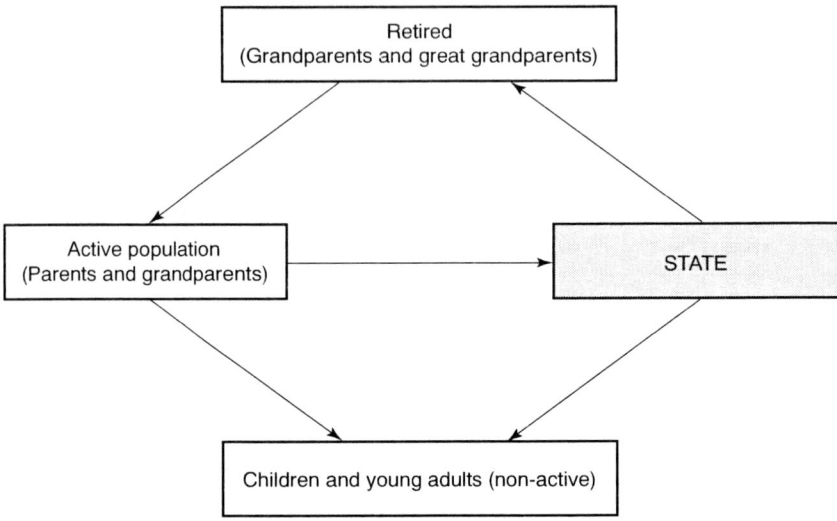

Figure 1.2 The cycle of generational public and private financial transfers.

public systems) that serve to compensate for incomplete and low-income careers; this privatisation contributes to the feminisation of poverty in later life. Ginn and Arber show how British pension reform in the 1980s, by reducing the value of public pensions in favour of occupational and private pensions, has led to a greater gender inequality in incomes in later life.

The analyses presented in Chapters 2 to 8 offer a wide-ranging comparison of different European societies. They show how systems of social protection interact with private transfers and how these two systems influence social inequalities. Public and private transfers flow between three and four generations in both an upwards and downwards direction which can be represented in the theoretical model in Figure 1.2.

Cultural change and the changing generational contract

Exchanges of care and finance between the generations within the family do not take place within a closed universe, but are largely determined by the social context. Chapters 2 to 8 show the influence of systems of social protection upon these forms of exchange, whereas later chapters focus on the impact of cultural change on generational transfers. The studies of migrant populations in Germany, France and Scotland shed new light on the impact of cultural traditions.

Lorenz-Meyer and Grotheer (in Chapter 11) compare the behaviour and attitudes towards the care of older parents among Turkish immigrants of the second generation with Germans of approximately the same age, gender, family status and occupation. The two groups, however, have unequal access to community care services for older people, since these services are not adapted to meet the needs of ethnic minorities. For both groups, there is a strong sense of solidarity towards the eldest generations, even when family relations are difficult. For the majority of German men and women, the traditional model is still in place: women take on the responsibility of caring for their elderly parents. The level of community services provided does not diminish the support given by the family who consider these services as complementary to the help that they want to give. For the second generation Turkish population, family norms of help remain firmly in place, despite the frequent geographical separation between generations within families and despite the financial help which is sometimes provided, because of geographical separation, instead of caring tasks (a new cultural phenomenon). In renegotiating the generational contract (a necessary process following migration), women experience a double workload. In addition to the support that they traditionally give to their parents-in-law, they must now also be responsible for the care of their parents. Thus tacit gender and generational contracts are redrawn, and they become all the more important because of the lack of social policies directed towards helping ethnic minorities.

Ethnic minority families have greater responsibilities for family support as they lack support from the host societies, which are either indifferent or even hostile. Catherine Delcroix in Chapter 10 shows another aspect of this problem based on her research among families with North African origins living in France. She focuses on efforts that young, second generation ethnic minority adults (who have often acquired French citizenship) make to integrate into French society. In these families, where there is an increased risk of marginalisaton, the transmission of a father's life history to his children is of paramount importance. In her analysis of two successive generations, Delcroix demonstrates how these families which lack 'capital' in all its meanings have recourse to a different form of 'capital' – one that is not objective and which she calls 'subjective resources'. The transmission of subjective resources enables children to appreciate the family history, and helps to combat educational failure and social exclusion. Situated at the bottom of the social ladder, fathers also risk losing their status within the family, a loss which is made more difficult given the patriarchal tradition within North African families. Communication and exchanges between the generations therefore are at risk of becoming 'blocked', and at the same time there is an increased risk of 'dis-affiliation' (breaking the bonds that tie the individual to family and society) for young adults. These risks, in some cases, are avoided through the transmission of memory – the memory of immigration, which reconstructs both the image of the father and the child's identity.

Gill Jones examines the interrelationship between migration and social mobility of adult children in Scotland (Chapter 9). The author followed a group of young people from a rural region (the Scottish Borders), comparing the lives of those who remained and those who migrated to other regions, often to secure better jobs. These young migrants were more likely to be from families where their own parents had also migrated. Jones reveals a family culture of migration whereby the young follow in the footsteps of their parents and, in some cases, a chain-migration pattern whereby younger siblings follow the older. However, the part that parents play in social mobility, together with the geographical mobility which often accompanies it, may be problematic. The parents' competence can be seriously challenged by the new environment of their children. Since the latter are eager to become independent, 'there is an ambivalence about giving and accepting'. Young people may be compelled to find support outside the family, support which is often inadequate. This study shows the importance of the quality of relations between parents and children in terms of the giving of support by parents, which appears as important as the cultural or social resources that parents have at their disposal and are able to transmit to their children.

The final chapter by Bernard *et al.* examines how intergenerational ties have developed since the Second World War. The authors present and analyse the transformations that have taken place among families since classic sociological studies in the 1940s and 1950s in three areas in England: Bethnal Green (in East London), a London suburb (Woodford) and a Midlands town (Wolverhampton). In each area, household size is substantially reduced, more older people live alone, family networks are smaller in size and the geographical dispersion of family members is greater, but intergenerational ties are still strong. Modern technology, the car and the telephone, allow family contact to take place despite the distances involved. Support between the generations is reciprocal, with the immediate family and close friends as the main sources of help. These results show both the strength and the limitations of intergenerational exchanges, and the authors conclude that in future, families must be firmly located within community care policies that take account of these social and cultural changes.

Conclusion

From the analyses in this book a strong statement can be made: European societies, in whatever context, do not show signs of generational conflict. Retirement pensions have not set the young against the old, but the research reported here suggests the opposite hypothesis. It is precisely because of welfare systems that relations between the generations have been reinforced, despite the increase in life expectancy. The public contract between generations is a model of collective solidarity from which private contracts between family generations are renegotiated. Regarding gender, women are the main mediators of relations between generations in the family, and they stand at a pivotal point where the public (i.e. professional care-givers and social services) and private sectors meet (i.e. co-ordinating care within the family and complementing professional support).

However, we should not be deluded by this somewhat optimistic statement about generational solidarity. The risks of a 'rolling back' of welfare systems threatens this equilibrium. If the trend of replacing public solidarities by private, market-driven systems increases in Europe (putting an end to the European model of society), as advocated by those who falsely state that the current systems set the generations up against each other, then it is likely that European societies may witness a confrontation of young and old in the future. Any such future conflict is likely to be intimately tied to changes in the gender contract and have implications for gender relations.

Acknowledgement

We are grateful to Jim Ogg for his help with the French version of this text.

References

AGE (1990) *Annual Report*, Washington DC: Americans for Generational Equity.

André, C. (1997) 'L'évolution des Retraites en France et dans l'Union Européenne: Aspects Statistiques', *Après-Demain*, 395–6: 15–18.

Arber, S. and Evandrou, M. (eds) (1999) *Ageing, Independence and the Life Course*, London: Jessica Kingsley.

Atkinson, A., Rainwater, L. and Smeeding, T. (1995) *Income Distribution in OECD Countries*, OECD.

Attias-Donfut, C. (1988) *Sociologie des Générations. L'empreinte du temps*, Paris: PUF.

——(1995) 'Transferts publics et Transports privés entre générations', in C. Attias-Donfut, (ed.), *Les Solidarités entre Générations: Vieillesse, Familles, Etat*, Paris: Nathan.

——(1997) 'Family Relationships in France: The experience of older people', *Ageing International* XXIV (1): 32–50.

Auerbach, A.J., Gokhale, J. and Kotlikoff, L.J. (1994) 'Generational accounting: a meaningful way to evaluate fiscal policy', *Journal of Economic Perspectives* 8 (1): 73–94.

Barrere-Maurisson, M.A. (1992) *La Division Familiale du Travail. La Vie en Double*, Paris: PUF.

Bawin-Legros, B., Gauthier, A. and Stassen, J.F. (1997) 'Solidarités intergénérationnelles: entre famille et Etat', in R. Cipriani (ed.) *Aux Sources des Sociologies de Langue Française et Italienne*, Paris: L'Harmattan.

Bengtson, V. and Achenbaum, W. (1993) *The Changing Contract Across Generations*, New York: Aldine de Gruyter.

Blanchet, D., Lenseigne, F. and Ricordeau, P. (1996) 'Les Transferts Intergenerationnels', Paris: INSEE, Mimeo.

Castel, R. (1995) *Les Métamorphoses de la Question Sociale : Une Chronique du Salariat*, Paris: Fayard.

Chambaz, C., (1997) *La Pauvreté en France et en Europe*, Paris: INSEE Première n°533.

Coenen-Huther, J., Kellerhals, J. and Von Allmen, M. (1994) *Les Réseaux de Solidarité dans la Famille*, Lausanne: Réalités Sociales.

Cohen, D. (1997) *Richesse du Monde, Pauvreté des Nations*, Paris: Flammarion.

Commaille, J. (1994) *L'Esprit Sociologique des Lois*, Paris: PUF.

Comte, A. (1880) *Cours de Philosophie Positive*, t. IV, leçon 51, Paris: Schleicher.

Cournot, A.A. (1872) *Considérations sur la Marche des Idées*, Paris: Vrin.

Drew, E., Mahon, E. and Emerek, R. (eds) (1998) *Women, Work and the Family in Europe*, London: Routledge.

Dumons, B. and Pollet, G. (1994) *L'Etat et les Retraites*, Paris: Belin.

Durkeim, E. (1921) 'La famille conjugale', in textes, vol. 3: *Fonctions Sociales et Institutions*, Paris: Editions de Minuit.

Elder, G. (1974) *Children of the Great Depression*, Chicago: University of Chicago Press.

EPHESIA (1995) (Mission de coordination de la 4ème conférence mondiale sur les femmes, Pékin septembre 1995) *La Place des Femmes*. Paris: La découverte.

Giddens, A. (1992) *The Transformation of Intimacy*, Stanford: Stanford University Press.

Ginn, J. and Arber, S. (1996) Patterns of employment, gender and pensions: the effect of work history on older women's non-state pensions, *Work, Employment and Society* 10(3): 469–90

——(1998) 'When does part-time work lead to a low pension income?', in J. O'Reilly and C. Fagan (eds) *Part-time Prospects: An International Comparison of Part-time Work in Europe, North America and the Pacific Rim*, London: Routledge.

Glendon, M.A. (1977) *State, Law and Family Law in the United States and Western Europe*, Amsterdam, New York, Oxford: North Holland Publishing Company.

Goldsmith, A., Veum, J. and Darity, W. (1996) 'The impact of labor force history on self-esteem and its component parts, anxiety, alienation and depression', *Journal of Economic Psychology* 17: 183–220.

Halbwachs, M. (1950) *La Mémoire Collective*, Paris: PUF.

INSEE (1998) *Revenus et Patrimoine de Ménages*. Synthèse (19) Paris: Insee.

Kaeble, H. (1988) *Vers une Société Européenne. 1880–1980*, Paris: Belin.

Kertzer, D.I. (1983) 'Generation as a sociological problem', *American Sociological Review* 9: 125–49.

Kessler, F. (ed.) (1997) *La Dépendance des Personnes Agées*, Paris: Sirey.

Kohli, M. (1996) *The Problem of Generations: Family, Economy, Politics*, Collegium Budapest: Public lecture series.

Kotlikoff, J.K. (1992) *Generational Accounting – Knowing Who Pays, and When, for What We Spend*, New York: Free Press.

Künemund, H. and Rein, M. (1999) 'There is more to receiving than needing: theoretical arguments and empirical explorations of crowding in and crowding out' *Ageing and Society*, 19: 93–121.

Laslett, P. and Fishkin, J.F. (eds) (1992) *Justice between Age Groups and Generations*, New Haven: Yale University Press.

Lewis, J. (1995) 'Egalité, différence et rapports sociaux de sexes dans les Etats Providence du xxème siècle', in EPHESIA, *La Place des Femmes*, Paris: La Découverte.

Lye, N. (1996) 'Adult child–parent relationships', *Annual Review of Sociology* 22: 79–102.

Mannheim, K. (1952) 'The problem of generations', in K. Mannheim *Essays on the Sociology of Knowledge*, London: Routledge Kegan Paul.

Marshall, V. (1983) 'Generations, age groups and cohorts: conceptual distinctions.' *Canadian Journal on Aging* 2: 51–61.

Masson, A. (1995) 'L'héritage au sein des transferts entre générations: théorie, constat, perspectives', in C. Attias-Donfut (ed.) *Les Solidarités entre Générations*, Paris: Nathan.

Montigny, P. and Saunier, J.M. (1998) 'L'impact des transferts sociaux sur les revenus et niveaux de vie des ménages dans l'Union Européenne' *Dossiers Solidarité Santé, La Documentation Française*, 4: 119–36.

O'Reilly, J. and Fagan, C. (eds) (1998) *Part-Time Prospects: An International Comparison*, London: Routledge.

Parsons, T. and Bales, R.F. (1956) *Family Socialization and Interaction Process*, London: Routledge.

Piketty, T. (1997) *L'Economie des Inégalités*, Paris: La Découverte.

Pilcher, J. (1995) *Age and Generation in Modern Britain*, Oxford: Oxford University Press.

Pitrou, A. (1994) *Les Politiques Familiales : Approches Sociologiques*, Paris: Syros.

Preston, S. (1984) 'Children and the elderly: divergent paths for America's dependents', *Demography* 21(4): 435–57.

Rawls, J. (1971) *A Theory of Justice*, Cambridge: Harvard University Press.

Riley, M.W. and Riley, J.W. (1996) 'Generational relations: a future perspective' in T.K. Hareven (ed.) *Aging and Generational Relations. Life-Course and Cross-Cultural Perspectives*, New York: Aldine De Gruyter.

Rosenmayr, L. and Köckeis, E. (1963) 'Essai d'une théorie sociologique de la vieillesse et de la famille', *Revue Internationale des Sciences Sociales*, 3: 423–48.

Roussel, L. and Bourguignon, O. (1976) *La Famille après le Mariage des Enfants. Etude des Relations entre les Générations*, Paris: PUF, INED.

Roustang, G., Laville, J.L., Eme, B., Mothe, D. and Perret, B. (1996) *Vers un Nouveau Contrat Social*, Paris: Desclée de Brouwer.

Rubery, J., Smith, M., Grimshaw, D. and Fagan, C. (1998) *Women and European Employment*, London: Routledge.

Ryder, N. (1965) 'The cohort as a concept in the study of social change', *American Sociological Review* 30: 843–61.

Saint-Etienne, C. (1993) *La Génération Sacrifiée : les 20–45 ans*, Paris: Plon.

Samuelson, J.P. (1958) 'An exact consumption loan-model of interest with or without the social contrivance of money', *Journal of Political Economy* 66: 467–82.

Segalen, M. (1996) *Sociologie de la Famille*, Paris: Armand Colin.

Sen, A. (1997) 'L'inégalité, le chômage et l'Europe d'aujourd'hui', *Revue Internationale du Travail*, 136 (2): 169–86.

Sgritta, G.B. (1997) 'Solidarités étatique versus solidarité familiale. La question des générations' in J.Commaille and F. de Singly (eds) *La Question Familiale en Europe*, Paris: L'Harmattan.

Singly, F. de (1996) *Le Soi, le Couple et la Famille*, Paris: Nathan.

Tabah, L. and Maugué C. (1989) *Démographie et Politique Familiale en Europe*, Paris: La Documentation Française.

Thomson, D. (1989) 'The welfare state and generation conflict: winners and losers', in P. Johnson, C. Conrad and D. Thomson (eds) *Workers Versus Pensioners: Intergenerational Justice in an Ageing World*, Manchester: Manchester University Press.

Walker, A., (1996) *The New Generational Contract*, London: UCL Press.

21

2

THE REDISTRIBUTIVE EFFECTS OF GENERATIONAL TRANSFERS

Claudine Attias-Donfut and François-Charles Wolff

Introduction

Conflicts between generations are a part of the history and mythology of modern societies. The social explosion of the 1960s has become the major reference point, but it was preceded by a series of generational conflicts, some stronger than others, that have marked out western history during the last two centuries. The most famous are the youth movements that erupted in Vienna at the turn of this century, and the wealth of literature that they inspired has played a specific role in the renewal of the very notion of 'generation' (Schorske 1978). Modern reflections on 'generations', from Mannheim (1952) to the present, are in some ways an inheritance of the intellectual currents that were stimulated by these periods of rapid social change, from the French revolution of 1789 to the international uprising of young people in the 1960s.

The idea that a generation affirms itself in opposition to the preceding generation forms part of our collective mentality, structuring modern representations of the family or society. When the history of literature, arts or sciences is examined according to generations, it usually follows a rhythm of opposition from one generation to the next. Did not Gaston Bachelard remark, reflecting on the origins of scientific thought (1938), that new knowledge has to be constituted against previous knowledge? The tremendous impact of the 'Generation Gap' thesis that Margaret Mead (1970) applied at a global level shows the strength of this idea in the public imagination. Generational conflict is one of the components in the mythologies of modernity. The Oedipus myth, as a structural model which has often been evoked to interpret the revolts of young people (Mendel 1968), is one of the most evident of these myths.

In hindsight, the student movements of 1968 appear to have been as much to do with gender relations as to relations between the generations. The profound transformations that have since taken place bear witness to the success of these movements. Women have greater access to paid employment, to the means of contraception, and have gained the freedom to choose abortion – all of which are new rights that promote more gender equality. Educational models have become more flexible, and authority no longer reigns supreme in the family or in educational establishments. This success has led to a certain softening of relations between the generations, both in private and public life. But the past has not been forgotten, and the spectre of new conflicts still remains latent and at large in public opinion, especially public opinion that the media claims to reflect. This anxiety can be seen from time to time through the fears of young people and, to a greater extent, through those of older people. The ageing of the population has reactivated the menace of generational conflicts which could result not only in an uprising of young people, but also in a 'grey revolution'.

Today, behind the anxiety over the financing of pension schemes, an anxiety fuelled by unemployment, the slowing down of the economy and demographic ageing, lies the spectre of a new conflict in which the generations will argue over the allocation of social benefits.

From the myth to the reality of intergenerational solidarity

It is a paradox to think that social protection schemes, based upon public solidarity between the generations, would become a new field of generational conflict. The question to ask is whether the conflict or the solidarity will triumph. The numerous studies on intergenerational relations undertaken in different countries, as exemplified by the chapters in this book, show no indication of such a conflict in the attitudes and behaviour of populations. This demonstrates the myth at work and how it adversely affects social debates. Its symbolic power in modern society permits an argument to be formed that has a deep impact on people, and one that can be manipulated for ideological ends, that is against welfare systems, as has been discussed in Chapter 1.

Numerous research studies undertaken in Western countries (referred to in Chapter 1) show the vitality of solidarity between the generations. The purpose of this chapter is to underline the importance of intergenerational transfers within the extended family and to characterise the nature of private assistance between households in France, using data from a large survey on three different generational members of the same family. The uniqueness of this survey is that it allows us to empirically establish the complex links between diverse transfers which circulate between two or three generations, and to thereby show their regulatory social and economic role in the family and in society. The methodology which shaped the definition of the three generations that were interviewed allows us to operationalise the notion of generation and to study the interaction of private and public transfers.

The three-generational study

The contemporary family is multi-generational. Each one of these generations belongs to a specific birth cohort whose destiny was shaped by a particular history, set of beliefs and values, level of economic growth and stage of development regarding social welfare policies. This destiny is influenced by the social conditions encountered at the time of entry into occupational life, notably concerning the educational system and the labour market. Successive cohorts do not have at the outset the same possibilities of employment or the same chances of social mobility. Research on cohorts, which represents a key to the understanding of social change (Riley et al. 1972), shows the evolution of beliefs, political behaviour, social structures and social mobility (e.g. Inglehart 1990; Drouin 1995; Baudelot and Gollac 1997). It also shows the discontinuity of social destinies according to the period of history through which cohorts live.

It is not enough, however, to place individuals within their cohort, since one must also take into account family or kinship ties which bond the cohorts, as the interdependence of the generations contributes in turn to shaping the destiny of individuals. Forms of solidarity between generations have been studied using methodologies which entailed three generations, among the most noteworthy are Mangen et al. (1988) and Rossi and Rossi (1990). But in these studies, lineages were composed of persons from diverse age groups, which means that at a statistical level, it is not possible to link a family generation to a social generation defined by birth cohort.

It is necessary to distinguish clearly the different definitions of generations (see Chapter 1). However, all these meanings of generation are present for the same individual and together they mould social identity and patterns of sociability. Each person is defined both by his or her birth cohort and by family and kinship ties. The French three-generational study was devised precisely to examine these empirical links. It reunites the different meanings of generation by bringing together family generations and birth cohorts. The main methodological innovations of the study lie in the point at which the lineage is anchored and the mode of selection of the three generations.

This cross-sectional survey was undertaken in 1992 and involved families where there were at least three adult members of different generations living in France. The anchor for the data set was a 'pivotal' generation and these middle-aged individuals had to be born between 1939 and 1943 (aged 49 to 53) and to have at least one parent alive and one adult child (aged 18 or above and non co-resident or co-resident if older than 22 years and not a student). When there was more than one parent or one adult child, the interviewee was selected on a random basis. The underlying methodology therefore allowed the same comprehensive questions to be put to one 'pivot' generation member, to one grandparent and to one adult child, all of whom belonged to the same lineage.

The three generations in this research represent relatively homogenous age groups clearly differentiated in respect of historical periods and in the stages of their life course.[1] The young are entering adult life (jobs for some, further education for others), the 'pivot' generation are for the most part in paid employment, and the eldest generation have been in retirement for some time and are at risk of experiencing disability. Within this context, the different definitions of 'family', 'historical' and 'welfare' generations are made visible and allow an analysis which entails observation of the interface between the private and public spheres.

Social mobility and intergenerational transfers

Social mobility is an important dimension in the exchanges and relations between generations in the family, as shown in Gill Jones's chapter. But this dual perspective has been neglected in the vast literature concerning social mobility. Macro-social trends have largely mobilised researchers, such as structural mobility linked solely to changes in social structure, or 'fluidity' resulting from 'net mobility' which assesses the relation between the social position of a son (rarely a daughter) with that of his father, independently of the effects of structural mobility (cf. the review of social mobility research by Merllié 1994). More rare are researchers, such as Bertaux, who analyse in detail social mobility through an entire lineage using qualitative data from life stories (Bertaux 1974; Bertaux and Bertaux-Wiame 1988).

The central role of the family in social mobility is a well-established fact. Cultural and material heritage, as well as family support, are essential in the acquisition of a social position. Together they condition access to education and influence types of employment. Bourdieu and Passeron (1970) have shown how schooling acts as a system of social reproduction, whereby success is more frequent among children from families belonging to higher social levels. But inequality of opportunity does not stop at the attainment of different levels of education. The action of families extends beyond into areas such as access to employment and the beginnings of a career. This effect of the *'dominance du milieu'* (Boudon 1973) can either hinder or promote social mobility. As shown by Spilerman *et al.* (1993) in the United States, 'life chances' are also gained by those who have inherited wealth and have received family transfers, thereby exposing the myth of the self-made man. In contrast to the American dream, social success does not come solely from personal merit.

Reciprocally, social mobility has many effects upon the entire family. The social gap which it introduces can sometimes compromise family ties and result in a 'class neurosis' for those who have climbed the social ladder (de

Gaulejac 1987). This social gap can also be reduced through upward generational transmissions, when children share their advantages with their parents (Attias-Donfut 1993). The differences in social status between generations in the same family influence the nature of their relations, together with the direction and form of transfers that circulate between them. More generally, the social destiny of children is a crucial challenge for parent/child relations, where the education and help given to children is all-important. Interacting with family origins, birth cohorts (as stated above) also have unequal chances of structural mobility. Each one of the three generations studied in the three-generational research is clearly distinguished from the others in terms of its trajectory and chances of social mobility.

The older generation, most of whom were born between 1910 and 1920, have lived through a period of full employment and experienced little unemployment. They did not benefit from the expansion in education but have witnessed the rise of the salaried class and, in France, the 'end of peasantry' (Mendras 1967). In the cohorts to which they belong, the lower class represents the larger part. The mean income of this generation is quite low because of the number of widows, most of whom have very low levels of retirement pensions. However, they have in later life benefited from the expansion of social protection, and are much better off than their parents were at the same time of life.

The intermediate generation, born between 1939 and 1943, which we have called 'pivot', benefited from the expansion of education and a period of full employment from the 1950s to 1970s. The mean income of individuals in this generation is much greater (almost double) than that of their parents. They have important assets (80 per cent are home-owners). This generation has had an exceptional destiny when compared with that of their parents or adult children, having benefited the most from the post-war period of growth (from 1945 to 1975) and from the fruits of social welfare schemes.

The young people in the survey were aged between 19 and 32 years, and therefore were in a transitional phase. Many had not yet fully attained their occupational status. Their level of education is higher than that of their parents. Those who are no longer in the educational system are already experiencing a higher level of unemployment. Their mean incomes are higher than those of their grandparents, but they remain, as expected, lower than those of their parents.

A French study comparing the successive trajectories of birth cohorts from 1910 to 1970 in 10-year age groups has shown that net social mobility has changed little despite the fact that the 'baby boomers' have experienced a higher rate of upward mobility than other cohorts (Chauvel 1998).[2] It is because of this structural mobility that more of the 'pivot' generation were able to attain middle or higher social class occupations than preceding generations, thereby giving 'the impression that upward social mobility is the norm'. But the relative deterioration in employment opportunities that has followed the period of the '30 Glorious Years' (1945–75) risks seriously compromising the chances of young people repeating this pattern. According to projections by Chauvel (1998), irrespective of different hypotheses about the growth of occupations in middle and higher social class groups, there will be less upward social mobility in the next 20 years. This will result in a greater risk of downward social mobility, especially for the children of intermediate professions (middle and middle to higher groups).

In our survey, social mobility (defined by a comparison of the occupational status of successive generations) can be measured for the older and pivot generations, but not for the younger generation whose occupational status is still uncertain. In order to compare the three generations, we have introduced a subjective evaluation[3] of social mobility arising from the following question: 'Do you feel that you have socially succeeded in life (for the younger generations – you will succeed): more than your parents, less than your parents, or the same as your parents?' The replies to this question confirm the analyses and projections of cohort studies. The feeling of having socially moved upwards is held much more by the older and pivot generations (59 per cent), whereas it is the minority view among the younger generation (32 per cent).

Gendered generations

The value of self-assessed measures of social mobility can be confirmed by a symmetrical question asking parents to assess the social success of each of their children compared with themselves. The replies of parents demonstrate the same trends: the young are seen less frequently as being upwardly mobile and are considered more at risk of descending the social ladder than their parents or grandparents.

However, there are also gender differences, related both to the gender of parent and child. Mothers are more likely than fathers to favourably assess their daughters' social mobility. This corresponds with a true upward mobility of daughters compared with their mothers, although this has still left them at a level inferior to that of their fathers. Sons are regarded the same by fathers and mothers, the reference point for both parents being the social status of the father. Overall, fathers acknowledge the success of their sons more than their daughters. This result reminds us that the generations are gendered, and that there are inequalities between female and male lineages. These inequalities persist (as shown by employment statistics) in the careers of the youngest generation, among whom women are on average less favoured than men, despite the undeniable advances that have been made.

Exchanges between the generations, the roles of giving and receiving, and the flux and nature of transfers are articulated around gender. The gender division of roles and the social norms which give rise to them endure most strongly within the family, which acts to reinforce these norms.

Transfers across three generations

In this section we examine different types of both ascending and descending private transfers and their socio-economic determinants. Our analysis does not include inheritance, but it is focused on transfers which circulate between living generations, namely *inter vivos* transfers. An assessment of the balance of private transfers remains a difficult task to achieve since the survey only takes into account retrospective data based on financial gifts and other economic aid, either in nature or in kind, received regularly or occasionally. The difficulty of measuring instrumental transfers within the family are often emphasised by sociologists and economists. Our results mainly focus on the circulation of financial transfers and in-kind services between the three generations, which is likely to provide an underestimated picture of private assistance.

Empirical results provide evidence of the importance of financial gifts made by the pivot and older generations. The combination of responses received from three generations of the same family makes possible a more realistic measurement of the different forms of support. When the data is presented in this way, among grandparents (the older generation) 33 per cent have given money to their adult children and 30 per cent have given money to their grandchildren (the younger generation) in the last five years. In total, almost one in two older people (49 per cent) gave money to either their adult children or grandchildren. As far as the pivot generation is concerned, the proportion of donor households is 64 per cent for financial help to children and 9 per cent for financial help to their parents. In contrast to these primarily downward financial transfers, services are widely distributed between each generation, both downwards and upwards. For example, 89 per cent of pivots provide at least one domestic service to their parents, and 49 per cent of the older generation to their mid-life children (Attias-Donfut 1995).

The recognition of private assistance is necessary for the understanding of the generational contract. Therefore, we now analyse transfers given and received within the family. By considering different types of help, our purpose is to draw up a large panorama of exchanges that documents their heterogeneity. Specifically, we look in greater detail at the determinants of various financial and in-kind support to understand the characteristics of the households involved and the motivations behind the help given. The results show the significant redistributive nature of familial assistance.

Financial transfers from parents to their adult children

Young adult respondents were asked to report the existence and value of financial gifts from parents during the last five years. As far as the pivot generation is concerned, both financial gifts and donations received from parents were analysed. These cash gifts from pivot to young and from elderly to pivot are separated in an econometric analysis in order to demonstrate their different objectives across the life-cycle. In economic terms, the former mainly correspond to human capital investments and are targeted towards liquidity-constrained young adults (Cox 1990), whereas the latter may be referred to as a transmission of wealth in advance.[4]

Table 2.1 shows that financial transfers from pivots are mainly directed towards well-educated non co-resident adult children. Completion of graduate or postgraduate studies is associated with an increased probability of the receipt of financial transfers by respectively 12.3 and 14.5 percentage points. These transfers are earmarked for children with low current earnings, but since the expectation of future earnings is higher for the well educated, they have a high economic earning potential. Besides the positive effect of the child's qualifications, currently being a full-time student exerts a strong effect on the probability of being helped by 18.6 additional percentage points. Financial gifts are also more often provided by higher-educated parents, which supports the argument that transfers are human capital investments. Financial gifts are more frequent in families characterised by a low number of children, and they are more often directed towards a young female family member.

The redistribution of income, in the form of gifts and donations, from elderly parents to pivots ensures the transmission of wealth between generations. Such flows of income are made later in the life-cycle as indicated by the positive effect of the donor's age (see Table 2.2). In France, donations are most likely to be made by farmers and to a lesser degree by the self-employed in order to give their professional assets to their children, which may also be encouraged by tax incentives. In particular, the probability of donations increases by 13.7 percentage points when the donor is a farmer, and financial gifts more frequently benefit well-educated pivots. We have also examined the distribution of transfers among different siblings as indicated by the older generation, since the number of living pivots within a family exerts a negative impact on transfer decisions. According to the French data, equal sharing among siblings is observed in about 90 per cent of cases, and about one half of the elderly mention the desire to avoid intra-sibling conflicts.[5] This type of financial transfer therefore corresponds to an advanced inheritance.

We next turn to examine how parental and child resources affect the pattern of downward cash gifts. In both cases, transfers are more likely to be directed from rich donors to poor recipients. Concerning pivot–child pairs, a rise in the pivot's income or wealth significantly increases the probability of familial support. Conversely, the receipt of transfers is more frequent when they are directed towards children with a low level of resources (in terms of income and wealth). The results appear rather different when elderly–pivot pairs are examined. Financial transfers from the elderly to their pivot children are a way of transmitting wealth rather than helping to improve the recipient's

Table 2.1 Financial transfers from pivot generation to young in last five years

Variables	Probability of gift	
	coefficient	t-value
Constant	0.409	0.30
PIVOT'S CHARACTERISTICS		
Female respondent	−0.095	−1.17
Age	−0.014	−0.52
Married	−0.093	−0.79
Number of children	−0.146	−4.08
Education		
Primary school	0	—
Secondary school	0.120	1.20
Baccalaureate	0.106	0.82
Graduate – Postgraduate studies	0.299	2.03
Income (10E-4)	0.124	2.36
Wealth (10E-6)	0.138	2.32
Financial transfers from parents	0.226	1.83
YOUNG'S CHARACTERISTICS		
Female	0.169	2.03
Age	−0.008	−0.46
Marital status		
Alone	0.157	1.19
Non married couple	0.250	2.44
Married couple	0	—
Presence of children	0.039	0.38
Education		
Primary – Secondary school	0	—
Baccalaureate	0.176	1.55
Graduate studies	0.361	2.95
Postgraduate studies	0.425	3.20
Activity status		
Fully active	0	—
Unemployed	0.114	0.75
Student	0.545	3.18
Inactive	0.067	0.39
Income (10E-4)	−0.325	−3.54
Wealth (10E-6)	−0.325	−2.21
Subjective social mobility		
Same as parents	0	—
Better than parents	−0.104	−1.06
Worse than parents	0.285	1.99
Unknown response	0.168	1.49
Number of observations	1,312	
Number of young recipients	414	
Log likelihood	−657.59	

Source: Survey CNAV Three-Generations Study 1992.
Note: Probit analysis of financial gifts received.

Table 2.2 Financial transfers from elderly to pivot generation in last five years

Variables	Probability of gift	
	coefficient	t-value
Constant	–2.977	–4.32
ELDER'S CHARACTERISTICS		
Female respondent	–0.022	–0.20
Age	0.030	3.79
Widowed	0.088	0.88
Number of children	–0.067	–3.84
Education		
No diploma	0	—
Primary school	0.053	0.50
Secondary school	0.092	0.57
Higher education	–0.133	–0.60
Social status		
Farmer	0.450	2.87
Self-employed	0.018	0.10
Executive	0.185	0.92
Employee	0.018	0.12
Worker	–0.148	–0.95
Inactive	0	—
Income (10E-4)	0.073	0.60
Wealth (10E-6)	–0.041	–0.45
Financial transfers from parents	0.377	4.16
PIVOT'S CHARACTERISTICS		
Female	–0.097	–1.16
Married	–0.052	–0.44
Number of children	–0.032	–1.02
Education		
Primary – Secondary school	0	—
Baccalaureate	0.191	1.77
Graduate studies	0.258	1.83
Postgraduate studies	0.586	3.73
Income (10E-4)	–0.177	–3.21
Wealth (10E-6)	0.254	4.18
Subjective social mobility		
Same as parents	0	—
Better than parents	–0.216	–2.26
Worse than parents	0.012	0.07
Unknown response	–0.463	–2.23
Number of observations	1,217	
Number of pivot recipients	315	
Log likelihood	–614.25	

Source: Survey CNAV Three-Generations Study 1992.
Note: Probit analysis of financial gifts received.

standard of living. This explains why the level of donor resources appears to have no effect on the probability of financial gifts. *Inter vivos* donations and gifts from the older generation have redistributive effects and these transfers are higher for pivots with less income, whereas the probability of financial gifts increases with the wealth of pivot generation members, the latter certainly being richer after the receipt.

The estimation of the overall redistributive effect of private transfers has to take into account both their diffusion and the gift values. Among the recipients, the higher their level of wealth and income, the larger the amount of money they received. However, the greater the wealth and income of the recipients, the less often they received gifts. Among the donors, the richer they are, the more often they give, but the amount of money given is not directly related to the income and wealth of the donors. It is also important to note that the amount of money given represents a higher percentage of the total donor's revenue for poorer donors than it does for richer donors – twice as much for the lowest quintile of income than for the highest quintile among the pivot generation.

To understand the process of familial transfers, it is necessary to examine the impact of intergenerational social mobility. In the survey, each respondent was asked their opinion about their social position compared to that of their parents. This intergenerational comparison gives information about the existence of two specific channels of redistribution within the extended family. Concerning young adults, individuals who expect a lower social success compared to their parents are characterised by a greater probability of gift receipt with 9.7 additional percentage points. Thus, private transfers to young generations are given so as to reduce the likelihood of downward social mobility. In the same way, pivots who perceive themselves to be in a better position than their parents receive less financial transfers with a fall of 6.6 percentage points. On the contrary, they tend to provide more upward help, which may represent compensation for the assistance given in the past by their parents to achieve their social promotion.

Financial and time transfers to the older generation

Assistance from parents to adult children therefore seems the most widely used redistributive network within the family in France, a result attributable to the specific division of economic resources between the three coexisting generations. The tri-generational survey also indicates the existence of upstream transfers benefiting the older generation, with young adults providing a very limited degree of support to their parents. Middle-aged adults use two different types of assistance in order to improve the well-being of their elderly parents, namely financial support and the provision of services. The latter is especially important for older people with disabilities. First, we study financial and in-kind assistance from pivots to their parents. As both forms of support are likely to be interdependent (since children with a high time-price may prefer to transfer money even if the recipients are wealthy) the probabilities of both types of transfers are jointly estimated using a bivariate probit specification. Results indicate that money and time transfers are used by two different populations of households (see Table 2.3).

Financial support is mostly provided to the older generation by rich pivots (as indicated by the positive effect of their level of income), and the probability of a financial gift is also greater when the donor is from a middle management or higher occupational category. These variables show that mid-life children's time-prices matter to the extent that individuals with a higher wage offer more money to their parents. The fact that financial difficulties encountered by donors in their youth give rise to an increased probability of upstream assistance is more intriguing. One interpretation deals with an inter-temporal adjustment of redistributive behaviours, such that pivots who suffered in the past from financial difficulties have the desire to help their own parents in return. The intention to improve the financial position of recipients is also captured by the variable related to subjective social mobility. The probability of financial gifts slightly increases when middle-aged adults have a better social position compared to their parents, although the effect is insignificant at the 5 per cent level.

The results also show a gender gap in intergenerational assistance to parents. Men give financial help more often than women, whereas women more often give time-related and hands-on help, a finding that reflects the implicit gender contract. Many studies have shown the greater involvement of women than men in care-giving to dependent parents. The role of caring is mainly ascribed to women. Even when men are involved in the support of their elderly parents, the kind of activities and care they give is different from that which is given by women. For example, they give less physical care and support tends to be centred on activities such as shopping, going to the bank, etc. In addition, the act of caring for elderly parents, according to the responses of care-givers, causes less emotional difficulties for men than for women (Attias-Donfut and Rozenkier 1996).

Older women have more needs and greater levels of disability than men. Living alone is much more common for older women than for men, because women tend to marry men who are older and because women's life expectancy is longer. Women also receive more financial help from their children because of the lower level of pensions they receive in widowhood. Older women, therefore, represent a larger percentage of the recipients of assistance than men. Consequently, caring (from both the care-giver and the care-receiver's perspective) appears to be mainly a female activity.

In contrast to financial gifts, time-related assistance is not affected by differences in the donor's economic resources. In fact, most of the covariates (except the geographical distance separating the generations) exert no significant impact in the regression equation, which suggests that upstream

Table 2.3 Financial and time transfers given by pivots to elderly

Variables	Probability of financial gift		Probability of time transfer	
	coefficient	*t-value*	*coefficient*	*t-value*
Constant	−1.962	−6.34	−0.890	−4.81
ELDER'S CHARACTERISTICS				
Parents alive (number)	0.022	0.35	0.070	1.77
Co-resident parent (mean)	−0.096	−0.45	0.172	1.38
Institutionalised parents (mean)	0.611	3.04	0.240	1.45
Social status (mean)				
Farmer	−0.234	−1.28	0.108	0.90
Self-employed	−0.285	−1.31	0.217	1.48
Executive	−0.948	−2.56	0.192	1.10
Employee – Worker	−0.461	−3.19	0.001	0.01
Inactive	0	—	0	—
PIVOT'S CHARACTERISTICS				
Female respondent	−0.233	−2.29	0.468	7.18
Presence of spouse	−0.002	−0.01	−0.122	−1.11
Education				
Primary school	0	—	0	—
Secondary school	−0.058	−0.46	−0.051	−0.65
Baccalaureate	0.075	0.46	0.117	1.08
Graduate – Postgraduate studies	0.068	0.38	−0.053	−0.44
Social status				
Farmer – Self-employed	0.104	0.59	−0.215	−2.07
Executive	0.375	1.87	−0.017	−0.13
Intermediary	0.114	0.71	0.027	0.28
Employee	0.279	1.65	−0.027	−0.27
Worker	0	—	0	—
Income (10E-4)	0.213	1.95	0.019	0.23
Income squared (10E-8)	−0.013	−0.99	0.006	0.54
Wealth (10E-6)	0.134	0.91	0.177	1.86
Wealth squared (10E-12)	−0.018	−0.57	−0.028	−1.41
Financial difficulties in the youth				
No difficulties	0	—	0	—
No trouble – poor family	−0.016	−0.12	0.040	0.51
Occasional or regular troubles	0.337	2.68	0.079	0.92
Transfers from parents and step-parents				
Financial gifts	−0.101	−0.66	0.092	0.92
Donations	0.236	2.07	0.103	1.40
Bequests	−0.066	−0.58	−0.028	−0.38
Distance from parents (mean – 10E-2)	0.004	0.15	−0.167	−9.51
Subjective social mobility				
Same as parents	0	—	0	—
Better than parents	0.179	1.43	0.005	0.06
Less than parents	0.119	0.52	−0.085	−0.57
Unknown response	0.193	0.87	0.018	0.13
Number of observations	1,955		1,955	
Number of pivot donors	155		608	
Residual correlation (t-value)		0.151 (2.47)		
Log likelihood		−1,608.52		

Source: Survey CNAV Three-Generations Study 1992.
Note: Bivariate Probit analysis of money and time transfers from pivots to their parents.

transfers to older generations emanate from motives probably associated with strong norms of obligation. This also probably affects the lack of substitutes for family support in the marketplace since the family provides an affectional solidarity (Bengtson 1975) which can scarcely be replaced by a professional.

Second, we examine the existence of in-kind assistance received by the older generation from pivots in order to determine the characteristics of recipients. Table 2.4 shows that the probability of services is greater for female respondents, and the age and widowhood variables are also associated with increased help given by the pivots. The number of pivot siblings (i.e. the elder's number of children) is negatively correlated with the likelihood of upstream assistance given by each sibling since assistance is likely to be shared among them. This regression equation indicates the probability of being helped by a specific child, but the probability of help increases with a rise in the number of children when we consider assistance given by all children.

Whilst time transfers do not depend on the education level or the economic resources of older generation members, they do appear mainly directed towards elderly people with poor health, who also receive some form of professional help. The effect of the income of the older generation does not appear in the equation in Table 2.3, since it is neutralised by the social and economic characteristics of care-givers. But this effect clearly appears when considering the older generation on its own (Table 2.4). The lower their income, the more support they receive; the support rate is 50 per cent among the lowest quartile of income and falls to 21 per cent among the highest quartile. Again, upstream transfers are rooted in an intergenerational redistributive process of familial resources. Moreover, the empirical results show that elders who themselves cared for their own parents in the past are characterised by a greater probability of receipt from their own children.

Care of grandchildren

Half of the middle 'pivot' generation are grandparents. These young grandparents provide important help to their adult children by looking after their grandchildren. Two out of three give care (i.e. spend time with their grandchildren in the absence of the parents) – whether on a regular basis or occasionally – during the entire year and also often during vacations. In addition, 18 per cent of grandparents give care solely during vacations. In sum, 82 per cent of grandparents provide some form of care for a grandchild. Help given by this group of young grandparents is more intensive than the help that was given in the past by the two previous generations (Attias-Donfut and Segalen 1998). Of course, a young parent can receive help from either their parents or their parents-in-law. However, our analysis only takes into account the characteristics of the lineage of the person who has been interviewed, where 60 per cent of young parents receive help from their own parents.

The frequency of care given was recorded in the survey (i.e daily, weekly,

Table 2.4 Probability of in-kind assistance received by dependent elderly from pivot generation

Variables	Help from pivots		Help from economically active pivots	
	coefficient	t-value	coefficient	t-value
Constant	−3.909	−2.45	−4.313	−2.29
ELDER'S CHARACTERISTICS				
Female	0.349	3.01	0.302	2.22
Age	0.056	6.32	0.063	6.12
Widowed	0.211	2.00	0.298	2.37
Number of children	−0.082	−4.15	−0.076	−3.29
Education (end of school age)	0.008	0.55	0.003	0.20
Living within the family	0.172	1.35	0.140	0.93
Existence of professional help	0.304	3.06	0.318	2.77
Poor state of health	0.319	3.11	0.457	3.81
Help to dependent parents in the past	0.176	2.03	0.217	2.13
Income (10E-4)	0.460	1.61	0.321	0.95
Income squared (10E-8)	−0.100	−0.97	−0.017	−0.14
Wealth (10E-6)	0.019	0.08	0.218	0.77
Wealth squared (10E-12)	−0.229	−1.66	−0.306	−2.03
PIVOT'S CHARACTERISTICS				
Female	0.490	5.53	0.384	3.74
Age	−0.040	−1.34	−0.044	−1.26
Living alone	0.276	1.96	0.455	2.82
Number of non co-resident children	−0.027	−0.73	−0.022	−0.48
Number of co-resident children	−0.033	−0.68	−0.094	−1.54
Education (end of school age)	0.004	0.23	0.007	0.34
Income (10E-4)	−0.105	−1.10	−0.031	−0.28
Income squared (10E-8)	0.018	1.62	0.011	0.88
Wealth (10E-6)	0.203	1.58	0.082	0.56
Wealth squared (10E-12)	−0.044	−1.54	−0.020	−0.65
Distance from parents (10E-2)	−0.028	−5.58	−0.029	−4.86
Subjective social mobility				
Same as parents	0	—	0	—
Better than parents	0.118	1.17	0.090	0.76
Less than parents	0.123	0.63	0.062	0.27
Unknown response	0.091	0.44	0.131	0.52
Number of observations	1,217		948	
Number of elder recipients	309		221	
Log likelihood	−577.55		−424.62	

Source: Survey CNAV Three-Generations Study 1992.
Note: Probit analysis.

monthly, ...) and converted into a numerical value representing the amount of annual contact, following Cox and Rank (1992).[6] As underlined by Cardia and Ng (1998), the main feature of childcare is that it can be given by all families regardless of their economic status, unlike monetary gifts which are mainly given by high-income families. Childcare provides two financial advantages to these adult child recipients, who can then devote a greater amount of time to the labour market or to their own free time activities, and save the costs of placing children in a day nursery or employing a nanny.

According to Table 2.5, grandmothers devote more time to their grandchildren than grandfathers. However, the role that grandfathers play is important in two respects. First, they stimulate the grandmother's role in support (87 per cent of married grandmothers take care of the grandchildren compared with 78 per cent of grandmothers living alone). Second, grandfathers often give their time directly to their grandchildren (77 per cent of married grandfathers and 36 per cent of grandfathers living alone). When a divorce or separation occurs among young parents, there is an increase in help given to the single parent by his or her parents. The family environment has a significant effect: young parents receive support more often when both of their parents are still married to each other. In the case of remarriage in the grandparent generation, there is a fall in the amount of childcare given to the children from a previous marriage. Generally, grandparents are closer to their daughters than to their sons and this finding confirms the dominance of the female lineage which highlights the privileged mother–daughter bond in families.

Grandparenting appears more frequent when the pivot is characterised by a low level of education. Although the employment participation of both the pivot respondent and their spouse exerts no significant impact on the probability of childcare, the amount of time is lower for employed pivots who suffer an additional time constraint. Concurrently, grandparenting is mainly directed towards full-time-employed young mothers who need more help to look after their own progeny. This type of in-kind assistance is mainly given to young adults characterised by a higher social status than their parents. The probability of the care of grandchildren increases by almost 7.6 percentage points in the latter case, whilst young respondents who consider that they have a lower social status than their parents receive significantly less informal assistance in the form of childcare, with a fall of 11.6 percentage points.[7]

Because of the pivot's time constraint, their ability to offer childcare and the amount of childcare provided to a given child significantly decreases with the number of adult children. Distance is strongly negatively related to the provision of childcare. For example, a hundred kilometres in distance is associated with a fall of 6.0 percentage points at the sample mean. In contrast to monetary transfers which are characterised by low transactional costs, the geographical distance separating the pivot and young generations greatly increases the cost of grandparenting, and this variable may be considered as a good proxy of the price of services (Cox and Rank 1992). Finally, help given to grandchildren derives from family strategies oriented towards the social promotion of adult children rather than from redistributive processes. It is noticeable that the employment participation of the young is more decisive

Table 2.5 Childcare given by pivots to their grandchildren

Variables	Probability of childcare		Time of childcare (Log)	
	coefficient	t-value	coefficient	t-value
Constant	1.180	2.61	3.586	3.79
PIVOT'S CHARACTERISTICS				
Female respondent	0.304	3.48	0.793	4.34
Married	0.320	2.97	0.735	3.18
Number of children				
Having at least one child	−0.090	−2.67	−0.226	−3.10
Having no child and living apart	−0.075	−1.69	−0.147	−1.55
Having no child and living in parental home	−0.063	−1.95	−0.127	−1.86
Education				
No diploma	0	—	0	—
Primary school	0.283	2.68	0.701	3.20
Secondary school	0.238	2.15	0.524	2.27
Baccalaureate	0.058	0.32	0.361	0.97
Graduate – Postgraduate studies	−0.145	−0.73	−0.221	−0.52
Respondent employed	−0.088	−0.99	−0.379	−2.08
Spouse employed	−0.059	−0.69	−0.153	−0.86
Income (10E-4)	0.120	1.94	0.132	1.10
Wealth (10E-5)	0.161	2.43	0.328	2.39
YOUNG'S CHARACTERISTICS				
Female	0.204	2.20	0.539	2.83
Filiation with both pivots spouses	0.195	1.77	0.512	2.12
Age	−0.066	−4.75	−0.145	−4.99
Marital status				
Alone	0.466	2.57	1.315	3.60
Non-married couple	−0.051	−0.53	−0.031	−0.16
Married couple	0	—	0	—
Number of children	0.113	1.95	0.108	0.88
Education				
Primary school	0	—	0	—
Secondary school	−0.149	−1.25	−0.295	−1.19
Baccalaureate	−0.126	−0.80	−0.340	−1.07
Graduate – Postgraduate studies	−0.233	−1.43	−0.482	−1.42
Employed	0.243	2.34	0.545	2.51
Spouse employed	0.134	1.17	0.415	1.73
Distance from parents (10E-2)	−0.156	−9.60	−0.453	−11.95
Subjective social mobility				
Same as parents	−0	—	0	—
Better than parents	0.198	2.17	0.386	2.07
Less than parents	−0.300	−2.28	−0.643	−2.28
Unknown response	−0.208	−1.33	−0.451	−1.34
Sigma			2.583	35.03
Number of observations	1,263		1,263	
Number of young recipients	750		750	
Log likelihood	−722.84		−2,158.46	

Source: Survey CNAV Three-Generations Study 1992.
Note: Probit analysis of childcare from pivots and tobit analysis of childcare time amount.

than the paid employment of grandmothers influencing the existence of this type of care. Grandmothers in general arrange to spend time with their grandchildren whether they work or not.

Co-residence

Another way of redistributing resources concerns home sharing. In addition to financial transfers, individuals can also provide support by having either their adult children or their elderly parents living in their own household.[8] Home-sharing sometimes expresses the desire of both generations (where there are close ties and good relationships) to live in the same household, but this pattern has become less frequent since the norm has become 'intimacy at a distance' (Rosenmayr and Koeckeis 1963). Home-sharing seems to result mostly from economic necessity as it occurs at the expense of privacy of both co-resident generations. Economic links within the family through help with housing are highly important, since this type of support can be of great benefit to poorer households who cannot afford to redistribute money. We have used two models in the analysis, depending on whether middle-aged adults co-resided with their adult children or their parents.

First, we consider the situation where young adults live in the parental home, a feature which has increased during the last two decades (Desplanques 1994). In the three-generational survey, each pivot member was asked about the housing situation of each adult child. Therefore, the relationship between the resources of the child and the benefit of home-sharing is examined within the household by constructing a new sub-sample where each respondent-child pair is counted as a single observation. By restricting the econometric analysis only to families with more than one child, we are able to examine this type of support within the family by using a family fixed effect. Since most unobserved characteristics of the siblings are highly correlated within a given family, the estimations are based on a conditional logistic regression on the sample of siblings for which the dependent variable (home-sharing decision) varies across observations. The results of the conditional maximum likelihood technique are reported in Table 2.6.

For young adults aged at least 20 years, home-sharing principally concerns students and children with an economic disadvantage. Recipients are not yet established in their life course as is shown by the negative effects of the age, presence of spouse and number of children variables. The child's education exerts no significant impact on the probability of living with their parents, which is partly explained by the high proportion of students. We therefore consider a more restricted sample by excluding all the individuals currently enrolled in higher education, and the estimates remain relatively unchanged for level of education, although the achievement of graduate or postgraduate studies significantly reduces the probability of co-residence. The lack of significance also diminishes if the sample is restricted to older young adults

Table 2.6 Probability of an adult child living with his or her parents

Variables	Child over 20		Non student child over 20		Employed child over 20	
	coefficient	t-value	coefficient	t-value	coefficient	t-value
YOUNG'S CHARACTERISTICS						
Female	−0.561	−2.83	−0.687	−2.55	−0.493	−1.25
Age	−0.257	−6.19	−0.273	−5.45	−0.228	−3.92
Presence of spouse	−3.582	−9.83	−3.949	−8.54	−3.540	−7.25
Number of children	−1.097	−2.96	−1.015	−2.64	−0.757	−1.66
Diploma						
No diploma	0	—	0	—	0	—
Primary – Secondary						
school	−0.207	−0.58	−0.343	−0.83	−0.230	−0.40
Baccalaureate	−0.135	0.32	0.066	0.12	0.444	0.63
Graduate – Post-						
graduate studies	−0.481	−1.03	−1.053	−1.65	−0.556	−0.68
Occupational status						
Employed	0	—	0	—		
Unemployed	1.363	3.73	1.406	3.35		
Student	0.701	2.39				
Inactive	0.910	2.11	0.434	0.90		
Social status						
Self-empoyed					−0.010	−0.02
Executive					−1.485	−1.41
Intermediate					−0.191	−0.38
Employee					−0.289	−0.69
Worker					0	—
Subjective social mobility						
Same as parents	0	—	0	—	0	—
Better than parents	−0.713	−2.00	−0.762	−1.59	−1.135	−1.83
Less than parents	−0.571	−1.29	−0.747	−1.37	−0.041	−0.05
Unknown response	−0.092	−0.24	0.204	0.37	−0.673	−0.88
Number of young adults	1,880		1,214		730	
Number of families	637		402		257	
Log likelihood	−203.73		−118.32		−81.17	

Source: Survey CNAV Three-Generations Study 1992.
Note: Fixed Effect Logit analysis of co-residence with adult children. Estimation based on groups of children for which the dependent variable varies across observations.

(older than 25), and the likelihood of co-residence with parents decreases in the latter case with the child's level of education. It seems, therefore, that most children characterised by low-opportunity costs have little alternative option than to live with their parents.

Examining the social status of young adults provides valuable information about individual needs for co-residence. Table 2.6 shows that the probability of home-sharing is higher for the unemployed, students or inactive young adults. Of course, such recipients have the lowest level of economic resources among siblings. Because children in higher education are likely to have lower current incomes but higher permanent income expectancies, we also estimate the model with two restricted samples by excluding first the students and then the inactive adults. The coefficients confirm the increased probability of co-residence for unemployed young adults and suggest a lower likelihood for those who are in middle manager or above occupational groups among siblings who have jobs. Whilst money transfers mainly correspond to help in the case of promotion, living with parents primarily occurs in the case of necessity and the probability significantly decreases for adult children characterised by an ascending social mobility.

Concerning co-residence in later life, the population census in France shows that since the 1960s, the proportion of elderly couples living with others has declined over time. This decrease is the sharpest for persons or couples aged over 75 years, 16.6 per cent of whom were still living with other people according to the 1990 census (Baraille 1993). Our study reveals approximately the same proportion of elders living with one of their children (not necessarily the one who was interviewed). Two contrasting patterns stand out from the many different forms of home-sharing – one where parents and children have always lived together, the other where parents in their old age revert to a pattern which was discontinued as their children reached adulthood and sought independence (Arber and Gilbert 1989). In the older generation, these two situations surprisingly occur in roughly equal - proportions, with 54 per cent having always lived with a child with whom they are currently sharing a home, and the remainder having gone to live with a child (or children) following a prolonged period of independence, referred to as re-cohabitants (Attias-Donfut 1997).

Permanent shared residence is found in two out of three cases in the countryside, while re-cohabitation is more of an urban phenomenon. The rural nature of a lifelong shared residence is strong among groups with a particular occupational identity, with 46 per cent being former farmers, in contrast to 23 per cent for those who re-cohabit. Among the latter, there are a greater number of manual workers (49 per cent re-cohabitants compared with 39 per cent lifelong cohabitants), some former clerical-level employees (12 per cent and 9 per cent respectively), but a very small number of former management-level employees (2 per cent re-cohabiting, and none in lifelong cohabitation). Widowed mothers are the majority in both situations, while parents living as a couple and widowed fathers are numerically greater among those living with an adult child who has never left home.

The characteristics of mid-life children sharing the residence distinguishes these two situations of co-residence. The most outstanding distinction is that between sons and daughters. Sons never leave their parents' home in two out of three life-long cohabitation cases, while parents live with daughters in nearly three out of four cases of re-cohabitation. These two distribution systems explain why the national statistics show almost as many sons as daughters living with their parents. The number of sons living with parents is in fact slightly higher. The overwhelming majority of children who never leave home are single, while re-cohabitation involves mostly married children, but also a significant proportion of divorced and widowed children.

Levels of education of the pivot generation are on average higher in the case of those who re-cohabit. Intergenerational social mobility measured by the subjective indicator is far more evident where a return to home-sharing follows a period of prolonged independence than where it has been un-interrupted. Re-cohabitation is more likely where the younger generation has achieved more than their elderly parents, which is a probable manifestation of the return-effect of social mobility, since the co-residence raises the parental standard of living. Conversely, uninterrupted home-sharing is characterised by social immobility between generations. The social position of the adult child who primarily cohabits, in relation to siblings who do not, is disadvant-aged (socially, occupationally and educationally) and this is also confirmed by the subjective indicator of social mobility. This type of co-residence benefits the cohabitant child, since this child is the main recipient of the 'gift' of the shared home.

However, both types of co-residence are associated with supporting parents who have partly lost their autonomy. This is corroborated by the fact that compared to the elderly population in general, a greater proportion of elderly parents living with their children need the latter's help to perform daily activities of living. Co-residence therefore expresses a reciprocity between parent and child, whether it is a direct one in the case of lifelong co-residence or is delayed in time, in the form of re-cohabitation.

Conclusion

The empirical results presented in this chapter show that family transfers are mainly directed towards kinship members who have the greatest needs. Economic transfers, whether financial or in kind, circulate from richer to poorer generations, whether flowing upwards or downwards. Consequently, *inter vivos* transfers significantly reduce inequalities between generations.

Middle-aged parents provide important economic support to their young adult children, which helps these children in the transition to adulthood. The three-generational data has shown the importance of financial help given to young people by both their parents and grandparents. This redistribution of resources within the family substantially increases the standard of living of the younger generation, whether they are inactive or at the beginning of their careers. Moreover, the members of the pivot generation who receive financial transfers from their elderly parents are more likely to give financial help in turn to their own children.[9] For example, if we consider financial gifts or loans, 66 per cent of pivots helped by their own elderly parents provide such support to their adult children whilst the proportion is only 44 per cent concerning non-recipient pivots. Evidence argues in favour of a generalised process of family redistribution, such that cash gifts flow downward within the extended family, either directly from parents to children or from grandparents to grandchildren, or indirectly from elders to pivots and then in turn from pivots to young adults. In this way, the less well-off generation across the life-cycle is economically supported.

By giving financial gifts to their descendants, older people reduce their own financial resources. This circular flow, upwards from the pivot generation towards the poorest among the older generation and downwards from the richest among the older generation to the pivot generation, exerts an effect which diminishes gaps in the standard of living between middle-aged adults and their elderly parents. However, the full impact of these compensatory processes remains undoubtedly underestimated in terms of non marketable transfers in the form of caring activities or co-residence.

A French cross-sectional survey from INSEE conducted in 1994, the Budget Survey of Families, confirms our findings and illustrates the overall reduction of intergenerational inequalities through private cash gifts (de Barry *et al.* 1996). First, financial transfers between generations within families significantly increase the incomes of household members aged under 40 years and in particular they sustain the income of young disadvantaged households. Second, for households where the members are aged above 40 years, the transfers they make reduce their disposable income. The net effect of these *inter vivos* transfers is therefore to reduce inequalities in income that are age related. The flows of private financial transfers, however, are noticeably different as far as inheritance wealth is concerned. In fact, because of the increase in longevity, the mean age at which an individual can expect to inherit parental wealth increased from 48 years in 1984 to 51 years in 1994 for France (Accardo 1997). But the rise in the mean age that one can expect to inherit would probably be partly compensated by a greater frequency of cash gifts and other forms of financial help, as well as the expanding new phenomena whereby the older generation gives financial support directly to their less well-off grandchildren.

In this detailed study of the economic flow of exchanges between the generations, it is possible to see, simultaneously, various kinds of logic behind transfers which, although they may have the same form, differ completely in their objectives and significance. Two principal processes can be seen to be at work. On the one hand, forms of support, in money or time, are above all directed towards those who are in need, and therefore have a redistributive function within the family. On the other hand, support given by the eldest and the middle generations to the youngest generation, is mostly directed towards preventing a lowering of their social status. The financial transfers and help in the form of housing that are received by the younger generation is principally to minimise the risk of a downward slide in social mobility. In contrast, childcare of grandchildren (a practice largely undertaken by the middle generation) has the function of helping young mothers in the upward path of social mobility. This is an expression of female solidarity towards promoting the professional career of women.

Generational exchanges are firmly articulated upon gender roles. Inter-generational ties and gender divisions in turn demonstrate the gendered nature of generations. The strong mother/daughter bond both structures the forms of support given to descendants (childcare of grandchildren) and support given to ascendants (care tasks for disabled elderly parents). Men and women both make a contribution to family solidarity, but through different patterns of transfers. Men more often give financial help, women more often give time-related support. But gender roles are not always so clearly dis-tinguished, as, for example, the new role that young grandfathers play in looking after grandchildren. Could this be an aspect of more equal gender relations for generations to come?

In conclusion, the interaction of ascending and descending flows ensures a redistribution of resources between the generations and achieves a relative degree of harmony between their standards of living and wealth.

Acknowledgements

We are grateful to Jim Ogg for his translation from the French text.

Notes

1 The French tri-generational research concerned 1,958 individuals of the pivot generation aged between 49 and 53 years, 1,217 parents of the pivot generation aged between 66 and 92 years, and 1,493 children of the pivot generation aged between 19 and 32. The age range of 49 to 53 was determined according to demographic tables in order to maximise the probability of having at least one living parent and one adult child. This research was undertaken at the Research Unit of CNAV, by C. Attias-Donfut, A. Rozenkier and S. Renaut, and with the co-operation of INSEE. The first results have been published in Attias-Donfut (1995; 1997).

2 Chauvel's (1998) research has confirmed the hypothesis that social fluidity remains constant (Erikson and Goldthorpe 1992) but it also reveals a slight tendency, pro-gressive and tangential, to increase, which can only be perceived over a long period of time and not in the short term.

3 The validity of this question is shown by its significant correlation with categories of occupations. The correlation is not perfect, which can in part be explained by the imprecision of classifying occupational groups and by the fact that they are only one aspect of a social position, the others being income, level of education and standard of living. We include this subjective indicator in the analysis because of its explana-tory power.

4 Arrondel and Wolff (1998) also point out that *inter vivos* intergenerational trans-fers within the extended family follow strong life-cycle variations – firstly human capital investments, then redistributive help in case of necessity, and finally advanced transmission of wealth. This evidence argues in favour of a life-cycle framework analysis of interactions between parents and children.

5 The prevalence of the equal division of *inter vivos* transfers to sibling pivots may be explained by the cost associated with unequal transfers, since parents would otherwise have compensated the earnings differences among their children.

6 Econometric results concerning the discrete choice and the amounts of care using Probit and Tobit models are reported for the full sample of young adult parents where each child is counted as one observation. As the results may be biased because of unobserved factors correlated between siblings, non reported estimates are controlled for unobserved familial heterogeneity using fixed-effect models for families with two or more children.

7 We can also note that the probability of care increases with the number of grandchildren.

8 As Rosenzweig and Wolpin have shown (1993), co-residence would appear to be a cheaper mechanism by which parents can make transfers because of the public's good nature regarding housing services.

9 Parents have a higher probability of helping children after having received transfers from their own parents in the past, but they also tend to favour the same way of transmission that they themselves benefited from (Arrondel and Wolff 1998).

References

Accardo, J. (1997) 'Successions et donations en 1994', *Insee Première* 521.

Arber, S. and Gilbert, N. (1989) 'Transitions in caring: gender, life course and the care of the elderly', in B. Bytheway, T. Keil, P. Allatt and A. Bryman (eds) *Becoming and Being Old: Sociological Approaches to Later Life*, London: Sage.

Arrondel, L. and Wolff, F.C. (1998) 'La nature des transferts inter vivos en France: investissements humains, aides financières et transmission du patrimoine', *Economie et Prévision* 135: 1–27.

Attias-Donfut, C. (1993) 'Coéducation des générations et effets en retour de la mobilité sociale', in G. Pronovost, C. Attias-Donfut and N. Samuel (eds) *Temps Libre et Modernité. Hommage à Joffre Dumazedier*, Paris: L'Harmattan.

——(1995) 'Le double circuit des transmissions', in C. Attias-Donfut (ed.) *Les Solidarités entre Générations. Vieillesse, Familles, Etat*, Paris: Nathan.

——(1997) 'Home-sharing and the transmission of inheritance in France', in M. Gullestad and M. Segalen (eds) *Family and Kinship in Europe*, Washington: Pinter.

Attias-Donfut, C. and Rozenkier, A. (1996) 'The lineage-structured social networks of older people in France', in H. Litwin (ed.) *The Social Networks of Older People*, London: Praeger.

Attias-Donfut, C. and Segalen, M. (1998) *Grands-parents. La Famille à travers les Générations*, Paris: Odile Jacob.

Bachelard, G. (1938) *La Formation de l'Esprit Scientifique*, Paris: Vrin.

Baraille, J.P. (1993) 'L'âge de la retraite', in *Données Sociales*, Paris: Insee.

Barry, C. de, Eneau, D. and Hourriez, J.M. (1996) 'Les aides financières entre ménages', *Insee Première* 441.

Baudelot, C. and Gollac, M. (1997) 'Le salaire du trentenaire: question d'âge ou de génération?', *Economie et Statistique* 304/305: 601–24.

Bengtson, V.L. (1975) 'Generation and family effects in value socialization', *American Sociological Review* 51: 358–71.

Bertaux, D. (1974) 'Mobilité sociale biographique: une critique de l'approche transversale', *Revue Française de Sociologie* 15: 329–62.

Bertaux, D. and Bertaux-Wiame, I. (1988) 'Le patrimoine et sa lignée: transmissions et mobilité sociale sur cinq générations', *Life Stories/Récits de Vie* 4: 8–25.

Boudon, R. (1973) *L'Inégalité des Chances*, Paris: Armand Colin.
Bourdieu, P. and Passeron, J.C. (1970) *La Reproduction*, Paris: Editions de Minuit.
Cardia, E. and Ng, S. (1998) 'How important are intergenerational transfers of time? A macroeconomic analysis', unpublished manuscript, Boston College.
Chauvel, L. (1998) *Le Destin des Générations*, Paris: Presses Universitaires de France.
Cox, D. (1990) 'Intergenerational transfers and liquidity constraints', *Quarterly Journal of Economics* 105: 187–218.
Cox, D. and Rank, M.R. (1992) 'Inter vivos transfers and intergenerational exchange', *Review of Economics and Statistics* 74: 305–14.
Desplanques, G. (1994) 'Etre ou ne plus être chez ses parents', *Population et Sociétés* 292.
Drouin, V. (1995) *Enquêtes sur les Générations et la Politique*, Paris: L'Harmattan.
Erikson, R. and Goldthorpe, J. H. (1992) *The Constant Flux. A Study of Class Mobility in Industrial Societies*, Oxford: Clarendon Press.
Gaulejac, V. de (1987) *La Névrose de Classe*, Paris: Hommes et Groupes.
Inglehart, R. (1990) *Culture Shift in Advanced Industrial Society*, Princeton: Princeton University Press.
Mangen, D.J., Bengtson, V.L. and Landry, P.H. (eds) (1988) *The Measurement of Intergenerational Relations*, Beverly Hills: Sage Publications.
Mannheim, K. (1952) 'The problem of generations', in K. Mannheim (ed.) *Essays in the Sociology of Knowledge*, London: Routledge and Kegan Paul.
Mead, M. (1970) *Culture and Commitment: A Study of the Generation Gap*, New York: Garden City.
Mendel, G. (1968) *La Révolte contre le Père*, Paris: Payot.
Mendras, H. (1967) *La Fin des Paysans*, Paris: Sedeis (réédition 1984, Arles: Actes Sud).
Merllié, D. (1994) *Les Enquêtes de Mobilité Sociale*, Paris: Presses Universitaires de France.
Riley, M.W., Johnson, M. and Foner, A. (1972) *A Sociology of Age Stratification*, New York: Russell Sage Foundation.
Rosenmayr L. and Koeckeis E., (1963) 'Propositions for a sociological theory of aging and the family', *International Social Science Journal* 15: 410–26.
Rosenzweig, M.R. and Wolpin, K.I. (1993) 'Intergenerational support and the life-cycle incomes of young men and their parents: human capital investments, coresidence and intergenerational financial transfers', *Journal of Labor Economics* 11: 84–112.
Rossi, A.F. and Rossi, P.H. (1990) *Of Human Bonding: Parent–Child Relations across the Life Course*, New York: Aldine DeGruyter.
Schorske, C.E. (1978) 'Generational tension and cultural change: reflection on the case of Vienna', *Daedalus* 107: 111–22.
Spilerman, S., Lewin-Epstein, N. and Semyonov, M. (1993) 'Wealth, intergenerational transfers, and life chances', in A. Sorensen and S. Spilerman (eds) *Social Theory and Social Policy*, New York: Praeger.

3

COMPLEMENTARITY BETWEEN PRIVATE AND PUBLIC TRANSFERS

Claudine Attias-Donfut and François-Charles Wolff

Introduction

State-funded welfare in the form of social protection schemes have a profound effect on the very foundations of society. They impact upon social structures and, more generally, social ties. They represent a formidable stake for societies, and the problems that they pose should never be reduced simply to financial questions. It is important not to ignore the sociological aspects in debates on the welfare state. Retirement pension schemes have largely contributed to the shape of modern life (Kohli 1986) and, as we show in this chapter, they have also contributed to redefining intergenerational relations. The purpose of this chapter, therefore, is to contribute towards a better understanding of the impact of social benefits on the functioning of families and society, through an analysis of their interaction with intra-family support. We also aim to show the moderating effects of these intergenerational exchanges on social inequalities.

There has been little empirical research to date on the interaction between public and private transfers. To understand the underlying process of this interaction is difficult because of its dynamic nature. In addition, the interaction is no longer observable in most industrial countries, because their social welfare systems were established long ago and public flows have already replaced or complemented private forms of solidarity. The results of any such research would therefore reveal a *'fait accompli'* as Cox and Jimenez (1995) have noted, since the replacement of private exchanges by public flows has already taken place and is difficult to detect.[1] However, research conducted in the United States on this issue, using either cross-sectional or longitudinal analyses, leads to the same conclusion and suggests that the two types of transfers are rather independent of each other.

During the period 1935–79, evidence reported by Lampman and Smeeding (1983) revealed only a modest decline in intergenerational private transfers in the United States despite the large growth of the public sector. Econometric results based on various data sets concerning financial support from parents to children are quite similar (Rosenzweig and Wolpin 1994; Cox and Jakubson 1995; Schoeni 1996), pointing to a slight decline of family solidarities in response to the growth in social benefits. Rosenzweig and Wolpin (1994) have shown that parents view a dollar of income earned by their daughter as equivalent to a dollar rise in the welfare benefits of that daughter. However, there exists only a small trade-off between the generosity of government aid and the incidence of transfers from parents to children. The case of informal care for older people leads to similar results: for example, according to Pezzin *et al.* (1996), the large increase in public residential care provision from 1982 to 1985 resulted in only a small reduction in care provided by informal care-givers.[2]

The flow of transfers between living family members can be distinguished according to three main characteristics: the type – private or public; the direction – either upward or downward; and the form – either financial or in kind (Kessler *et al.* 1991). Although aggregate transfers of each kind may be evaluated from a macroeconomic perspective, the relevance of such an approach remains limited since it does not allow an understanding of the dynamics of these flows. The French three-generational data set (discussed in Chapter 2) sheds light on the microprocesses at work in these transfers.

The importance of private transfers and their redistributive effects were shown in Chapter 2. We now consider the directions and forms of intergenerational transfers when private and public transfers are distinguished. Young adult and mid-life generations contribute towards finances dispensed by the state, mostly in the form of taxes, and receive in return support in the form of family allowances and help with education fees for their children. The resources of the eldest generation are mostly made up of pensions and this group makes only modest contributions in the form of taxes. The older generation give much more to their mid-life children than to their grandchildren, since their gifts to the former represent a part of their wealth which is to be inherited. Most middle-aged parents still give support to their adult children and these transfers, together with financial gifts from grandparents, enable the young adult generation to cope with difficulties in relation to paid employment, education and housing. Parallel to these descending flows, there coexists ascending financial assistance, although these transfers are less frequent. The same processes occur in other developed countries (see the chapters by Kohli *et al.* and Gulbrandsen and Langsether).

This approach enables us to bring to the fore two channels of intergenerational transfers. On the one hand, public support benefits mostly the older generation, who, in turn, are the just beneficiaries of a pension system into which they paid when they were economically active. On the other hand, flowing from this ascending pattern of state transfers, there are private transfers which, for the most part, benefit descending generations. Older generations redistribute their financial resources not only to their adult children (namely the mid-life pivots) by way of gifts and inherited wealth, but also to their grandchildren in the form of timely offers of financial help and gifts. However, in contrast with public transfers which are visible and paid regularly, the total amount of private support remains invisible in most cases and not all households display this type of solidarity. Moreover, the informal and sporadic character of familial support makes it impossible to establish the exact amounts which would enable a precise comparison between public and private assistance.

Taking into account the redistributive action of the family demonstrates the existence of circular mechanisms of support whereby public solidarities in the form of pensions largely supplement and add to the private solidarities between the three generations. This finding calls into question the idea of generational conflict which is suggested by methods of generational accounting, and which mainly originates from considering only public transfers. The cycle of extended exchange shows the interdependence of the generations and the sustaining elements of this reciprocal process between private and public solidarities. With the provision of pensions, the state has put into place a new structure of family solidarity. Whereas in pre-industrial societies younger generations took responsibility for their ageing parents, today it is parents and grandparents who support and financially help their descendants. This marked bias towards descendants, which is a feature of modern society, is the product of a social process and should not be considered as a universal fact which is historically common to all kinship relations.

These circular mechanisms, with their descending flow of familial distribution, appear only possible today because older people now enjoy a quality of life that was previously unknown. Not only can they remain independent without having to rely upon financial help and co-residence with their adult children, but they can also generously provide for their descendants. The expectation of retirement pensions also allows employed parents to help their adult children instead of exclusively saving for their own future. This argues in favour of the maintenance of pensions in the public sector. Finally, the importance of all social policies which benefit older people should be emphasised since a significant proportion of retired people contribute towards and supplement family solidarities.

Analysis of the complementarity model

Our purpose in this chapter is twofold. First, using the French three-generational survey, we present a detailed analysis of the underlying process of three types of assistance. We focus on financial support from middle-aged adults to younger generations, then on practical and financial support given to older people, and finally on cash transfers both upwards and downwards between the mid-life generation and their older parents. Each of these exchanges is considered in the context of the interaction between public and private transfers. Second, since changes in intra-familial assistance may have already occurred in the past and cannot be examined using our survey, we turn to an examination of a society where systems of social protection are currently being introduced. An ideal case for exploring this process is that of Guadeloupe, where the French system of social protection has recently been introduced. This research is particularly insightful and emphasises the value of not only quantitative analysis, but also qualitative analysis to further an understanding of the evolution of both private and public systems of redistribution.

Financial support received by adult children

Young adults are the main recipients of private support given by the two ascending generations. The French three-generational survey (discussed in Chapter 2) shows that 32 per cent of non co-resident children can rely on regular financial payments from their parents, 14 per cent of them are given some form of allowance and 80 per cent receive at least one type of household service. However, these figures correspond to an underestimated balance of private assistance, since help and gifts from parents-in-law, paternal or maternal grandparents as well as the spouse's grandparents have not been taken into account.[3] Alongside these transfers, 50 per cent of young people receive some form of social allowance from the state. This state-provided assistance principally flows to them in the form of education grants, housing allowances for students, unemployment-related benefits and family allowances for those with children.

At first sight, the data set does not support the notion that generous public welfare programmes erode private solidarities since the latter remain of high importance. In fact, it seems that familial support does not diminish when public help is given additionally to younger generations (Paugam and Zoyem 1997). In total, 15.6 per cent of young adults receive both gifts from parents and regular payments from the state, a fact which confirms the coexistence of the two supports. The characteristics of recipients according to whether they receive public support, private support, or both forms of support, and descriptive statistics are given in Table 3.1. Private transfers are essentially orientated towards those who need them the most and at the same time aimed at those who obtain higher levels of education.

Motives of parents in such cases therefore need to be examined since parents may invest in those adult children who show the greatest probability of moving up the social scale. Social mobility among adults at the start of their career is, however, difficult to measure, but a subjective evaluation shows that parents give more help to adult children who are at risk of sliding down the social scale than to those who are more likely to move up (see Chapter 2). Young people's attitudes towards their future are also characterised by a certain apprehension. Only one in three young people believe that they will

Table 3.1 Proportion of young adults receiving private and public transfers

Characteristics of young adult	Private	Public	Private and public
Age			
Less than 23 years	57.7	46.0	29.9
23 to 25 years	37.4	42.3	19.0
26 to 28 years	26.2	44.4	10.9
29+ years	21.7	60.0	13.2
Marital status			
Alone	47.1	29.7	18.0
Non married couple	34.4	43.5	16.3
Married couple	20.2	61.1	13.7
Number of children			
No child	38.9	25.0	13.1
One child	25.5	62.2	19.4
At least two children	18.7	91.6	17.9
Education			
Primary – Secondary school	18.2	57.9	11.9
Baccalaureate	28.4	48.8	16.1
Graduate studies	40.9	38.3	17.4
Postgraduate studies	48.4	37.2	19.6
Activity status			
Employed	27.0	41.1	11.8
Unemployed	35.8	78.9	23.2
Student	75.7	54.4	41.7
Non active	28.1	79.8	21.3
Occupational status			
Independent	15.5	58.6	3.4
Executive, manager	38.4	29.6	12.8
Intermediate	33.9	37.9	13.3
Employee	25.2	48.3	13.5
Worker	21.7	57.1	14.2
Non active	64.8	64.8	39.8
Income per month			
< 4,200 FF	64.7	60.8	36.6
4,200 < 7,500 FF	34.0	56.3	19.9
7,500 < 10,800 FF	28.4	46.9	15.4
10,800 < 16,700 FF	25.3	44.2	10.6
> 16,700 FF	20.9	34.4	5.1
Wealth			
< 20,000 FF	40.4	49.2	21.8
20,000 < 50,000 FF	33.6	41.8	15.0
50,000 < 100,000 FF	28.5	35.0	8.9
100,000 < 500,000 FF	22.1	45.6	10.8
> 500,000 FF	17.1	58.1	8.6
Mean	31.6	47.5	15.6

Source: Survey CNAV Three-Generations Study 1992.
Note: Descriptive statistics indicate the proportion of young adult recipients. Private transfers are received from parents during the last five years.

achieve more than their parents – 24 per cent of those who receive financial support from their parents and 35 per cent of those who are not being financially helped by their parents.

Public assistance mostly benefits economically inactive children, whether they are students, unemployed or in other inactive categories. Furthermore, young people with few or no qualifications are more likely to receive financial help from the state. As they leave the education system earlier, they are more likely to start a family at an early age and therefore become eligible for family allowances. Most public support is means-tested, as is indicated by the higher proportion of adult children with lower incomes that receive benefits. For example, among young people whose income per capita is less than 4,200FF per month, 61 per cent receive at least one form of state benefit, but the proportion falls to 46 per cent for those with incomes above 7,500FF per month.

Analysing the characteristics of young adults that receive both public and private transfers supports the idea that these two forms of solidarit complement each other. These younger adults are mostly to be found in single-person households, and they have higher levels of education or are still full-time students. Whereas the mean proportion of households receiving both forms of support is 15.6 per cent, it rises to 23.2 per cent among the unemployed and 41.7 per cent among students, but the level of assistance is only 11.8 per cent among employed young adults. Whether the support given to students is provided mostly by the state or from within the family, it represents a considerable investment in human capital. Young adults in poorer households also benefit significantly from the combination of public and private financial support. Among those whose monthly income is less than 4,200FF per month, 36.6 per cent receive both types of support compared with less than 20 per cent among those whose monthly income is between 4,200FF and 7,500FF per month. Despite their coexistence, further evidence is required in order to understand the complexities of both types of flow.

In the substitution hypothesis, it is expected that parents would give less money to their children in response to increased public transfers which are given to them. According to the three-generational study, the total amount of family aid is given largely independent of any public allowances received by young people. When the two groups of young people are separated into those who receive some form of state allowance and those who do not, the rate of private aid is 30 per cent in the latter group, with a mean total of 37,600FF of private aid given over the last five-year period. For those young people in receipt of state allowances, the comparable figures are 33 per cent and 36,650FF of private aid respectively. This result shows that these two forms of support are complementary.

It could therefore be argued that the presence of public forms of benefit serves to stimulate private support and to prepare the young person for leaving the parental home or for higher education, and that the family continues to give support even when state allowances are paid, contributing to the reduction of the overall costs of the transition into adulthood. Above all, families with limited resources are enabled to make choices concerning education or independent housing for young adults that they would have been unable to make in the absence of state support.

If we examine the forms of financial help received by young adults according to the level of their parental resources, descriptive statistics again suggest that private and public support complement each other irrespective of the level of parent's income. Evidently, the amounts of public and private aid differ according to the level of income of their parents, such that state benefits are more common and private sources of assistance are less likely for low-income parents. The redistributive aim of public support is at work in this relationship which proves its importance for the adult children of parents with limited resources. However, irrespective of the level of parental income, parents are slightly more likely to give financial help to children who are receiving some form of state allowance than to those who do not. The proportion of those who do not receive any form of support varies comparatively little with the level of parental income. When the young adult recipients are in need during early adulthood, both the state and the family attempt to provide economic resources to the less well-off. Public support would therefore seem to act as a stimulus for the circulation of private support at all levels of income.

We also estimate the effect of public allowances on private transfers using an econometric two-stage procedure separating the probability of cash gifts and the value conditioned on the actual event of the transfer. A negative impact of public subsidies on private support within the family is expected in the event of substitution between these types of support (Cox and Jakubson 1995). While the recipient's income from paid employment significantly decreases the probability of receiving cash gifts from parents, the receipt of state allowances increases at the same time as the probability of being financially helped by parents.[4] Starting from a mean estimated probability of private transfer at 28.7 percentage points, a rise in income for young people of 1,000FF per year decreases the probability of parental support to 26.1 per cent, whereas parental support rises to 32.9 per cent for those young people who receive public support. The hypothesis of 'crowding out', therefore, can be rejected since the total amount of state allowances exerts no significant effect (in both the probability and amount equations) upon the value of support given by parents to the younger generation.

Using these econometric estimates, we also simulate the impact of a withdrawal of state allowances given to young people, based on the assumption that these withdrawn funds are not redistributed elsewhere in society.[5] The money saved could, for example, be put towards decreasing the current public expenditure deficits. On the one hand, such a policy would result in a substantial erosion of private solidarities from 28.7 per cent to 25 per cent, and on the other hand, a reduction in the total amount of private transfers to the value of 3,040FF per year. Therefore, the withdrawal of public transfers would result in a reduction of parental generosity of the order of 26 per cent. The simulation-based results clearly argue in favour of a reinforcement, such that public support to young people also encourages private support through cash gifts from parents to their adult children.

On the whole, empirical results reveal the mistake of assuming that the family can replace the state if public expenditure on welfare is cut back, since such a policy has the effect of reducing the amount of assistance exchanged within the family. Furthermore, in families characterised by a limited level of economic resources, where public allowances more often represent the only form of financial support, reducing or withholding such benefits does not lead to an increase in financial help given by the family. A reduction in public resources received by mid-life parents and grandparents has the net effect of being disadvantageous to young people. Consequently, contrary to the common idea of generations in conflict for public resources, the young would not benefit from any reduction in public spending directed towards the retired.

It could be argued that the dynamic process of the interaction between both public and private assistance may not be fully taken into account since the preceding conclusions emanate from a cross-sectional survey. Fortunately, recent French longitudinal research conducted by Paugam and Zoyem (1997) provides additional results in favour of the complementarity hypothesis. Studying the impact of private transfers from parents to adult children, the authors confirm that familial assistance exerts a substantial effect on the budgets of the most impoverished households as do means-based state benefits. Following the introduction of minimum income support, this survey concludes that both state and family transfers are cumulative rather than being perfect substitutes. In particular, financial gifts from parents are more frequently distributed among long-term recipients of minimum income support than among those who are no longer receiving income support, an empirical result which is in accordance with the idea of cumulative private and public assistance.

Support given to older people

The interaction between family solidarities and social policy raises a particular problem for the care of dependent older people, since support given by middle-aged adults to their elderly parents is not normally in the form of financial help, whereas it is for help given to the younger generations. Older people are more likely to receive domestic help and, where necessary, daily help with activities of living when they are no longer able to live independently. These different forms of practical support can equally be given by professionals financed for the most part by the public sector.

The relationship between the public and private care of older people has been the subject of numerous studies which have emphasised the political implications of the state reneging on its responsibilities by substituting family care for state welfare programmes; see for example, Twigg (1993), Johansson and Thorslund (1993) and Lesemann and Martin (1993). Several of these studies show that by supplementing family care with public services the amount of private support given actually increases, for example Chapell and Blandford (1991) and Daatland (1992). When older persons are highly dependent, whether they live alone or with their mid-life children, it is unusual for them to receive only professional help without the addition of family support (Bouget and Tartarin 1990; Attias-Donfut 1993; Renaut and Rozenkier 1995).

Conversely, it is not unusual for private assistance from children to exist in the absence of professional service support. For example, among older people aged above 75 years, 60 per cent receive some form of daily support from their social network whereas only 30 per cent receive help from professional services (Renaut and Rozenkier 1995). This pattern is also found in the United States which confirms that informal support to older people is not eroded when there is an increase in public forms of support. The extent to which public subsidies of formal care substitute family care has been analysed using both longitudinal and experimental data, and the results show that the rise in public provision of care during the last decade has not resulted in any reduction in informal care-giving efforts by the family (Tennstedt et al. 1993; Pezzin et al. 1996).

The three-generational research clearly confirms the above results. As older parents reach an age where health problems increase, they are more likely to receive the services of a professional to supplement family support. According to the data, 27 per cent of the elderly report the benefit of professional help – 22 per cent of those with no familial in-kind assistance and 32 per cent for those receiving time transfers given by middle-aged children. In addition, the presence of public assistance does not affect the amount of time given by children. Older people receiving professional support do not receive lesser amounts from their descendants. On the contrary, the amount of private help received is comparatively of more significance when it complements public forms of support.

As expected, the quantity of family and professional support given to older people is determined by their degree of disability, but the increase in one form of support does not give rise to any decrease in the other form. Far from acting as a disincentive for family support, the presence of a professional carer acts to enhance family support, as previous research has confirmed (Hagestad 1995). Nonetheless, analysing only upward in-kind transfers leads to an incomplete balance of *inter vivos* transfers since a substantial proportion of elderly people provide money to their adult children.

Reciprocal financial exchanges between the middle aged and their parents

We therefore turn to an analysis of two-sided exchanges between mid-life 'pivots' and their older parents. In response to a change in the intergenerational wealth distribution, we anticipate that modifications to intergenerational transfers would occur in two directions. On the one hand, in so far as the older generation redistributes part of their retirement pension and their assets downwards within the family, a decrease in the level of pensions should also have the effect of reducing the amount of financial help that the older generation gives to their descendants. On the other hand, as upward financial assistance is mainly directed towards the poorer elderly, the decrease in pensions should also be accompanied by a rise in cash support and time assistance bestowed by middle-aged adults.

Such a hypothesis is tested by examining the reciprocal support between the pivot generation and their elderly parents. For this analysis, we focus only on financial help through gifts of money and occasional loans made during the last five years, as well as any supplementary finance given on a regular basis, whilst inheritance wealth is excluded. If we consider family support only from the viewpoint of the recipients (which gives an underestimated picture of the total amount of this type of support), we find that 18 per cent of the pivot-elderly pairs are involved with financial family support. As analysed in Chapter 2, these financial transfers are principally in a descending direction: 11 per cent of the pivot generation receive financial support from their elderly parents, while 7 per cent of the pivot generation give financial help to their elderly parents (reciprocal supports are insignificant and concern only 0.4 per cent of the sample population).

The provision of private financial help is determined mostly by the level of economic resources of the two generations. Gifts to the pivot generation are, above all, characteristic of the wealthiest older-generation members. Among all the donors belonging to the older generation, 42 per cent are part of the richest quartile, whereas 12.5 per cent are in the poorest. Financial help which ascends the generations shows a similar trend and it is for the most part determined by the level of wealth and income of the pivot generation. Almost half of the pivot generation members who give such financial help belong to the richest quartile of households. Additionally, the greater the wealth of older-generation members, the less money they receive from their mid-life children. The existence of compensatory financial transfers between the eldest and pivot generations would be magnified by the inclusion of in-kind services and co-residence.

In order to understand the dynamic process of redistributive transfers within the family, we estimate the effect of a reduction in retirement pension on the circulation of financial gifts between these two successive generations. For this purpose, we have simulated quantitatively what would happen if there is a reduction of 10 per cent of the value of retirement pensions, assuming that no compensatory public payments occur to either of the generations.[6] The objective of the underlying simulation is restricted to extracting the main effects associated with such a scenario. We estimate a bivariate probit model for the two transfers in order to control for the interaction between them. The econometric estimates enable the calculation of the mean probabilities of upward and downward transfers to be made (at the sample means) and consequently the impact of an anticipated reduction in the level of retirement pensions.[7]

The simulation confirms the expected predictions that retired people decrease the amount of financial support given to their descendants and that the pivot generation have to increase the amount of help given to their elderly parents in order that the latter maintain an adequate standard of living. A reduction of 10 per cent in the value of retirement pensions would result in an increase of 6.9 per cent in the probability of cash gifts from the pivot to the older generation and a reduction of 2.1 per cent in the probability of financial help from the older to the pivot generation. The fact that the total amount of downward reduction is less than the total amount of upward increase may be explained by the omitted impact of such a reform on the circulation of inheritance wealth. If the latter is taken into account, the inheritance wealth from the eldest members expected by 'pivot' children will be reduced in the long term by an amount equal to the reduction in the value of retirement pensions, as the savings of these households will be reduced proportionately.

The impact of a simulated reduction in the value of retirement pensions is not only significant for the financial transfers between the pivot-generation members and their older parents, but also for the totality of exchanges in the form of in-kind transfers and co-residence, the latter support being expected to increase if pensions are reduced. Moreover, the subsequent alteration of intergenerational economic resources will have some repercussions on private transfers among the three co-existing generations within the family. Since the wealthiest households give the most, one would expect that the financial help given to adult children and grandchildren would reduce if the value of retirement pensions falls. Similarly, a reduction in both gifts and the value of expected inheritance wealth by the middle-aged adults would occur.

The forms of financial help within the family are mostly interdependent on each other. Therefore, the pivot-generation members would be exposed to a double disadvantage, receiving less financial help from their elderly parents and at the same time having to provide more financial resources to support them. If the pivot-generation members are to maintain their standard of living, they must, in turn, give less to their own adult children. Therefore, a reduction in the value of retirement pensions not only results in a reduction in the proportion of the pivot generation which would receive such transfers, but also leads to a decrease among the younger-generation members as well.

These younger-generation members would be deprived twofold of financial help, from both their parents and their grandparents. The net expected effect of the underlying process would be that, in wanting to address the increasing costs of supporting ageing populations, the economic consequences that follow would have a direct negative effect upon private transfers of wealth for subsequent generations.

The preceding analyses of familial supports mainly dealt with the factors influencing quantitative variations in the amount of public benefits or private sources of help. It did not take into account the consequences of state intervention for the structure of kinship relations, or qualitative changes in kinship relations. Examining societies where systems of social protection are currently being introduced therefore provides an ideal setting to explore the dynamic nature of the process of private and public transfers and brings to the fore its complementary, as shown by the case study of Guadeloupe.

The case of Guadeloupe[8]

Guadeloupe can be seen as a unique 'laboratory' in which to understand the effects of social policy upon the family in at least two important ways. As a society noted for its significant economic and social growth during the past two decades, it represents a unique historical moment characterised by the coexistence of both traditional and modern forms of economic, social and family life. At the same time, like other French overseas territories, Guadeloupe provides an example of a generous welfare state in a rapidly transforming society. Guadeloupe is an island in the eastern Caribbean with a population of about 420,000, and is a part of French territory. The study undertaken combines both qualitative and quantitative research (Attias-Donfut and Lapierre 1997).

The qualitative research concerns thirty lineages of three generations with the intermediate generation belonging to a cohort aged between 49 and 53 years, together with their elderly parents and their adult children, selected among the lower middle classes (non-professionals) that were receiving some form of social allowance (e.g. housing and family allowances, and/or un-employment-related benefits). The families are representative of the largest part of the population in Guadeloupe, since professionals and higher social classes represent a minority in the total population. Semi-structured interviews, together with a quantitative study of almost 360 members of the intermediate generation aged 49–53, have demonstrated the way in which private and public help is given and negotiated. Analyses of each of the three generations studied allows examination of a range of first-hand experiences. These life experiences correspond with the respective periods of transition to different forms of social protection in Guadeloupean society.

The history of the lives of older people in Guadeloupe reflects the recent past where people lived in large families in rural settings, and where the poor were engaged in self-sufficient modes of production. Even though children attended school, they still contributed at a very early age to domestic and agricultural labour until at least the 1950s, and therefore they represented an important economic resource to families. Older people had a strong hierarchical position and the respect of elders still remains the norm. They have led a long working life and in old age are supported by the family. In rural societies, such as the traditional and poorest parts of Guadeloupe, the seniority principle inherited from African culture is still in place. Older people today have lived through these conditions and they are sources of knowledge through which cultures of solidarity and resilience to poverty are transmitted to younger generations.

The introduction of social protection schemes has, however, led to significant transformations in Guadeloupean society, transformations which have occurred parallel to its modernisation and the decline in the agricultural-based economy. Two types of state benefits have had a decisive impact on families, namely the introduction of retirement pensions, on the one hand, and, on the other, benefits for children and young people through family allowances and grants for education. Because older people who have retired from paid employment now have free time and modest but sufficient pensions, they have begun to give both practical and financial help to their children and grandchildren. For example, whilst older people received little support from their parents when they were child-rearing, they are now able to give time to caring for their grandchildren. Above all, because they now have retirement pensions, older people no longer receive economic assistance from their adult children or grandchildren, but are able to give such help to them. Retirement pensions have therefore significantly contributed to reversing the directional flow of solidarity.

At the other end of the scale, the status of 'children as resources' has now been transformed to that of 'project children' (children as investments), because of the introduction of family allowances. Schooling and further education is financed through these allowances, and parents now invest in the education of their children in the hope that their children's future social mobility will benefit the wider family. In poor families, every family member that is offered substantial help is expected to reciprocate in a compensatory way, whether this is by domestic help, participation in the subsistence economy, or by bringing a wage into the household. When family allowances are provided for a child, families become more responsible for their child's welfare by investing in education. By investing in human capital, new visions of the future are created and families can now enlarge their time horizon. This investment is also encouraged by the fact that parents, during their working life, now anticipate a retirement pension which contributes to this enlargement of their perspective of time.

Consequently, the main direction of family solidarity has switched from the older person who is 'provided for', to the older person who 'provides', and from the child seen as a resource to the child seen as an investment for the future. The efforts of the family group are no longer directed mainly towards the elders, as was the case up until recently, but towards the young, as witnessed in Guadeloupe by a dramatic rise in the level of children's education within the last decade.

At the same time, the way in which the family group functions economically and through solidarities, is also experiencing change. In economies where survival is the main issue, solidarity is focused on meeting basic needs, the sharing of a roof and securing food. Such an economy operates only within the confines of the domestic household and immediate neighbourhood. The increase in financial resources that results from paid labour or social protection, together with an increase in free time, allows the domain of solidarities to encompass improvements in the quality of life. These improvements occur because of a wide variety of services given and received which extend beyond those that are the basic necessities. Improvements in the standard of living also result in the operation of 'solidarities at a distance', with the domain of solidarities no longer restricted to the same household or immediate neighbourhood. As the system of exchanges is enriched and extended in space, a reduced number of members are selected to participate in the giving and receiving of support. Whereas the solidarities of survival and proximity concern the extended family, solidarities of life-styles and 'at a distance' are confined to a limited number of potential family networks that are restricted and mainly characterised by direct lines of descent.

To conclude this discussion of Guadeloupe, it is important to emphasise that the impact of social benefits is not confined solely to supplementing existing resources. For the beneficiaries, they fundamentally add a further dimension to the sense of temporal and future time. As pointed out by Kohli (1986), social protection predetermines the life course by the institutionalisation and the temporalisation of social life. The effect of retirement on individuals is not confined simply to the period in which it is experienced. The anticipation of retirement has an effect upon the behaviour and life choices made by individuals throughout their life course. The same applies to public aid for schooling and further education of children. In situations of poverty, individuals are preoccupied with surviving on a day-to-day basis and they are confined to the present moment. The introduction of social protection schemes offers a future and transforms attitudes towards time, which is not necessarily the case if welfare is targeted only at the most destitute for a short period of time.

Finally, it should be noted that in Guadeloupe the passage from a rural to modern economy has neither fragmented family relations nor destroyed the ties between generations, as happened in Europe during the nineteenth century among poor working-class families. Segalen (1995) has shown how historically in France kinship relations experienced discontinuities. After the dispersion of families caused by migration towards towns and the ensuing urban squalor, families were reconstituted when the condition of the working-classes improved, a process which was largely brought about by the advent of retirement pensions.

The dynamics of inequalities and transfers

The preceding analyses allow us to draw an accurate picture of underlying macro-social process. The two forms of public and private transfers are shown to be complementary, but their direction and importance are mainly determined by the extent of inequalities between the generations. At the same time, the two forms of transfers deeply influence and transform these existing inequalities. We shall now restate the effects of transfers upon inequalities both within and between the generations in France, and then conclude with an interpretation of the processes involved.

Effects upon intergenerational inequalities

It is often stated that retired people today are seen as too rich and their presence is considered to be too costly for public finances to bear. But the common dichotomy of active versus inactive individuals, and the three age groups defined by childhood, middle-aged working and retirement provide an inaccurate division of the population. The situation in France is described by Hourriez and Legris (1995) who show that households whose members are aged under 40 years have lower standards of living than older households and that their overall situation has deteriorated in the last two decades. This contrasts with the current cohort of adults aged between 40 and 70 years who have the highest standards of living, whilst very old people, the majority of whom are widows, have low levels of income.

These intergenerational inequalities result in an overlapping of two phenomena, as pointed out by Baudelot and Gollac (1997). On the one hand, there exists the evolution of patterns of income throughout the life course which is common to members of the same age cohort. On the other hand, successive cohorts experience different economic climates so that each cohort does not have the same chance of achieving prosperity. These two phenomena occur simultaneously and are difficult to distinguish. Throughout the most recent period of economic growth, both career progression and levels of incomes have followed an upward pattern. However, in the current period of economic recession and high unemployment, the pattern of the life course is more chaotic and no longer follows the more traditional model of income and occupational careers improving with age. The two effects, namely the pattern of the life course and cohort effects, are mutually reinforcing and result in greater perceived differences between age groups (Baudelot and Gollac 1997). Private financial transfers operate in favour of elderly people in poor health and with low incomes. Among the elderly, family support and professional

61

services differ according to social class. In higher social classes, older people in need of support can turn more easily to the private sector whilst public support tends mostly to be targeted towards lower social class groups (Renaut and Rozenkier 1995). Transfers organised by the state are mainly means-tested and tend to be directed towards very old people, the latter recipients being mostly widows with low incomes. Family supports in the form of co-residence, cash gifts and the provision of informal care also tend to benefit the poorest and most vulnerable sectors of the older population, since each one of these forms of support decreases in volume when the income of older parents is high. This support results in an improvement of the standard of living of the poorest elderly which therefore contributes towards reducing inequalities.[9]

Effects upon intra-generational inequalities

Although the existence of inheritance wealth undoubtedly accentuates inequalities between members of a generation, the hypothesis that the same effect would apply to *inter vivos* transfers is not supported by research data. The effects of private transfers upon intra-generational inequalities have to be considered at the level of each specific generation. Two processes lead to a reduction of social inequalities among the elderly population. On the one hand, poorer elders receive cash or in-kind support from their mid-life children conditional on the level of income of the care-givers, and this supplements professional help. On the other hand, richer elders provide money in the form of an anticipated transmission of wealth to their children and also in the form of occasional cash gifts both to children and grand-children. The conjunction of these two phenomena overwhelmingly leads to a readjustment of standards of living within the grandparent generation, the poorer being relatively richer after the receipt of upstream transfers and the richer being relatively poorer after their downward transmissions.

The varying circumstances faced by young adults make it difficult to assess the degree of inequalities of income among young adults at a given moment in time. Several factors influence these inequalities, such as different levels of income among those who are working, differences in employment status between those who work and those who are unemployed, and the unequal stages of the transition to adulthood between those who are still in higher education, those who have just finished their education, and those who finished long ago. An assessment of the distribution of public and private forms of support and their effect upon the incomes of young adults needs to take into account all these factors and should be treated with caution.

Two reinforcing redistributive transfers are brought into play. First, it has been shown that public allowances benefit less well-off adult children. Second, we have demonstrated that private support in the form of financial gifts is also directed towards poorer adult children and tends to complement public assistance. Therefore, the two interwoven forms of redistribution should reduce inequalities among young adults, even if the compensatory impact is a short-term reduction in inequalities. We now provide empirical evidence from the three-generational data in order to test our hypothesis.

The approach that we have taken consists of comparing differences in current income according to its three main components, namely income from paid employment, from public transfers, and from private support in the form of financial gifts and loans. As our balance-sheet of private transfers only deals with money from parents, our results provide an underestimate of the impact of family support upon intra-generational inequalities among young adults. Figure 3.1 shows that the most important differences among young adults are in income from paid employment. Leaving aside those in the first decile who receive no income from paid employment, there is an income ratio of 7.8 between the second and tenth (highest) decile. The addition of public transfers to income from paid employment reduces significantly this ratio to 5.6.

The main result lies in the fact that the addition of private support to public transfers and employment income narrows the ratio between the second and tenth decile to 5, whilst the first decile now receives almost 2 per cent of the total income of the younger generation. This narrowing of differences is effective for the whole of the younger generation. The lower half of the

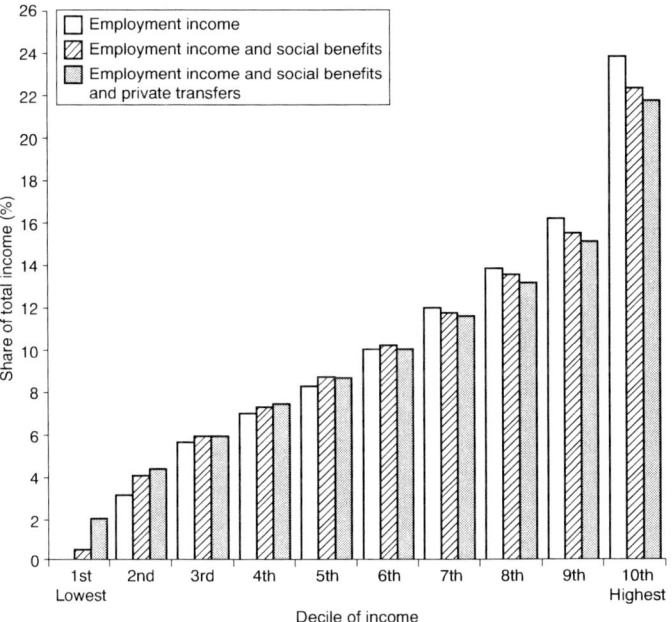

Figure 3.1 Income inequalities among young adults according to sources of income.

income distribution (lower five income deciles) receive 24 per cent of the total income from paid employment. If we add state benefits to paid employment, this proportion increases to 26.5 per cent, and to 28.2 per cent when private transfers are also included. Private transfers therefore result in a small reduction in income differentials among young people, thereby reinforcing the redistributive process of public transfers.

However, the redistributive effect of this financial help needs to be qualified since the least wealthy households only receive small amounts of family financial support, a finding which has also been emphasised by Barry *et al.* (1996). In fact, two different types of support to young adults can be distinguished: 'basic needs' orientated support and support that is concerned primarily with social advancement (Pitrou 1992). The former focuses on the prevention of poverty among recipients and therefore reduces inequalities, while the latter tends to benefit young people who are not in poverty and are starting to become established in adult life.

In fact, although the poorest households do not participate at all in financial transfers, there are certainly crisis periods in the family life-cycle which require other forms of support. In the poorest families, the ascending generations cannot contribute towards alleviating poverty. Here, poverty occurs throughout the generations and, in these cases, public subsidies are of the utmost importance. Whereas some parents can easily make up deficits in their children's income by making regular financial payments to them, this process is much more difficult to realise where children experience long-term poverty. In addition, cash support to the poorest family members has the negative effect of impoverishing those who make such transfers, thereby creating inequalities in the intermediate generation.

The generation of people in their fifties, whilst enjoying standards of living that are higher than both the younger and older generations, is also the generation which shows the most marked inequalities. Richer middle-aged adults are more frequently involved in assistance either to parents or adult children, and conversely poorer pivots cannot rely on the support from their elderly parents. Economic help that the middle generation provides to the two other generations can therefore increase inequalities within that generation in so far as the poorest pivots give a greater proportion of their income than the richest.

Conclusion

In order to fully understand the dynamics of intergenerational exchanges, it has proved essential to analyse both private and public transfers. Such an analysis, as demonstrated here, can be achieved using data from a three-generational study because of the convergence between family and welfare generations. An evaluation of the flow of exchanges using data from households shows that public transfers reshape and sustain family solidarities (such private transfers are 'forgotten' within generational accounting), and that these transfers today benefit subsequent generations. Within the life course, individuals begin by receiving support from their mid-life parents which they in turn indirectly repay in their economically active years through the provision of pensions. During this period they also provide support to their adult children and receive private transfers from their elderly parents who in turn benefit from care as they enter later life.

The complementarity of public and private forms of support has been shown for different categories of transfers. Whether these transfers are for financial help for young adults or care given to the eldest-generation members, the results are the same. In all cases, public benefits increase the recipient's chances of an additional and complementary form of support from members of their family lineage. This pattern is confirmed by a simulation of the variation in levels of public forms of support. If the amount of public benefits directed towards young people is reduced, then parental generosity also reduces. This would have negative consequences for the most needy young adults. If the amount of retirement pensions is reduced, this would directly affect the reciprocal exchanges between older people and their adult children. The latter would give more help to their parents and they in turn would receive less financial support in the form of gifts from their parents. The interdependence of the generations can be clearly seen in this scenario. A reduction in public or private resources for the oldest and youngest generations results, in turn, in a redistributed and weakened flow of transfers across the entire family lineage. As has been shown through macro-social data (see Chapter 1), the old and the young have linked destinies.

The theoretical model used to assess the interaction between private and public support, namely the complementarity *versus* substitution hypotheses, is not able to reveal the profound changes in the quality and structure of inter-generational relations. These changes have been directly observed in the qualitative research undertaken in Guadeloupe. The introduction of a social security system has reshaped the social status of different generations, together with modifying the functions of families and their economic modes of organisation. It has contributed to a reversal in the main direction of the flow of family transfers. Whereas they were previously ascendant, they have now become notably more descendant. The social security system has also played a decisive role in widening the temporal horizons of families. State benefits by their very existence, stimulate or make possible future life plans, for example in relation to educational benefits and retirement pension programmes.

The interaction of public and private *inter vivos* transfers between the generations results in a modest, but real, reduction in social inequalities, inequalities that exist both between the generations and within the youngest and oldest generations. This phenomena can be seen from the analysis of the composition and distribution of incomes within different generations. Help with housing and other types of material transfers, which as we have seen are directed towards those most in need, reinforce the redistributive function of public subsidies. These family dynamics of the generations, in turn, interact with the macro-social processes in two ways.

First, public help and support in the form of financial benefits have a redistributive effect upon households. They also act as an incentive for family solidarities, and families in turn operate a redistribute process within kinship relations. The overall result is an intensification through private transfers of the redistributive effect of public transfers, and in this way a relative reduction of inequalities is achieved. The second process is a result of the heterogeneity of the generations relating to the particular historical moments which have shaped them. Successive cohorts within society have experienced periods of strong or weak economic growth, of prosperity or decline, and as such they exhibit inter-temporal historical inequalities, but at the same time they influence each other. Exchanges between generations make adjustments for the economic prosperity of different historical periods. In the current interactions which are taking place between three or even four generations, those that have accrued the most wealth, which is currently the intermediate generation, appear to circulate their reserve wealth to both the ascending and descending generations. This diffusion serves both to reduce the disparities between the generations and to moderate inequalities among the two most disadvantaged generations, which are young adults and the very old. Whatever the inequalities of people of different ages and from different cohorts in society, diverse age groups are interdependent within families through whom the destinies of different generations are locked together.

Acknowledgements

We are grateful to Jim Ogg for his translation from the French text.

Notes

1 As pointed out by Cox and Jimenez (1995), it seems no longer possible to observe the transformations of private transfers in response to a modification of public assistance in societies where the welfare state has been long established.

2 Results reported by Pezzin et al. (1996) appear especially robust since they are derived from a social experiment. They found that an increase in publicly provided residential care results in a small reduction of care provided to unmarried persons whereas there is no significant reduction for married persons.

3 Some other family contributions should also be taken into account in the analysis, for example the regular support given in the form of household fixtures and fittings, help with the payment of rent, or free housing which occurs when financial help is given to the younger generation to buy their own homes.

4 The composition of the pivot generation's income (whether it is from public or private sources) is not relevant in the econometric equation.

5 The simulation focuses only on a change in state allowances received by adult

children since financial support to children is mainly influenced by the level of wage income of the child.

6 We are aware that such adjustments are likely in long-term policies where changes to the pension system are made due to a lower ratio of active to inactive members of the population, and that it would necessarily result in a decrease in the level of retirement pensions over future years.

7 The simulation only focuses on the frequencies of private support because of the limited available information concerning cash gift values. The results should be interpreted with caution especially on account of the low number of observations in the survey. However, they are highly informative when considering the altered pattern of the circulation of private transfers which results from a decrease in the level of retirement pensions.

8 The effects of social policy upon the family in Guadeloupe reported in this section summarise several conclusions drawn from research undertaken by Attias-Donfut and Lapierre (1997).

9 The frequencies of co-residence and daily domestic help from mid-life children are respectively 29 and 50 per cent when the transfers are directed towards an elderly parent among the least well-off quartile, whilst they are 16 and 37 per cent respectively among the most well-off quartile.

References

Attias-Donfut, C. (1993) 'Dépendance des personnes âgées. Pourvoyance familiale et pourvoyance sociale', *Revue Française des Affaires Sociales* 47: 33–52.

Attias-Donfut, C. and Lapierre, N. (1997) *La Famille Providence. Trois Generations en Guadeloupe*, Paris: La Documentation Française.

Barry, C. de, Eneau, D. and Hourriez, J.M. (1996) 'Les aides financières entre ménages', *Insee Première* 441.

Baudelot, C. and Gollac, M. (1997) 'Le salaire du trentenaire: question d'âge ou de génération?', *Economie et Statistique* 304/305: 601–24.

Bouget, D. and Tartarin, R. (eds) (1990) *Le Prix de la Dépendance*, Paris: La Documentation Française.

Chapell, N. and Blandford, A. (1991) 'Informal and formal care: exploring the complementarity', *Aging and Society* 11: 299–317.

Cox, D. and Jakubson, G. (1995) 'The connection between public transfers and private interfamily transfers', *Journal of Public Economics* 57: 129–67.

Cox, D. and Jimenez, E. (1995) 'Private transfers and the effectiveness of public income redistribution in the Philippines', in D. Van de Walle and K. Nead (eds) *Public Spending and the Poor: Theory and Evidence*, Baltimore: Johns Hopkins University Press.

Daatland, S.O. (1992) 'The public–private mix: the role of families and the public care system in the welfare state', *European Journal of Gerontology* 1: 2–6.

Hagestad, G.O. (1995) 'La négociation de l'aide: jeux croisés entre familles, sexes et politiques sociales', in C. Attias-Donfut (ed.) *Les Solidarités entre Générations. Vieillesse, Familles, Etat*, Paris: Nathan.

Hourriez, J.M. and Legris, B. (1995) 'Le niveau de vie relatif des personnes âgées', *Economie et Statistique* 283/284: 137–58.

Johansonn, L. and Thorslund, M. (1993) 'Importance et limites des ressources formelles', in F. Lesemann and C. Martin (eds) *Les Personnes Agées. Dépendance, Soins et Solidarités Familiales. Comparaisons Internationales*, Paris: La Documentation Française.

Kessler, D., Masson, A. and Pestieau, P. (1991) 'Trois vues sur l'héritage: la famille, la propriété, l'Etat', *Economie et Prévision* 100/101: 1–29.

Kohli, M. (1986) 'Social organisation and subjective construction of the life course', in A.B. Sorensen, F.E. Weinert and L.R. Sherrod (eds) *Human Development and the Life Course. Multidisciplinary Perspectives*, Hillsdale: Erlbaum.

Lampman, R.J. and Smeeding, T.M. (1983) 'Interfamily transfers as alternatives to government transfers to persons', *Review of Income and Wealth* 29: 45–66.

Lesemann, F. and Martin, C. (eds) (1993) *Les Personnes Agées. Dépendance, Soins et Solidarités Familiales. Comparaisons Internationales*, Paris: La Documentation Française.

Paugam, S. and Zoyem, J.P. (1997) 'Le soutien financier de la famille: une forme essentielle de la solidarité', *Economie et Statistique* 308/309/310: 187–210.

Pezzin, L.E., Kemper, P. and Reschovsky, J. (1996) 'Does publicly provided home care substitute for family care? Experimental evidence with endogenous living arrangements', *Journal of Human Resources* 31: 650–76.

Pitrou, A. (1992) *Les Solidarités Familiales. Vivre sans Famille?*, Toulouse: Privat.

Renaut, S. and Rozenkier, A. (1995) 'Les familles à l'épreuve de la dépendance', in C. Attias-Donfut (ed.) *Les Solidarités entre Générations. Vieillesse, Familles, Etat*, Paris: Nathan.

Rosenzweig, M.R. and Wolpin, K.I. (1994) 'Parental and public transfers to young women and their children', *American Economic Review* 84: 1195–212.

Schoeni, R. (1996) 'Does aid to families with dependent children displace familial assistance?', unpublished manuscript, Santa Monica Rand Labor and Population Program.

Segalen, M. (1995) 'Continuités et discontinuités familiales: approche socio-historique du lien intergénérationnel', in C. Attias-Donfut (ed.) *Les Solidarités entre Générations. Vieillesse, Familles, Etat*, Paris: Nathan.

Tennstedt, S.L., Crawford, S.L. and McKinley, J.B. (1993) 'Is family care on the decline? A longitudinal investigation of the substitution of formal long-term care for informal care', *Millbank Quarterly* 71: 601–24.

Twigg, J. (1993) 'The interweaving of formal and informal care: policy models and problems', in A. Evers and G.H. Van der Zanden (eds) *Better Care for Dependent People Living at Home*, Bunnik: Netherlands Institute of Gerontology.

WEALTH DISTRIBUTION
BETWEEN GENERATIONS
A source of conflict
or cohesion?

Lars Gulbrandsen and Åsmund Langsether

Relationship between the generations

During the past two decades, young adults in 'the establishment phase' (i.e. when they are normally undergoing higher education, acquiring their first home and starting a family) in many countries have experienced both growing unemployment and high 'admission prices' to the housing market, whereas old and middle-aged people at the same time have enjoyed the results of good economic conditions and a favourable economic and housing policy. Based on these disparities between age groups in contemporary society, theories have been put forward which suggest that these inequalities provide fertile ground for conflicts between the generations. It is likely that some of the much-used epithets in Norway, such as 'hard-working generation', 'the well-off 50-year-olds' and the less fortunate 'left to do the dishwashing generation', are motivated more by a desire to focus on differences than on actual conflicts over distributional policies between age groups. Age is an important distribution criterion in the modern welfare state since it is the criterion that distinguishes the occupationally active and 'providing' section of the population from the 'provided for' sections. Arguably the most important aspect of the modern welfare state is the construction of a public support system for elderly people.

The hypotheses advanced regarding growing conflict between the generations have focused both on the relationship between middle-aged parents and their children in the establishment phase, and on the relationship between elderly people and their descendants (adult children and grandchildren) in terms of older people's disposition of their accumulated wealth. Attention has, on the one hand, focused on generational inequalities as a basis for conflicts regarding public distribution policy. On the other, the potential for conflict has been linked to generational inequalities within individual families. The question of conflict or absence thereof between generations is not merely a question of the type and extent of economic inequality, but is also a question of the type and nature of transfers between the generations – both in the public and the private sphere – and of attitudes and norms regarding such transfers and inequality.

Economic inequality is one of the main dimensions giving rise to social and political conflict in society. The growing wealth accumulation (particularly of housing wealth) combined with the institution of inheritance, has been pointed to by many as a basis for new class divisions in society (cf. Saunders 1984; Hamnet 1991). Generational conflicts within the framework of the family arise and acquire their form from the existing societal context. Conflicts on the societal level often relate to economic and social policies, which in varying degrees affect some generations more favourably or unfavourably than other generations. Here, redistribution policy, above all the social security system for those without earned income, plays the most crucial role. However, the tax system, housing policy, education support and rules on inheritance tax are also central elements of a distribution policy which benefits people in certain phases of life, and which is normally paid for by people in other life-phases. While such measures may be of a universal nature and be justified by the norm of equality of opportunity for young persons irrespective of their social background, they also allow children to be independent of their parents during the establishment phase – irrespective of whether parents have the financial ability to help their children, e.g. with both housing and education.

In Norway, to date, there has been little conflict in the political arena regarding transfers from the working-age generation to the elderly. In fact there has been more disagreement about support schemes for the occupationally active (e.g. the level of compensation available under health insurance and unemployment insurance schemes and the level of support available under social assistance). The Norwegian social security system enjoys great legitimacy among the population in relation to transfers to the elderly, both in terms of benefit payments and in terms of free/low-priced care services (Øverbye and Eia 1995). As we shall show later, almost half the Norwegian population believe that nursing and care services for elderly people should be absolutely free of charge to users. Only 1 per cent advocate that such services should be fully paid for.

However, important changes in the redistribution policy have taken place during the recent past; changes that alter the significance of the societal and family spheres as arenas for distribution policy. These changes may create complex patterns of conflict between generations. The progressive nature of the tax system has been weakened, housing taxes have been reduced and, at the same time, there has been a reduced subsidy for housing consumption and rising house prices. Compared with the situation in the 1950s and 1960s, the progressive nature of inheritance tax has also been reduced. The socially motivated equalisation policy is being weakened, thereby also weakening equalisation across the life course, which has mainly had disadvantages for the younger generation. These changes have created conflicts in the political arena. However, it must be said that the generational element has been little in evidence in these conflicts, and that the level of conflict during this realignment of policy has been low.

A public policy which increases age-related economic inequality will concurrently increase the potential for private transfers between generations and increase the importance of the family as a potential arena for redistribution. However, the proponents of the 'increasing conflict hypothesis' have questioned the extent to which present and future generations of middle-aged and elderly people are willing to take into account the economic interests of their descendants, and have pointed to the family as an arena for increasing intergenerational conflict.

In a situation where elderly people spend all of their accumulated wealth, the stage could be set for conflicts with potential heirs. But neither great wealth differences between generations nor the unwillingness of middle-aged and elderly people to take their descendants' interests into account, will cause intergenerational conflict if these differences are accepted and enjoy legitimacy in all age groups. Key issues concerning the conflict hypothesis therefore relate both to wealth differences and differences in attitudes, norms, needs and behaviour between generations. Using Norwegian data from our own surveys we will illuminate some of the key issues related to this subject. The chapter mainly addresses the following questions:

1 To what extent and by what means do parents help their children in the establishment phase? Is there any evidence of conflicting attitudes about such assistance held by different age groups?
2 How do people make use of their wealth in old age? What do they leave as inheritance? What attitudes and norms are widespread in the population in relation to inheritance and use of wealth in old age?

Age-related economic inequality

In most countries of Western Europe there is evidence of wide differences in economic resources between different age groups. This applies to income (where those around age 50 are generally the most advantaged), and income in relation to maintenance burden (where the most advantaged are between 50 and retirement age, after their children have left home). In Norway, the middle-aged and older people possess the largest net wealth. These generations have accumulated their wealth through a life-span marked by a favourable economic climate, rising employment and negligible joblessness up to the end of the 1980s. Wealth accumulation in this period was strongly influenced by developments in the housing sector, where three factors are of particular importance: an increase in the proportion of owner-occupiers, a substantial rise in house prices, and an extensive subsidisation of housing – partly through low-interest loans for housing construction and partly through concessionary tax rules. Today, an important part of old people's wealth consists of non-liquid housing capital.

In order to examine the relative income and asset position of different generations in Norway, Table 4.1 shows how various aspects of Norwegian households' income and wealth are associated with age. As is clear from the first row, households' gross occupational income rises until the main household member (defined as the person with the highest income in the household) is aged about 50. Total income, which includes occupational income (row 1), public transfers (row 3) and capital income (row 4), is far more evenly distributed across the age groups, but is still highest in the 45–54 age group. The 67–79 age group receives the highest volume of transfers through the public social security system (row 3), and it also has the highest net capital income. (Net capital income comprises interest on bank deposits and return on other capital, also imputed capital income on the value of the owner-occupier's house. Debt interest is deducted.) Net capital income mainly reflects households' financial wealth. However, up to and including the age group with the highest income (45–54), net capital income and net financial wealth (e.g. bank deposits and shares) are negative (rows 4 and 6). Here, too, sizeable differences are evident among age groups; financial capital, for example, is on average NOK542,000 higher among the oldest than the youngest groups.

All income and financial wealth are, in principle, recorded in the data in Table 4.1 on the basis of households' tax returns. In view of the high share of owner-occupancy (see row 5) and high housing quality, the value of housing constitutes an important part of private wealth. Such wealth is subject to very low assessment for tax purposes in Norway. As a result, Statistics Norway's figures for households' total net wealth in row 7 of the table are unrealistically low, and real differences among age groups are larger than shown in the table. Two methods are available for revising the wealth estimates. One method is based upon information about market prices and tax assessment. Investigations have shown that the taxable value of housing is on average only one quarter of the market values (Gulbrandsen 1994). Row 8 of the table shows the results when the real property values used in row 7 are multiplied by a factor of four to bring the taxable value of real capital into line with market values. The second method, using sample surveys, is to ask people for their estimate of the market value of their housing and recreational property. Row 9 shows the distribution of net wealth based on our own national survey carried out in the autumn of 1995 (Gulbrandsen and Langsether 1997). This yields lower figures than if we multiply the official valuations by four. The revised figures in row 8 are probably more accurate, since people seem to

Table 4.1 Economic indicators by age of main household member, Norway 1995 (all figures (except in row 5) are averages in thousands of kroner)

	25–34	35–44	45–54	55–66	67–79	80+
1 Occupational income	249	334	372	240	24	2
2 Total income (= line 1+3+4)	264	360	399	320	193	115
3 Gross public transfers	32	41	35	69	147	103
4 Net capital income	−17	−15	−8	11	22	10
5 Owner-occupiers	67%	86%	93%	92%	87%	71%
6 Net financial capital	−299	−331	−207	102	272	243
7 Net wealth (Statistics Norway)	−149	−45	153	121	461	323
8 Net wealth (adjusted)	176	595	981	1,163	947	558
9 Net wealth (survey)	171	432	709	794	581	490

Source: (1997) Ukens statistikk, nr 17, Oslo: Statistisk sentralbyrå. This is a sample survey of about 10,000 households in which data are taken from household members' assessed tax returns. These data are linked to data on various forms of governmental transfers, providing highly reliable data on household incomes and financial wealth.
Note: Apart from rows 5 and 9, the figures in the table are taken from Statistics Norway's income and wealth survey from 1995.

understate their bank deposits in an interview situation, resulting in under-estimated financial capital in row 9.[1] But using either measure, the 55–66 age group has the greatest net wealth.

Inheritance and gifts in an historical and theoretical light

Inheritance and gifts are among the oldest institutions in our society. In historical times the giving of gifts was of special importance for transactions between persons and groups outside the realm of the family. Within the lineage/family, a duty of maintenance existed which means that the term 'gift' is inappropriate for the assistance and support that was exchanged among persons and generations in this sphere. Gifts were important both in political and social contexts, as an alliance-building element between ruling families, and between princes and subjects; in the building and maintenance of friendly relations; upon marriage (dowry, morning gift); and on ritual occasions. This giving of gifts was strongly controlled by principles of reciprocity (cf. Mauss 1969).

The institution of inheritance has played an equally central role in political, social, economic and kinship contexts. Both in the Germanic law tradition, where the right of inheritance and succession 'follows the blood', and the Roman law tradition, where testatory freedom was usual, the institution of inheritance has played a central role for the cohesion between, and wealth accumulation over, generations – and consequently for the establishment and maintenance of social classes and inequality in society.

Inheritance law

The Norwegian inheritance law bears the stamp of the Germanic inheritance tradition in which inheritance and advancement of inheritance are distributed to heirs based on the closeness of their kinship with the testator. The testatory freedom is strongly limited. Lineal descendants (i.e. children, grandchildren and so forth) have an unconditional right to receive two-thirds of the total estate of the deceased. Inheritance is, in principle, shared equally among the lineal descendants. If the testator has not made a will, and is not survived by a spouse, the lineal descendants receive the entire inheritance. A surviving spouse inherits one-quarter of the testator's estate when there are lineal descendants, one-half when there are heirs in the second class of heirs (testator's parents and the testator's children), and the entire estate when only more distant relatives of the testator exist. Under Norwegian inheritance law the surviving spouse also has the right to retain undivided possession of the estate, which is exercised in the great majority of cases.

Gifts to lineal descendants are regarded as advancement of inheritance, and are included when state inheritance tax is assessed. The tax is lower for lineal descendants than for other beneficiaries, and it increases with the size of the inheritance. Over the past 50 years, inheritance tax has been lowered, both through increases in tax-free amounts and lower progressive tax rates (Bliksvær 1996).[2]

Our surveys show that very few wills are drawn up in Norway compared with, say, the USA (according to our own survey only 7 per cent of Norwegian households in 1995). This is probably related to the difference in the inheritance law between the two countries and traditions of inheritance rights, but also to the longstanding Norwegian tradition of relatively independent farmers with allodial rights to farm property (the right of the first-born child to buy at a reasonable price). Drawing up of wills, as expected, increases with age and is most common among people without lineal descendants. But only among the over-80s without lineal descendants do a majority report having drawn up a will. We interpret the Norwegian modest recourse to wills as representing a high level of legitimacy of the law's rules on distribution of inheritance.

Motives for saving

Over recent years, particularly among economists, the so-called 'life-cycle hypothesis' for consumption and saving, launched by Modigliani and Brumberg (1954), has occupied centre stage in terms of understanding inheritance and wealth transactions between generations in modern capitalist, Western societies. This theory implies that people save during their economically active years with a view to equalising consumption over their lifetime.

In its 'pure' version this theory stipulates that inheritance-motivated saving does not occur, and that people consume their accumulated wealth in old age. If people leave an inheritance, it is because they 'miscalculate' how long they will live. Revised versions of this theory open the way for inheritance as a result of older people being more risk-averse than younger people, and possibly more likely to retain a larger volume of wealth than younger persons for prudential reasons, and it allows for saving motivated by altruism (Kotlikoff 1988; Modigliani 1988).

If the life-cycle theory in its narrow version was valid and elderly people used up their accumulated wealth, the stage could be set for conflict with potential heirs if the latter did not accept such behaviour. However, there is reason to consider what economic mechanisms, particularly what forms of house ownership, would make such spending possible – especially because significant parts of the wealth to be consumed would be in the form of an owner-occupied house.

The many studies of old peoples' asset management have not shown that elderly people in fact consume assets on any large scale, even in countries where the social security system is less well developed than in Western Europe. The life-cycle theory, with its focus on the individual and its behavioural assumptions, appears to take too little account of fundamental norms with regard to assistance and support between generations, the close relationship between the right of inheritance and private property rights (Knoph 1959) and of the motivation to save in more general terms. The life-cycle theory does not explain why people continue to save after becoming rich and have more than they manage to consume, or why older people save when they have no lineal descendants. Another factor is older people's ability to spend accumulated wealth (good health is needed in order to accomplish this), and their willingness to sell a house or recreational property which they have built themselves, or which the family has owned for several generations.

Using data for Norway in the 1990s, we examine behaviour and attitudes relating to assistance, support and inheritance transfers between current generations. These data are not suited to undertaking any form of complete testing, either of the life-cycle hypothesis or other theories about such transfers. Neither can these data say much about changes over time. However, by giving information about wealth differences and behaviour and attitudes relating to a wide range of transfers between current generations, they provide a good basis for discussing the question of intergenerational conflict.

Inheritance and gift transactions – data and analysis

In the past decade we have carried out several surveys of inheritance and gift transactions (Langsether 1993; Gulbrandsen 1996). These surveys form part of larger surveys of Norwegian households' economic conditions and behaviour in economic contexts. They were carried out because inheritance and gift transactions had previously been very poorly covered both in official statistics and in earlier surveys. However, surveys are a weak method of producing relevant, reliable data on inheritance and gifts. In the first place it is difficult to communicate to interviewees what it is we are looking for, and people may find it difficult both to remember and estimate values. Reliable data over time are particularly problematic and it is virtually impossible in an ordinary survey to elicit information both about (and from) the donor and the beneficiary relating to the same transaction. With these limitations in mind we now turn to some of our main findings with regard to assistance, support, inheritance and gift transactions between generations in present-day Norway.[3]

Who are the beneficiaries and who are the donors?

In a survey from 1990 we attempted to identify the *beneficiaries* of inheritances, gifts and unpaid assistance and support, and the volume (expressed in value estimates) of such transactions. The interviewees were asked to confine themselves to transactions that had taken place over the five years prior to the survey. Our data shows that the value of transfers received totalled about NOK42,000 per household over the preceding five-year period (and averaged NOK114,400 for each receiving household). Eighty-eight per cent of this figure was reported to have been given by parents and/or parents-in-law and 12 per cent by adult children to their parents and/or other private sources.

Although we make allowance for the fact that receipts of unpaid services, free housing, etc., are underestimated in this survey (this is especially the case for elderly persons' receipts of such services from their own adult children, cf. Lingsom 1985), our data shows that, apart from transfers between people with mutual maintenance responsibility, transfers in the private sphere, measured in monetary values, are mainly *transfers between parents and adult children*. Moreover, when receipt of inheritance is included, the flow of values from the parental generation to their adult children far exceeds the flow in the opposite direction (Langsether 1993).

This pattern of transfers is shown in Table 4.2, where the average value of *received* transfers and the percentage who have received transfers in the last five years are shown by the *beneficiary's* age, and Table 4.3, which shows the average value of *given* transfers (including assistance, support and advancement of inheritance, but not inheritance left) and the percentage who have made transfers, by the *donor's* age.

Table 4.2 shows that it is usually young persons in the establishment phase who receive transfers, but that the value of transfers received by young persons is smaller than transfers received later in life. The biggest transfers are received by people in their 40s and 50s – the period in life in which people usually receive both advancement of inheritance (around age 40) and inheritance (average age upon receipt of inheritance is just over 50). Only 12 per cent of the oldest interviewees report having received any form of transfer over the

Table 4.2 Beneficiaries: (a) average value of inheritance/gifts/support received by interviewee's household over preceding five-year period; and (b) the percentage of households in receipt of transfers, by interviewee's age (average values in thousands of kroner)

Transfers received	16–29*	30–39	40–49	50–66	67+	Total
(a) Average amount received by recipient households	73	102	192	129	61	114
(b) Percentage of households in receipt of transfers	50%	44%	39%	31%	12%	37%
n =	368	445	325	401	257	1,796

Source: Our own survey 1990.
* Children living at home in parental households in this age group are not included.

past five years. While we have reason to believe that this figure is on the low side, it does not alter the fact that elderly people both receive transfers less often and, on average, of less value than those persons in other life-phases.

Table 4.3 shows that the over-50s are the most likely to be donors, with the greatest frequency of such gifts from people aged 50 to 66. Transfers to one's own children appear to play an important role, both in the form of transfers from parents in the age range 40–60 (establishment support), and advancement of inheritance, which we assume constitutes the bulk of transfers from people over age 67. People in this oldest age group make the biggest transfers in value terms.

Table 4.3 Donors: (a) average value of advancement of inheritance, gifts and support provided from the interviewee's own household to persons outside the household in the last five-year period; (b) the share of households that have made such transfers; and (c) the share of households that have made transfers to their own children, by age of interviewee (average values in thousands of kroner)

Transfers received	16–29*	30–39	40–49	50–66	67+	Total
(a) Average value for households that have made transfers	10	11	84	54	133	62
(b) Proportion of all households that have made transfers	15%	12%	22%	40%	29%	23%
(c) Proportion of households that have made transfers to their own children	—	4%	13%	38%	27%	16%
n =	368	445	325	401	257	1,796

Source: Our own survey 1990.
* Children living at home in parental households in this age group are not included.

Parental support for young adults

In a 1993 survey we asked about various aspects of parental assistance and financial support to their children during the establishment phase. We focused on support for education, assistance in starting a home, allowing adult children to live at home free of charge and providing surety for loans. The following analyses are based, first, on information from parents (parents with at least one child over the age of 20 who had left home) about gifts/transfers made to their children after reaching the age of 20, and second, on information from young persons on what gifts/transfers they had received from their parents after reaching the age of 20. Table 4.4 shows gifts/transfers made by parents under the age of 65 and Table 4.5 shows gifts/transfers received by young persons in the age range 20–29. These tables illuminate the situation for Norwegian young persons today in the establishment phase and the behaviour of their parents' generation.

Table 4.4 shows that eight out of ten parents have given their child(ren) one or more form of establishment support, 49 per cent have allowed adult children over 20 to live at home free or cheaply (usually in connection with education), 43 per cent have given one or more children direct financial support for education and 19 per cent for home establishment. Sixty-three per

Table 4.4 Percentage of parents who gave various forms of establishment support to their children over age 20

Purpose/type of financial assistance	Percentage who have given such support
1 Direct financial support for education	43
2 Direct financial support for home establishment	19
3 Direct financial support for 'other purposes'	21
4 Surety (for children or grandchildren)	20
5 Free or cheap living at home	49
6 Combinations of types of financial support:	
● Direct financial support for home establishment, education or 'other purpose'	56
● Financial assistance in general; at least one of the five purposes	80
● At least two of the five purposes	45
● At least three of the five purposes	18
● Financial support or living at home during education	63
● Direct financial support or living at home	75
● Covered most or all costs connected with at least one purpose	19
n =	(544)

Source: Løwe (1995).

cent have given some form of support during education. Education appears to be the reason which most often triggers support from parents. This is confirmed by information from young persons about transfers made to them. It should also be noted that 19 per cent of parents aged below 65 assert that they have met 'most or all' of the expenses incurred in at least one establishment purpose. In this survey the interviewees were not asked about the value of the transfers, but whether they covered 'some', 'most' or 'all' of the costs of the establishment purpose in question (Løwe 1995).

Table 4.5 shows transfers reported by children aged 20–29. Fewer children in the establishment phase report having received transfers than is indicated by the parental generation's information on its gifts/transfers. Thirty-seven per cent of all children report having received direct financial support (so far) in the establishment phase. Support for education and home establishment are the dominant purposes. Forty-one per cent report having received transfers when free/cheap living at home is included. This is likely to be too low an estimate of the proportion who received transfers during the entire establishment phase, since the youngest (age 20) have only just entered this phase. However, more frequent transfers appear to be noted if parents are asked whether they have made transfers to their adult children than if adult children are asked whether they have ever received transfers from their parents.

Table 4.5 Receipt of support by young persons aged 20–29: (a) percentage who have received a house/plot, advancement on inheritance or support for education; and (b) percentage who have received various forms of support during their education*

All young persons	Percentage who have received support
(a) Received house/plot or advancement on inheritance/gifts	28
● also received education support	37
● also free/cheap living at home	41
n =	(493)
(b) Young persons undergoing education:	
Received support for accommodation and living expenses	24
Received support for tuition fees/materials	28
Lived at home free or cheaply	31
Received interest-free or low-interest loan for education	11
Received support in one of the above forms	55
Received any support, apart from living at home free	
or cheaply	41
n =	(326)

Source: Løwe (1995).
* Note that these estimates are calculated for young persons still in the establishment phase.

Analyses of this material by Løwe (1995) provide further information about the characteristics of parental support for young adults:

- Parents with high income and high capital wealth (income and capital in the top decile) provide financial support in various forms more often than other parents. Capital wealth is of particular significance for the support of home establishment.
- Parents who have themselves received an inheritance and/or gifts are more likely to make similar transfers to their children. Their own education, attitude to supporting children in the establishment phase and their number of children (having only one child increases the propensity to give) have a positive impact both on the propensity to provide support for educational purposes, and to the provision of direct financial support regardless of purpose.
- Providing surety for one's own child's loan is a form of support that is independent of parental income and wealth.
- Young persons in the establishment phase who are on a low income, are jobless or caring for small children do *not* receive support more often than other young persons, even after controlling for their parent's educational level.
- Young persons are more likely to receive support if they are pursuing studies, and markedly more support is provided if their parents have a high level of education.

The volume of support to young persons undergoing education (including support inherent in living free/cheaply at home) suggests a distribution in favour of children who undergo higher education. In general, the combination of universal public funding of educational studies, and the fact that highly educated parents provide financial support to their children more often than other parents, means that children of highly educated (and usually well-off) parents undergoing education are the best placed, as they usually enjoy financial support both from the state and from their parents.

Viewed against the background of state support and credit schemes developed in the post-war period, it is relevant to examine whether, and how, parental support has changed over time. Based on information from parents and their practice of giving financial support, it has become somewhat less common since the 1980s to help one's children with their first home establishment. This is interesting, for one thing because it coincides with the lifting of previous restrictions on the credit market, removal of price regulation on co-operative housing, fewer housing starts and wide fluctuations in – but in the long term, rising – house prices. There also appears to have been a growing tendency to allow children to live at home cheaply or free for longer periods, but this increase levelled off in the 1990s.

Just over 40 per cent of parents who had children around the age of 20, both in the 1950s and in subsequent decades, report having given financial support towards their children's education. Since the percentage undergoing education was previously far lower, it follows that those studying in the 1950s and 1960s were more likely to receive parental support for education. This is only partly confirmed by data regarding the support the interviewee him/herself received during education after the age of 20. Up to the mid-1980s the percentage that received financial support for education fell, but has risen since then. In the 1990s, 48 per cent of young persons undergoing education report that they receive financial support from their parents, and 18 per cent say that most or all their study costs are met by this means. The tendency to live at home, without paying the full cost involved while undergoing higher education, has been growing since the 1950s, and appears to have settled at a high level by the end of the 1980s, according to interviewees' information about their own receipt of transfers and support. Our data also show that young persons already living at home are now more likely to continue to do so free of charge.

Asset management

So far in this chapter we have sought to illuminate the scope of transfers in the form of establishment assistance, advancement of inheritance and inheritance. In this section we take a more general look at people's saving and asset management – especially old people's saving and motivation for saving, their attitudes to consuming accumulated assets and their attitudes to leaving an inheritance.

Table 4.1 showed that net financial capital grows steeply with increasing age up to the age group 67–79, with a somewhat lower (but still very high) level among the over-80s. This age distribution of wealth is the outcome of the interplay between life-phase and generational differences for the actual generations. Mention was previously made of Modigliani's and Brumberg's life-cycle hypothesis, and it is pertinent in that connection to ask to what extent older people deplete their assets after retiring from paid employment. To the extent that they do so, do they deplete only financial assets (savings) or also real assets (mainly residential property)? What attitudes do people have to depleting their assets in old age?

Two questions in our survey from 1995 provide some basis for answering these questions. First, a general question on households' financial situation. The question has five fixed-reply categories and the percentage of respondents choosing each alternative is indicated:

- 5% 'Money/income were insufficient'.
- 4% 'Must use some of my/our savings to manage'.
- 43% 'Just manage on my/our present income'.
- 39% 'Manage so well that I/we can save a little'.
- 7% 'Manage so well that I/we can save a lot'.

We assume that those who choose one of the last three alternatives are not depleting their financial assets. As shown in the first row of Table 4.6, this is roughly the case for nine out of ten in all age groups. Among pensioners this category breaks down into approximately equal groups of those who say they just manage and those who say they manage so well that they are able to save.

The answers to another question about saving are shown in the second and third rows of Table 4.6. The percentage answering that they actually save is shown in row 2, and is clearly larger than the percentage that – to the first question – replied that they were able to save. Those who saved were asked an additional question on how much they were likely to save in the current year, and a number reported 'nothing' (characterised as 'zero savers'). The third row in Table 4.6 shows the percentage of active savers within various age groups after excluding the 'zero savers'. Caution should be shown when interpreting the figures in Table 4.6. Their accuracy depends, among other things, on whether people view mortgage repayments as saving. If they do not, the percentage that save are underestimated while, on the other hand, if taking out a mortgage is not viewed as dissaving, the percentage reported as saving will be overestimated. However, these issues are of little importance for elderly people since few of them hold loans (cf. Gulbrandsen and Langsether 1997). The life-cycle hypothesis receives little support in this survey data. Nine out of ten pensioner households do not deplete their financial assets, while well over one-half reply that they increase their assets through saving.

Pensioners usually highlight two motives for saving: half of those who save say that they do so in order to secure their own future or to have money available for unforeseen expenses. However, one in four pensioners state that they save in order to secure their children's or grandchildren's future. Moreover, this is the only motive mentioned more often by the elderly than by middle-aged and younger people.

There is a reasonably good match between elderly people's views on depleting their assets and their own management of their assets, although the number who could conceive depleting their assets appears to exceed those

Table 4.6 Percentage who say they do not deplete their financial assets, and percentage engaged in saving by age group

	25–34	35–44	45–54	55–66	67–79	80+	Total
% not depleting financial assets	90	90	94	92	88	89	91
% who report saving	58	65	75	80	76	76	70
% who report saving excluding 'zero savers'	50	57	69	69	56	59	58

Source: Our own survey 1995.

who actually do so. Table 4.7 shows the age distribution on the following question: 'If you think about old age, could you see yourself spending your savings on yourself?' This question is probably perceived as relating to spending financial assets (money in the bank), rather than residential assets. Among pensioners, aged over 66, a majority either would not do so, or would only use a small portion of their assets. Perceived readiness to spend savings in one's old age is an attitude usually found among young persons, and clearly declines with increasing age. Whether this difference is due to age or is a difference between generations cannot be answered by our study.

A large proportion of Norwegian households' assets are tied up in residential property, therefore we asked people for their views on using part of their residential assets. Almost one-half, 44 per cent, would not deplete such assets, while the other alternatives we presented received little support. Fourteen per cent could conceive of freeing-up equity by buying a smaller dwelling, 10 per cent could conceive of borrowing against a mortgage on the house, only 3 per cent could conceive of selling and becoming tenants, and the same low percentage could conceive of selling their dwelling to a financial institution subject to being able to continue to live there. There was no difference among age groups as regards leaving residential assets intact. Buying a smaller dwelling had twice as many adherents among those between 45 and 79 years as among the under-45s and over-79s. However, 10 per cent of the pensioners had moved house during the last five years, and 20 per cent had moved after the age of 66. One in five of those who moved house switched from owner-occupancy to rental tenancy resulting in the release of residential capital. Half moved from one owner-occupied home to another – with the freeing-up of residential capital as a possible consequence. However, the freeing-up of residential capital does not necessarily entail increased consumption since such capital may be placed in a bank deposit or transferred to descendants.

Table 4.7 Attitude to depleting assets in old age by age of interviewee (column percentages)

	25–34	35–44	45–54	55–66	67–79	80+	Total
Use nothing	6	6	7	12	13	18	8
Use a little	28	38	43	38	46	48	37
Use more than half	30	21	19	19	15	17	22
Use most	29	27	27	23	18	11	25
Don't know	6	8	5	9	8	6	7
n =	100%	100%	100%	100%	100%	100%	100%
	(656)	(602)	(434)	(387)	(356)	(71)	(2725)

Source: Our own survey 1995.

Table 4.8 Perceptions of the importance of leaving wealth in the form of inheritance, by age of interviewee (column percentages)

	25–34	35–44	45–54	55–66	67–79	80+	Total
Very important	14	13	9	13	14	16	13
Somewhat important	25	25	30	36	39	37	30
Less important	23	26	28	30	24	28	25
No importance	18	18	22	18	19	17	14
Unanswered/ don't know	20	18	11	3	3	3	14
n =	100% (656)	100% (602)	100% (434)	100% (387)	100% (356)	100% (71)	100% (2725)

Source: Our own survey 1995.

A necessary consequence of old people's unwillingness to deplete their wealth is the leaving of an inheritance to descendants. Table 4.8 shows how perceptions of the importance of leaving an inheritance are distributed among various age groups. Just under one half of those interviewed considered it important to leave an inheritance to their heirs, while an almost equally large proportion consider this to be of less importance. It may be noted that while older people have a greater tendency than younger people to attach importance to leaving an inheritance, there is no difference in perceptions between those who have lineal descendants and those who do not. This is a rather unexpected finding. For the latter group it seems reasonable to assume a strong altruistic attitude in this respect.

A well-developed welfare state where older people are not required to deplete their financial assets in order to obtain care and nursing services, and where social security benefits/pensions make it possible for most people to maintain their earlier housing consumption as pensioners, has clear-cut consequences for how much inheritance older people will leave to the benefit of their potential heirs. This system, however, presupposes higher taxes to meet the required costs. Young and middle-aged taxpayers, especially people who do not expect to receive a large inheritance, may be thought to prefer lower taxes rather than public services free of charge to users. We have attempted to ascertain whether different perceptions of governmental responsibility for financing care and nursing services provide a basis for generational conflict in this field. We asked people to take a position on four alternative forms of user-payment for care and nursing services. Almost half the interviewees (42 per cent) agreed that such services should be free of charge to users, and be paid entirely from public budgets. Twenty-two per cent believed that people should pay a user-charge, 33 per cent favoured income-testing, i.e. that the size of the user-charge should vary with the means at people's disposal, while only 1 per cent considered that people should pay the entire cost of such services. The most generous perceptions in favour of public services free of charge to elderly users are to be found among the youngest.

Conclusions

There are substantial financial inequalities between generations in Norway today, and these inequalities have been the subject of speculation and predictions of increased generational conflict. However, we find little, if any, trace of such conflicts. The fact that the oldest people do not deplete their wealth (a significant portion of their wealth is, moreover, tied up in housing), reduces the likelihood of a possible conflict based on fear among their coming heirs that the older generation will squander their wealth, and their heirs' inheritance. Elderly people probably reduce their saving upon retirement, but they do not stop saving.

We have also shown sizeable voluntary transfers between generations, especially in the form of support for children at the establishment stage. Moreover, the extended support provided to children by the parental generation, after the parents no longer have any legal responsibility for providing for them, gives little support to notions of generational conflict. From a lifetime perspective such support appears to be far more encompassing and to benefit a far greater number of people than advancements of inheritance.

Our data indicate that different generations hold remarkably similar attitudes, whether we consider the significance of leaving an inheritance or parents' obligations towards their own children in the establishment phase. However, when it comes to the willingness to deplete accumulated wealth in old age, young people are more in favour of depletion than older people, but also more in favour of state welfare benefits that will make such depletion less likely.

A well-developed pension system, and care and nursing services which are cheap for the users, means that most pensioners do not need to deplete their financial assets; these important elements of a well-developed welfare state also enable older people to retain their dwellings. Another contributory factor is the very modest taxation of the housing stock. With such a well-developed welfare state – and these arrangements enjoy great legitimacy among all age groups – there must necessarily be a close link between welfare state measures for elderly people and the inheritance that falls to the heirs. Formulation of government policy with reference to the interests of the respective age groups could be a viable approach here.

Younger and middle-aged persons might be expected to prefer lower taxes rather than have to contribute to old people's asset accumulation. On the other hand, paying tax could also be seen as an insurance premium for receiving an inheritance in middle age. Without care services that are strongly subsidised by the state, so that elderly people's assets remain intact, a large number of future heirs would risk losing all inheritance if their parents were to need nursing care, and were compelled to pay for it themselves. However, in such situations one might expect intergenerational alliances within families against the state authorities in order to secure the provision of inheritance rather than intergenerational conflict across families.

The transfer patterns between generations that our studies have brought to light do not provide a basis for generational conflict. In the period ahead they may, however, in combination with universal transfer and assistance schemes, amplify and maintain economic and social inequality both within and between the generations. This is especially likely in the context of the current trend towards growing, but increasingly skewed distribution of, prosperity among private households.

Notes

1 In addition to the fact that interviewees tend to understate their bank deposits, Statistics Norway measures wealth components that are not covered by our survey, e.g. the value of shares and securities. The relative value of shares as saving mediums are changing. In 1997, for the first time in Norway, saving in shares and securities is outstripping saving through bank deposits.
2 A child can inherit NOK200,000 from its parents without paying inheritance tax. For inheritances between NOK200,000 and NOK800,000, tax is charged at 8 per cent and for inheritances above NOK800,000, at 20 per cent.
3 We are using data from three surveys carried out in 1990, 1993 and 1995 respectively. The surveys are based on representative samples (using a cluster sampling technique) of Norwegian households interviewed in their own home. The sample sizes were 2,000 in 1990 and 3,000 both in 1993 and 1995.

References

Bliksvær, T. (1996) *Arvelovgivningen i Norden*. Notat 96:5. Oslo: Institutt for sosialforskning.
Gulbrandsen, L. (1994) 'Takst og verdi', *Eiendomsmegleren* 11: 15–18.
——(1996) *Norske husholdningers økonomiske situasjon. Resultater fra en undersøkelse høsten 1995*, Oslo: Institutt for socialforskning.
Gulbrandsen, L. and Langsether, Å. (1997) 'Eldres formue og formuesforvaltning', Paper presented at 9 Nordiske socialpolitiske forskerseminar, Køge, Danmark, nov. 1997.
Hamnet, C. (1991) 'A nation of inheritors? Housing inheritance, wealth and inequality in Britain', *Journal of Social Policy* 20 (4): 509–36.
Kotlikoff, L. (1988) 'Intergenerational transfers and saving', *Journal of Economic Perspectives* 2 (2): 41–58.
Knoph, R. (1959) *Norsk arverett*, Oslo: Aschehoug.
Langsether, Å. (1993) *Arv, gaver og levekår*, Rapport 93:4. Oslo: Institutt for sosialforskning.
Lingsom, S (1985) *Uformell omsorg for syke og eldre*, SØS:59, Oslo: Statistisk Sentralbyrå.
Løwe, T. (1995) *Etableringsassistanse*, Rapport 95:5, Oslo: Institutt for sosialforskning.

Mauss, M. (1969) *The Gift*, London: Routledge.

Modigliani, F. (1988) 'The role of intergenerational transfers and life cycle saving in the accumulation of wealth', *Journal of Economic Perspectives* 2(2): 15–40.

Modigliani, F. and Brumberg, R. (1954) 'Utility analysis and the consumption function: an interpretation of cross-section data', in R. Kurihara (ed.): *Post-Keneysian Economics*, New Brunswick: Rutgers University Press.

Øverbye, E. and Eia, H. (1995) *Oppfatninger om velferd*, Notat 95:5, Oslo: Institutt for sosialforskning.

Saunders, P. (1984) 'Beyond housing classes: the sociological significance of private property rights in the means of consumption', *International Journal of Urban and Regional Research* 8(2): 202–27.

5

FAMILIES APART? INTERGENERATIONAL TRANSFERS IN EAST AND WEST GERMANY

Martin Kohli, Harald Künemund, Andreas Motel and Marc Szydlik

Introduction

In most modern societies, there is little co-residence between adult family generations, but relations and transfers between them usually remain strong. Are East and West German families different in these respects? For East Germany, as for Eastern Europe more generally, there are two conflicting expectations: family ties can be hypothesised to have weakened through the four decades of socialist rule with its attempt to break the family transmission of cultural and material capital; alternatively, family ties may have strengthened through reliance on the family as the only remaining vestige of the private sphere and the most viable network of informal exchange.

Intergenerational transfers through the family – transfers between adult members of family lineages not living in the same household – represent one of the most interesting and neglected fields of modern welfare societies. They have been neglected because sociologists, in tune with the classical tradition from Durkheim to Parsons, have assumed that with the nuclearisation of the family and the advent of public social security, family transfers beyond the nuclear household would wither away, and be substituted (or crowded out) by the emerging public systems (Künemund and Rein 1999). They are interesting because they challenge the received notions of the family and the welfare state, and have substantial and surprising consequences for well-being and social cohesion (see Chapters 2 and 3; Attias-Donfut 1995; Kohli 1999; Szydlik 1998).

Family transfers are particularly salient for cohesion or conflict among the generations (see Chapters 2–4). One of their surprising features is that their net flow is clearly downward, from the older to the younger generations in the family. A second feature is their dependence on public transfers: the elderly rely, to a large extent, on their pension incomes from which to make transfers to their descendants. The public transfers from the working population to elderly pensioners are thus partly 'returned' by the latter by way of family transfers. This clearly reduces the potential for conflict over public transfers; it is an important reason for the high legitimacy, shown by many surveys, that public pension systems (still) enjoy among all parts of the population, including the younger generations (Kohli 1993). As to the family, transfers – both *inter vivos* and as inheritance – are obviously themselves a potential source of family warfare, and may thus create generational conflicts; more often, however, they complement and reinforce the pattern of cohesion that is typical for adult family generations.

In this chapter, we document and discuss current private intergenerational transfers in East and West Germany. This addresses more than simply an internal interest in the process and problems of the unification of the two Germanys. Examining intergenerational transfers in East and West Germany presents a revealing pattern of comparative research: that of the contrast between two societies which had become separated for 45 years but which are now moving closer together again, to the point where it is questionable as to whether they still *are* separate societies.

We might focus on West Germany as a special case among Western societies; and in fact, there are good reasons to assume that West Germany *is* (still) special to some extent. For example, it has recently been shown (Attias-Donfut 1998) that intergenerational relations among adults are less close in West Germany than in France in terms of shared values and conflicts over values (one obvious explanation being the intergenerational rupture due to the Nazi past). In the present chapter, however, we will follow another logic of comparison: we will treat West Germany as representative of the normal Western pattern, and focus on the specifity of East Germany.

Examining intergenerational transfers in East Germany is not simply the application of a special research topic to yet another society. It is highly salient in two ways:

1   The German Democratic Republic (GDR), like the other state socialist (or 'communist') societies of Eastern Europe, presented a special regime of intergenerational transmission which warrants analysis as a regime type, i.e. an articulated set of properties closely linked to the basic structural features of these societies. Two such features that were especially salient for intergenerational transmission were, on the one hand, the centralised (and partly totalitarian) power structure of state socialism (Meuschel 1993) with its tendency to lower the impact of the family, and, on the other hand, its shortage economy (Kornai 1980) which made consumption largely dependent on one's inclusion in interpersonal networks.

2 The GDR was highly influenced by its specific generational history, and it can be argued that the latter was one of the major causes of its implosion in 1989 (Kohli 1994; Mayer and Solga 1994; Zwahr 1994). One aspect of this history was the increasing closure of social space for upward mobility (including the rates of admission to university education) during the 1970's and 1980's which resulted in massively growing disillusion and discontent among younger cohorts – a trend clearly demonstrated by the GDR surveys over the 1980's. Another aspect was the increasing attempts by the political elite to transmit their status to their children, which was seen as especially illegitimate and repugnant in a system that ideologically disavowed all forms of private inheritance and dynastic privileges.

Today, East Germany presents a difficult causal attribution problem. Any difference to the West that we find – for example, in rates of intergenerational transfers – can be attributed either to the persistent influence of the socialist past or to the conditions of the present transformation period. The cross-sectional data that are available today – including our own – do not permit a clean empirical differentiation between these two causes. The differentiation must instead rely on theoretical arguments.

In some dimensions, especially those of family formation, it is the dramatic – and historically unprecedented – consequences of the transformation period that stand out. Thus, fertility in East Germany between 1989 and 1995 dropped from a Total Fertility Rate (TFR) of 1.56 to one of 0.84, and nuptiality showed an even larger drop (Grünheid and Mammey 1997). In other areas of life, it is reasonable to assume that the socialist period still has an impact. Intergenerational relations over the entire life course have been shown to depend on the long-term socialisation history between parents and children (Rossi and Rossi 1990), and they may also depend to some extent on long-term cultural preference patterns. It is therefore still warranted for family studies to focus more on the GDR past, or on state socialist societies generally, even though they have now become 'only history' (as the phrase goes). Moreover, these systems have been highly interesting societal specimens; for reasons of intellectual curiosity and even more of socio-diversity we should not let them slide into analytic oblivion.

Hypotheses

How have the patterns of private intergenerational relations and transfers evolved in the GDR? We could hypothesise that family ties had been weakened during the four or more decades of state socialist rule because of the regime's tendency, following from its totalitarian elements, to break up the power of the family, first by taking the socialisation of the young out of the hands of the family, and second by making it difficult for parents to transmit status and material capital to their descendants. On the other hand, we could hypothesise that the family had been strengthened, first because it became the only possible counter-world to the official one of state and party, and second because it was indispensable as a network of exchange. The most interesting theoretical model here is that of 'communist neo-traditionalism' (Jowitt 1983; Walder 1986). It concerns the mechanisms through which positions and goods were distributed and loyalties assured: through networks of clientele-ship and exchange, often on the basis of traditional identities such as ethnic-ity or family. The latter were thus paradoxically strengthened, even though the aims of official policy were to make them less salient.

Most of the evidence so far seems to favour the second hypothesis. For example, it has been shown that relations between parents and their adult children were closer in East than in West Germany (Szydlik 1996). Scattered comparisons between families in Eastern and Western countries before 1989 point in the same direction (Andorka 1997; Huinink 1997).

For the transformation period (since 1989), there is again a negative and a positive hypothesis. We could hypothesise that the transformational stress has weakened family ties because a crisis leads to de-solidarisation, and the lack of economic resources impedes transfer-giving. The dramatic changes with regard to fertility and nuptiality mentioned above point to a demo-graphic involution that, were it to continue, would threaten the survival of the family as the normal life form. On the other hand, we could hypothesise that the transformation crisis has increased the need for family help, and strength-ened the tendency to rely on and retreat to the family. Thus, while family formation has been strongly compromised, existing families may have moved closer together; their transfer capacity has decreased, however.[1]

Taking both periods into account, we expect that there are more inter-generational transfers in East than in West Germany, but only among those groups which still have sufficient resources. Here, again, the impact of the East German past comes into play. Whatever the 'legacy' of that past in terms of values, attitudes and practices, there is a clear legacy in terms of available resources, or lack of them. On the aggregate level, there are still important income differences between East and West Germany, and even more import-ant wealth differences. For home ownership, the relation between East and West is about 1 to 2, for mean household wealth, 1 to 3.5. However, since major wealth is not usually picked up in surveys, the actual contrast would be even more dramatic. East Germany still has very few large owners and controlling elites; in important ways, it now has capitalism without capitalists. These differential resource constraints need to be taken into account when comparing the transfer patterns between East and West.

Data and results

The data presented here come from the German Aging Survey, a large representative survey of 40–85-year-old German nationals living in private households, collected in the first half of 1996. The sample (n = 4838) was stratified according to age groups, gender, and East and West Germany. The survey programme comprises sociological measures of the various dimensions of life situations and welfare – among them, intergenerational relations and transfers – as well as psychological measures of self and life concepts (see Dittmann-Kohli et al. 1997).[2]

Within the aggregate picture of income and wealth sketched above, we can identify age groups and cohorts that have been (relative) winners and losers of the transformation process. The losers are those in mid-life, who have been especially hard-hit by the transformational recession and labour market crisis, and do not yet have access to retirement provisions (Kohli 1997). The winners are the pensioners, most of whom have profited from being incorporated into the West German pension system. The pensions paid in the East are still somewhat lower than those in the West, but the difference is smaller than for work incomes. Pensions, moreover, follow the logic of publicly guaranteed transfers rather than that of privately contracted incomes, and are therefore more reliable and secure. In our survey, the third age group, the 70–85-year-olds, have the lowest mean equivalence income in the West and the highest in the East. All three age groups have lower incomes in the East than in the West, but the difference is smallest in the 70–85 age group, with Eastern incomes reaching 79 per cent of Western levels for men, and 83 per cent for women. The 70–85 age group in the East is also the one with the most positive evaluation of how the situation has evolved over the last ten years. A majority of 58 per cent state that their living standard has (much or somewhat) improved during this period, with 35 per cent seeing no change and only a small group of 8 per cent stating that it has (much or somewhat) worsened. In contrast, among their age peers in the West, the large majority (74 per cent) have experienced no change, while only 12 per cent see a change for the better, and 14 per cent for the worse.

Previous studies, as well as our own results, have shown that transfer giving is strongly dependent on available resources. So it seems appropriate for our comparison to concentrate on the 70–85-year-olds, the relative winners of the transformation where the resource difference between East and West is smallest, because it is there, if at all, that we can expect the hypothesised tendency of East Germans to give more transfers to manifest itself. This older age group will be closest to the 'true value' that would be expected under equal resource constraints.

Family transfers are of two kinds: between living family members (*inter vivos*) or as bequests (inheritance). Bequests are more important in size; but *inter vivos* transfers are more interesting in terms of social policy (they reach their beneficiaries earlier in life when their needs are larger) as well as in theoretical terms (they are part of an ongoing interaction process and open up a broader range of motives and negotiations). For this reason, our discussion will focus on *inter vivos* financial transfers.

As a backdrop to the East–West differences, we need to outline the general transfer patterns. To what extent do transfers to and from persons occur, to what extent do they remain in the family, and which direction do they take? Figure 5.1 presents some of the answers. The first key result is that transfers among the 40–85-year-olds are highly asymmetrical: 31 per cent have made large gifts of money or commodities, or given regular financial assistance to at least one other person during the 12 months before the survey, while only about 8 per cent have received such material transfers.

Figure 5.1 also shows that the transfer process is concentrated in the family lineage. The transfers go mainly downward, from the older to the younger generations. Among the transfer givers, almost 70 per cent give to their adult children. ('Adult children' are defined as biological children as well as step-children and adopted ones of at least age 18). In 7 per cent of the cases, transfers are given to grandchildren, and in 8 per cent, to parents(-in-law). Other relatives are the beneficiaries for 15 per cent of all transfer givers, and non-relatives for 10 per cent. The sources of transfers to our respondents corroborate this pattern. Among the 8 per cent who have received transfers, almost 70 per cent have benefited from their parents(-in-law), and 17 per cent from their adult children. Grandchildren do not play a role here: only one of our respondents received a transfer from a grandchild.

In the East, the concentration on the family descendants is even stronger than in the West. Seventy-five per cent of the 70–85-year-old East Germans who give transfers give them to their adult children compared to 61 per cent in West Germany; for transfers to grandchildren, the proportions are 45 and 32 per cent, respectively. By contrast, other relatives and non-relatives are

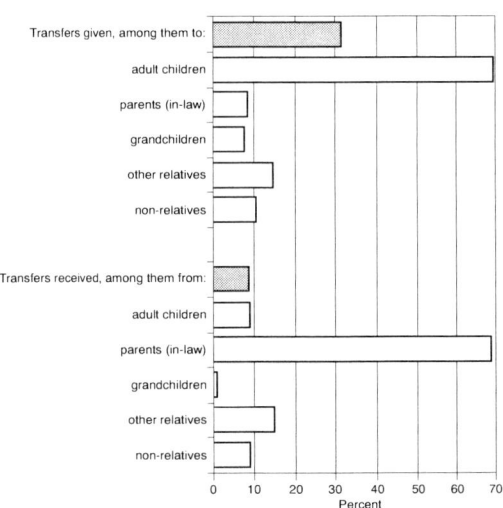

Figure 5.1 Private transfers given and received by 40–85 year-old Germans.

Source: German Aging Survey 1996, n = 4838.

more frequent receivers of transfers in the West. Thus, for East Germans of this age cohort, solidarity within the family lineage is higher, and there are less resources available for those who do not have first priority. (This difference between East and West also holds if the analysis is restricted only to those respondents who have living adult children or grandchildren.)

Figure 5.2 shows the proportions of respondents who have given transfers to (at least one of) their adult children in East and West Germany according to age groups.[3] The results support our expectations. The Western transfer rates are somewhat higher in the youngest group and considerably higher in the middle group, while in the oldest group, those aged 70–85, the pattern is reversed, with 30 per cent of East German parents giving transfers compared to 23 per cent of those in West Germany. The asymmetry of the transfer process is even larger among this group than for the sample as a whole: only 3 per cent of the 70–85 year olds in the West and 5 per cent in the East have received transfers.

The transfer amounts given by parents aged 70–85 to each child (Figure 5.3) are clearly higher in the West. In East Germany, more than two-thirds of the transfers are less than 1000 DM, while in West Germany, the most frequent category (mode) is that from 2000–5000 DM. Thus, elderly parents in the East give more transfers to their children but smaller ones.

How transfers depend on available resources is demonstrated in Figure 5.4. In order to make resources directly comparable between East and West, the income quartiles are calculated for Germany as a whole, rather than for each of the two parts separately. In both regions, transfer rates from elderly

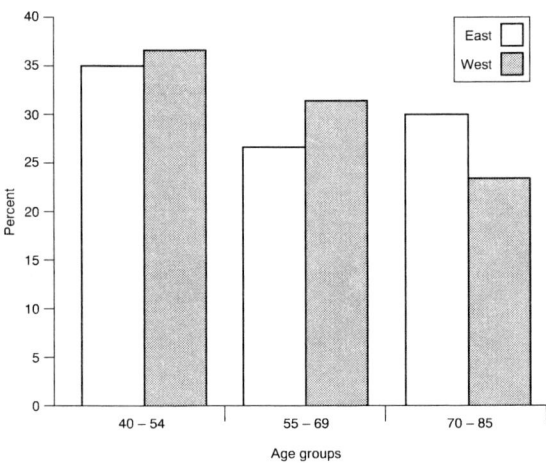

Figure 5.2 Transfers given to adult children in East and West Germany by parents' age group.

Source: German Aging Survey 1996, n = 3192.

94

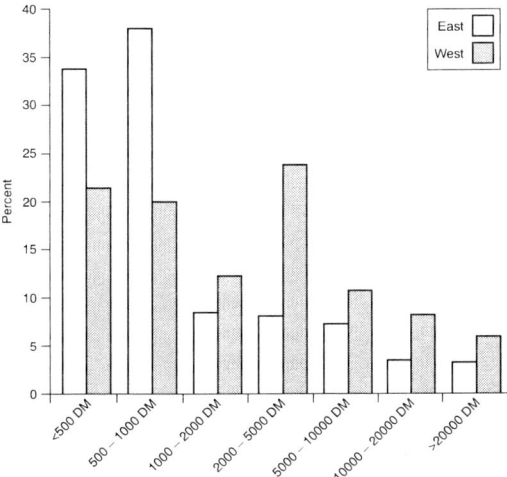

Figure 5.3 Amount of transfers given to children in East and West Germany (parents born 1911–1926).

Source: German Aging Survey 1996, n = 204.

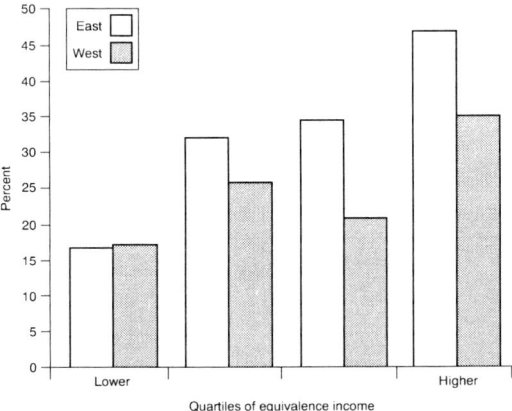

Figure 5.4 Transfers given to adult children in East and West Germany by equivalence income of the parents (parents born 1911–1926).

Source: German Aging Survey 1996, n = 1112.

parents to their children increase with higher equivalence income, but the association is stronger and more regular in the East. This may on the one hand, be due to the fact that West Germans have more other resources in the form of wealth at their disposal (see page 91); or the other hand, constraints may not have the same impact over the whole income scale. In the lowest quartile, East and West German parents give in almost equal proportions; the very limited resources override other factors. In the upper three quartiles, where resource constraints are less painful, the hypothesised tendency of East Germans to give more transfers is confirmed.

Figure 5.5 gives an example of how the age-specific needs of the receivers and resources of the givers come into play, based on the data for the whole age range of our sample. In both regions, children in early adulthood have the highest chance of receiving transfers. Many of them are still in education, and/or are faced with the demands of setting up a family at a time of limited or even erratic income. In such a situation of 'life-course squeeze', family transfers are especially important. Previous research has predominantly shown that *inter vivos* transfers are targeted to those children who are most in need (while bequests are overwhelmingly given equally to all children), and our results corroborate this pattern. About half of the adult children still in education (and not living at home) in our sample, and about a quarter of the unemployed receive transfers from their parents. Why, then, is the support for children in their early adulthood lower in East Germany? Their life-course squeeze is as hard if not harder than in the West. The answer relates to the lack of resources of their parents, usually in their 40s and 50s where, as noted earlier, the employment and financial situation is particularly tight. Conversely, this may explain why children between 45 and 55 are much more likely to receive transfers in East than in West Germany.

The patterns described so far on the basis of bivariate data are confirmed by multivariate modelling with logistic regressions (not shown here). In the

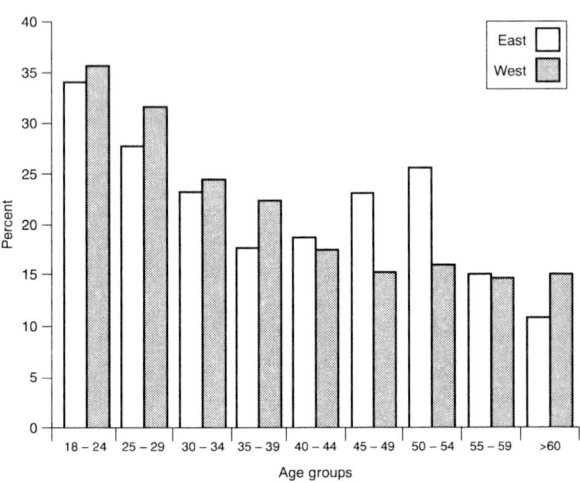

Figure 5.5 Children receiving transfers in East and West Germany by age groups.
Source: German Aging Survey 1996, n = 6476.

70–85 age group, Western parents are one-fourth less likely to give transfers than Eastern ones; this difference is significant at the 0.05 level. The strongest determinants of transfers are the resources of the parents (income and wealth), the needs of the children and the frequency of contact between them.

In the current debate on the welfare state, a key question is whether private transfers between generations have been crowded out by the public old-age pension system, and conversely, whether a retrenchment of the latter would result in increased private transfers. A careful analysis of the public–private link (see Kohli 1999; Künemund and Rein 1999) yields the opposite conclusion: the private transfer system would be weakened if pensions were to be decreased (also shown in France, see Chapters 2 and 3). On the aggregate level, there is an obvious and surprising pattern: part of the public transfers from the employed population to the elderly in the form of pensions are handed back by them to their family descendants. On the individual level, the pattern comes out still more clearly. We have seen that family transfers depend heavily on the availability of resources; since the resources of the elderly consist to a very large extent of pension incomes, the latter are a precondition for transfer giving. This is even more true for East than for West Germany, given the fact that in the East, where the welfare state is used to cope with (part of) the transformation crisis, public transfers make up a larger part of total income and wealth is lower.

Conclusion

The results of our analysis of the transfer patterns in East and West Germany lead to three conclusions:

First, even though resources are lower in the East than in the West, the proportion of transfer givers among elderly parents is higher. This reflects both a stronger family solidarity and a higher need among adult children.

Second, the amounts of transfers in the East are rather low, which would seem to indicate that most of them cannot do much good in terms of material support. However, the transfer flows demonstrate that support relations do exist and it is likely that they can be counted on to function above their current levels if a real crisis occurs. Moreover, family transfers are embedded in a multi-dimensional exchange process of which money giving is just one dimension. This is what makes intergenerational transfers in the family important for the well-being and social inclusion of lineage members, above and beyond their incidence and amount at a given moment.

Third, in East Germany the public/private interface is especially salient. Public pensions make up a larger proportion of the resources of the elderly than in West Germany, and thus have a stronger impact on their capacity to give transfers. As a consequence, public pensions in the East are even more important for the well-being of the younger generations.

Acknowledgements

Previous versions of this chapter were presented at the 92nd Annual Meeting of the American Sociological Association (August 9–13, 1997, Toronto, Canada) and at the 3rd Conference of the European Sociological Association (August 27–30, 1997, University of Essex, UK). We are grateful to the participants of these sessions and especially to the editors of the present volume for their critical comments and suggestions.

Notes

1 In one of the very few (cross-sectional) comparisons over time, Harcsa (1996) shows that in Hungary, the proportion of households that receive services and financial support from their parents considerably decreased between 1984 and 1995.
2 The German Aging Survey has been designed and analysed jointly by the *Research Group on Aging and the Life Course* at the Free University of Berlin and the *Research Group on Psychogerontology* at the University of Nijmegen (Netherlands) in collaboration with *infas Sozialforschung*, Bonn, and financed by the Federal Ministry for Families, the Elderly, Women and Youth. The sole responsibility for the content of this chapter lies with the authors. For a more complete account of intergenerational transfers, see Motel and Szydlik (1998) and Kohli (1999); a full report of the sociological results is given by Kohli and Künemund (1998).
3 We speak of 'age groups' here even though with our cross-sectional data we cannot, of course, exclude the possibility of cohort effects. However, our analyses so far have given few indications that would suggest the likelihood of cohort effects. The data in Figures 5.2 and 5.4 are based only on those respondents who have at least one adult child living outside their household.

References

Andorka, R. (1997) 'Functions and problems of families during the totalitarian system and the present transition to a market-based democratic system', in L. A. Vaskovics (ed.) *Familienleitbilder und Familienrealitäten*, Opladen: Leske + Budrich.
Attias-Donfut, C. (1995) 'Le double circuit de transmission', in C. Attias-Donfut (ed.) *Les solidarités entre générations: Vieillesse, familles, État*, Paris: Nathan.
——(1998) 'Generationenverhältnis und sozialer Wandel', in R. Köcher and J. Schild (eds) *Wertewandel in Deutschland und Frankreich*. Opladen: Leske + Budrich.
Dittmann-Kohli, F., Kohli, M., Künemund, H., Motel, A., Steinleitner C. and Westerhof, G. (1997) 'Zusammenarbeit mit infas-Sozialforschung', in *Lebenszusammenhänge, Selbst- und Lebenskonzeptionen – Erhebungsdesign und Instrumente des Alters-Survey*, Forschungsgruppe Altern und Lebenslauf (FALL), Forschungsbericht 61, Berlin: Freie Universität.
Grünheid, E. and Mammey, U. (1997) 'Bericht 1997 über die demographische Lage in Deutschland', *Zeitschrift für Bevölkerungswissenschaft* 22: 377–480.
Harcsa, I. (1996) *Habits of Interfamilial Support*, Budapest (mimeo).
Huinink, J. (1997) 'Vergleichende Familienforschung: Ehe und Familie in der ehemaligen DDR und der Bundesrepublik Deutschland', in L.A. Vaskovics (ed.) *Familienleitbilder und Familienrealitäten*, Opladen: Leske + Budrich.
Jowitt, K. (1983) 'Soviet neotraditionalism: The political corruption of a Leninist regime', *Soviet Studies* 35: 275–97.

Kohli, M. (1993) 'Von Solidarität zu Konflikt?', in G. Verheugen (ed.) *60 plus. Die wachsende Macht der Älteren*, Köln: Bund-Verlag.

——(1994) 'Die DDR als Arbeitsgesellschaft? Arbeit, Lebenslauf und soziale Differenzierung', in H. Kaelble, J. Kocka and H. Zwahr (eds) *Sozialgeschichte der DDR*, Stuttgart: Klett-Cotta.

——(1997) 'What comes after enterprise-centred social protection? The case of East Germany', in M. Rein, B. L. Friedman and A. Wörgötter (eds) *Enterprise and Social Benefits after Communism*, Cambridge/New York: Cambridge University Press.

——(1999) 'Private and public transfers between generations: Linking the family and the state', *European Societies* 1, forthcoming.

Kohli, M. and Künemund, H. (eds) (1998) *Die zweite Lebenshälfte – Gesellschaftliche Lage und Partizipation. Ergebnisse des Alters-Survey, Band I*, Berlin: Freie Universität.

Künemund, H. and Rein, M. (1999) 'There is more to receiving than needing: theoretical arguments and empirical explorations of crowding in and crowding out', *Ageing and Society*, forthcoming.

Kornai, J. (1980) *Economics of Shortage*, Amsterdam: North-Holland.

Lye, D. N. (1996) 'Adult child–parent relationships', *Annual Review of Sociology* 22: 79–102.

Mayer, K. U. and Solga H. (1994) 'Mobilität und Legitimität – Zum Vergleich der Chancenstrukturen in der alten DDR und der alten BRD oder: Haben Mobilitätschancen zu Stabilität und Zusammenbruch der DDR beigetragen?', *Kölner Zeitschrift für Soziologie und Sozialpsychologie* 46: 193–208.

Meuschel, S. (1993) 'Überlegungen zu einer Herrschafts- und Gesellschaftsgeschichte der DDR', *Geschichte und Gesellschaft* 19: 5–14.

Motel, A. and Szydlik, M. (1998) *Private Transfers zwischen den Generationen. Ergebnisse des Alters-Survey*, Forschungsgruppe Altern und Lebenslauf (FALL), Forschungsbericht 63, Berlin: Freie Universität.

Rossi, A. S. and Rossi, P.H. (1990) *Of Human Bonding: Parent–child Relations Across the Life Course*, New York: Aldine de Gruyter.

Szydlik, M. (1996) 'Parent–child relations in East and West Germany shortly after the fall of the wall', *International Journal of Sociology and Social Policy* 16, 12: 63–88.

——(1998) *Lebenslange Solidarität – Beziehungen zwischen erwachsenen Kindern und Eltern*, Freie Universität Berlin: Habilitationsschrift.

Szydlik, M. and Schupp J. (1998) 'Stabilität und Wandel von Generationenbeziehungen', *Zeitschrift für Soziologie* 27: 297–315.

Walder, A. (1986) *Communist neo-traditionalism*. Berkeley: University of California Press.

Zwahr, H. (1994) 'Umbruch durch Ausbruch und Aufbruch: Die DDR auf dem Höhepunkt der Staatskrise 1989. Mit Exkursen zu Ausreise und Flucht sowie einer ostdeutschen Generationenübersicht', in H. Kaelble, J. Kocka and H. Zwahr (eds) *Sozialgeschichte der DDR*, Stuttgart: Klett-Cotta.

6

GENERATIONAL RELATIONS
AND THE LAW

Marjatta Marin

The law, either in the form of written statutes or of other legal (juridical) expressions, practices and interpretations, is a social phenomenon which shapes the life course. In nineteenth-century classical sociology the law was denoted as having many different meanings and roles in social life. The term 'law' was used to refer to social norms that concerned socially important matters (e.g. Sumner 1957). The law was also seen as a way of binding individuals into society, signalling at the same time that social solidarity existed in society (e.g. Durkheim 1938, 1947). In addition, the law (especially 'good law') was seen as a way of supporting the individual's own happiness (Hegel 1961). The law could also be seen as a political or rational way of arranging public control, with the result that certain ways of behaving were politically legitimised through legalisation. The law itself was conceptualised as emanating through governmental actions and enforced by functionally specialised agencies, such as judges, prosecutors, and administrative officials (e.g. Rheinstein 1954).

These classical views about legal rules still exist today; for example, in a newer form, these ideas are presented by Parsons (1962) and Luhmann (1986). To Parsons the law was considered as a generalised mechanism of social control that operates diffusely in virtually all sectors of society. He sees the primary function of the legal system as integrative; it serves to reduce potential elements of conflict and to improve social integration: 'only by adherence to a system of rules systems of social interaction can function without breaking down into overt or chronic covert conflict' (Parsons 1962: 58). Luhmann emphasises somewhat different aspects of the law, seeing it not just as a series of technical formulae which judges or lawyers dispense but as providing answers to fundamental problems of social order. Law is seen as providing the framework of the state, with lawyers acting as the main human resource for the state, and legal theory providing a basis for theorising about the nature of society. In this respect, Luhmann comes close to the theories of Durkheim, for whom the law provided the fundamental expression of the state of society (Durkheim 1938).

Following these theorists, one could argue that the relations between the generations, i.e. the generational order, could be inferred from reading legal texts. The aim of this chapter is to show how the law can play an active role in shaping cultural understandings of ageing, as well as relations between age cohorts and generations. This chapter will analyse the mechanisms by which legal rules and legal order influence generational relations and describe the generational ideas that are implicit within the legal system. However, it is important to recognise that whatever the legal setting, intergenerational relations and cleavages can take on various concrete forms and patterns within a society: the 'one-to-one' relationship between law and social order exists only at a theoretical level.

Law as data

This chapter is based on a systematic analysis of empirical data concerning the Finnish law (Finnish Law Collections I and II from 1973–4, 1978–9, 1983–4 and 1995–6). The aim is primarily theoretical, with the empirical data serving as examples to illustrate theoretical ideas.

The focus is on laws which can be called 'age-laws', i.e. laws that specifically mention a certain age or ages. In 1978–9, there were 251 separate Finnish laws (statutes, acts) that mentioned a specific age or ages, and within these laws ages were mentioned over 1,000 times (Marin 1984). Within the ten-year period 1974–84, the number of times a specific age was mentioned in law (in future referred to as 'age-mentionings') had increased, thus signalling increasing age categorisation or age consciousness in Finland. Since then age-mentioning in law relating to younger ages have decreased while the mentioning of older ages in laws has increased. The latter is due to changes mainly in laws dealing with pensions, employment, unemployment and social security.

Age-mentioning laws are the focus of this chapter because they operate both in relation to family and other generational relations. They regulate the relationships between parents and their children, as well as affecting the ways societal generations differ from each other. Because family issues are emphasised, examples are taken from recent laws concerning marriage and the family, protection of children and the disabled, employment, education, and children's rights, regardless of whether they include age-mentionings within them.

There are major differences between countries in their legal systems and the centrality of the law in social life. Finland is often said to be a country of many laws and directives: when something is a problem, it is solved by a law. Finland belongs to the Scandinavian family within the Nordic welfare model where the state and public sector together play an important role in society (Esping-Andersen 1990; Gross 1991; Karisto *et al.* 1998). Laws are passed to regulate the relations and contracts both between citizens (i.e. private law) and between the citizens and the public sphere (mainly the state). The Nordic welfare model emphasises the latter in order to define the rights and obligations of both citizens and the state and the power-balance between them. The public sector, which is usually well organised and comprises strong professional groups, is regulated by legitimising the rights of citizens (especially in the role of consumers). In fact, Parsons expressed this as: 'law has a special importance in a pluralistic liberal type of society. It has its strongest place in a society where there are many different kinds of interests that must be balanced against each other and that must in some way respect each other' (1962: 72). Thus citizens can refer to law when negotiating contracts both with private and public partners. The law forms both the moral and reference basis for socially appropriate behaviour.

However, in relation to age-mentioning laws, there exists the possibility of a citizen not conforming to the legal age regulations: her/his actual behaviour does not have to follow the legally written life course. This is one aspect of the loose relationship between law and social order. This possibility of non-conformity particularly relates to younger ages where rights can be actualised later than the age at which they legally begin. Under the age of 18 (the age of full citizenship) the utilisation of legal rights is dependent on their parents' will and on the child's negotiations with their parents. For example, a child aged 12 is legally allowed to go to certain films or by the age of 16 can legally drive a moped, but whether (s)he actually can utilise this right may depend on negotiations with her/his parents.

The concept of generation

Though this chapter deals mainly with family generations, it is important to clarify the differences and interlinkages between family generations and societal generations. *Family or kinship generations* consist of the biological generational lineage running from grandparents through parents to their children (Kertzer 1983; Bengtson *et al.* 1985). The age difference and seniority between these generations is accepted only within the family system. However, on the societal level, each family generation (children – parents – grandparents) can belong to several societal generations due to the great age variation in child-bearing. Some women become a grandmother by the age of 40, while others only reach this status by their seventies.

Societal or historical generations comprise age cohorts which have experienced the same kind of things at about the same age during their life course (e.g. the 'biographical communities', illustrated by Thomas and Znaniecki (1951) in their research on Polish peasants), or those age cohorts which have shared experiences or interests and through them shared feelings of togetherness that can be called an organization of a collective mind (Braungart and Braungart 1986, 1987; Mannheim 1952). There also exists the concept of a partial generation (see Becker's chapter) which is related to Bourdieu's idea of a life-style generation occupying the same habitus (Bourdieu 1979; Roos 1986). The habitus (life-styles) of a generation are developed and reproduced through historical and contemporary processes, but the features of these life-styles are dependent on the social positions and social capital of their occupants, not only their chronological age. Thus, at the same time there can exist several different 'generations' in a society, whose members may be of approximately the same chronological age.

Legal regulation can affect both family and societal/historical generations and their relations. People may belong to both of them at the same time – they may for instance be both parents and members of a 'baby-boom' generation. Therefore they are targets of two kinds of legal effects: those targeted at family members and those focused on societal generations.

The mechanisms of legal influence

One way of looking at the relations between the law and generations is to pay attention to the multiple ways through which the law can affect generational relations. These effects can be grouped into historical, normative and resource effects.

Historical effects of the law

An historical effect is generated by the law when it influences the timing of central life events (marriage, education, work and retirement) in a different way for different birth cohorts. Laws may also change the core features of these events. These historical effects take place (a) when the laws change in such a way that they offer the next cohort different possibilities in relation to various life events, or (b) when the laws change the age-mentionings in such a way that certain life events become 'normal' or possible at a different age than in the past. In this way, the law may either be a generator of a new age structuration or life-course pattern in society, or a reflection of those changes which have already taken place in social life and structures. Which of these is the case can only be tested by comparing (over a period of time) age-related laws with the actual behaviour of individuals or with the existing organisation in society.

The rationale of this historical effect is illustrated in Table 6.1, by contrasting the renewal years of certain laws against historical time. This table indicates some of the laws (or their renewals) that are likely to affect the shaping of the individual's life course, i.e. laws on marriage and the family, child protection, education, employment and unemployment, and pensions and retirement. The oldest living generation comprises two larger age cohorts: those born during the first two decades of this century, and those born between 1920 and 1940. These birth cohorts, in family generational terms, comprise the current generation of grand- and great-grandparents. Typical of

Table 6.1 Dates of selected laws* and historical time in Finland

1900	1910	1920	1930	1940	1950	1960	1970	1980	1990
Ed		Ed	M	US	CP	EP	Ed	CP	
1866		1921	1929	1934	1952	1961	1970	1982	
						1962			
				CP	NP	1966	Em	M	
				1936	1956	1967	1970	1987	
						1969			
							US		
							1971		

BIRTH COHORTS
  (1900–1919)   (1920–39)
                          (1940–54)
                            (1955–64)
                              (1965–80)

* Types of laws: CP = Child protection
                  Ed = Education
                  Em = Employment
                  EP = Employment pension
                   M = Marriage
                  NP = National (public) pension
                  US = Unemployment security

the life course of these cohorts has been inequality in education, hard work, poverty, drastic life experiences including a war, poor health conditions and early entry into the labour force. During their earlier years there was the renewal of the marriage code in 1929 and also laws on unemployment and children's protection and care. Thus, these changes began to affect the adult life choices and possibilities of these age cohorts.

The next generation (age cohorts born in 1940–54) experienced during their lifetime rapid urbanisation, unemployment, day care problems for their children (mainly because of women's increased participation in paid employment), the necessity to save for housing (due to the Finnish ownership-centered housing policy) and the importance of education. Legal changes between 1961 and 1971 concerning pensions, retirement, employment and unemployment, affected and will affect their welfare level during middle and later life.

The cohorts born in the late 1950s and 1960s have been influenced by new laws on education, employment and unemployment, child protection, and the 1987 marriage code. The laws dealing with education, especially basic schooling, have resulted in one major change this century: the 1970 law gave the whole eligible age cohort the possibility (and obligation) of nine years of basic schooling. This obligation resulted in greater opportunity to acquire higher levels of schooling. Before that, education after four primary school years clearly differentiated people into different social strata, allowing only

10–20 per cent of the relevant age cohorts to receive higher education. This major change to the school system, together with the fact that in Finland education has had an important role in leading to upward mobility, explains why the 1950–64 birth cohort gave special weight to education: it was not easy for them to receive it. The 1965–80 birth cohort are the first generation in Finland where everyone has the same possibility of receiving secondary-level education and about half of them have been entitled to receive higher education. In this respect, they and their parents differ from each other: their parents only had hopes for better education, while they had the obligation and right.

The marriage code changed radically in 1987, allowing easier divorce and securing better children's rights, which were also altered in the renewed statutes of child protection and care in the 1980s. These laws, together with the increased divorce rate, have changed family relationships. Children born since the late 1970s are living in a more unstable family situation than former generations. Their parents are experiencing higher instability in parenthood relations and the role of grandparents may change with increased divorce, step-families and non-blood grandchildren.

The 1960s changes in pension and retirement laws have radically changed the role of paid work in people's lives. The Finnish pension scheme is based primarily on salaries (employment pensions), though there is also a national (public) pension system which provides financial security for older people who have not been engaged in paid work. These laws have, in spite of securing the socio-economic welfare of the elderly, also led to older people having to leave the labour market at younger ages than before. One of the consequences of the changes to the pension scheme is that recent cohorts of older people have more money and time to spend than former cohorts. Looking narrowly from the viewpoint of legally created chances, the current generation of younger elderly could provide an important 'caring potential' for their parents' generation.

The laws mentioned in Table 6.1 have had an influence on the position of different age groups (children, adolescents, middle-aged and older people) in relation to each other, but have also influenced their generational experiences. These laws may have generated within these age cohorts feelings of togetherness or at least given the opportunity for these feelings to arise.

Normative legal effects

A normative effect follows from the fact that some laws state rights and obligations for different age groups, especially in relation to how the relations between children and their parents are constituted by law. Table 6.2 examines all Finnish laws in 1978–9 that provide certain rights or obligations at specified ages. The laws that give rights to younger people (children and adolescents) construct at the same time their relation both to their parents and to the wider society. At various specified chronological ages their opportunity field is widened and opened to their own control under general citizen rights.

Eighteen is the age of full citizenship in Finland. This can be seen from Table 6.2, which shows how this specific age, as compared to other ages, is the age of increasing opportunities in the form of setting new rights. At ages below 18, at 18 and at 21, age restrictions are gradually removed and new rights set up. There exist two models (rationales) behind these legal changes: one is the intergenerational model, the other is the model of growing up as a citizen. The intergenerational model relates to the legal obligation that children and adolescents are tied to their parents in a one-way power-relationship until specified ages. Legal restrictions mean that children are not allowed to do certain things without the permission of their parents until they reach a certain age. By the age of 18 most of these restrictions are removed and the young person is provided with a set of citizenship rights.

The legal power of parents over the activities of their children is ex-emplified by the following legal paragraphs (it should be noted that instead of parents the powerholders can also be guardians who have custody of the child):

- a person is able to marry at age 18 without asking permission from her/his parents (Marriage Law, Si 201,4);
- a child who is 15 years old has the right to take part in or be heard in

Table 6.2 Contents of age-mentioning paragraphs in Finnish laws relating to selected age groups, 1978–9 (column percentages)

Age groups	Opening the opportunity field		Closing the opportunity field		
	Ending former restrictions	Setting new rights	Ending former rights	Setting new obligations	Ending obligations
0–17	24	17	24	23	4
18	36	41	18	16	4
19–20	11	13	6	4	—
21	24	2	8	—	—
23–25	3	7	3	—	8
26–55	2	7	13	22	24
56–65	1	15	26*	13*	56
66+	—	—	—	23*	4
Total	101	101	99	101	100
n =	(89)	(244)	(84)	(62)	(25)

Source: Marin 1984: 10.
* These legal paragraphs deal mainly with the obligation to retire in order to be entitled to an old age pension.

negotiations where the question of who is her/his real father is being investigated; at this age the child can also prevent the starting of this procedure (Fatherhood Law, Si 210,43);

- a child cannot be adopted against her/his will if she/he is 12 years old. In an adoption process the court should also hear a younger child if she/he is mature enough (Adoption Law, Si 215,8);
- by age 15 a child can make or cancel a work or schooling contract. However, when the child is under 18 years of age, the parents have the right to cancel these contracts if they find it necessary for educational, developmental, or health reasons (Law on Young Workers, Ty 407,3; Law on Educational Contracts, Ty 107,11);
- in divorce cases it is the parents who decide about the division of property, including the personal belongings of their children under 18 years old (Marriage Law, Si 201,39).

The third column of Table 6.2 shows legal paragraphs that state the ending of certain rights at specific chronological ages. Concerning childhood and youth, these rights are mainly economic ones and often relate more to the rights of their parents rather than of younger people themselves. The family is entitled to certain monetary benefits as long as children are under 16 or 18 years of age (e.g. child allowance or monetary benefits in different life situations such as divorce, widowhood and unemployment). In these cases it is up to the parents to decide who uses this money.

On the other hand, this legal one-way power-relationship puts parents in a position where they are obliged to take care of their children. This obligation may arise from the economic support given by the state to parents: the state has the right to expect relevant childcare in return. This obligation can also be seen as a moral one: children are vulnerable (powerless) in relation to their parents and thus entitled to receive relevant care from them.

The parents (or child's guardians) are legally obliged to take care of their children until they reach 18 years of age. Until the age of 18, parents legally have to promote the development and welfare of the child by respecting her/his needs, opinions and wishes, by giving her/him the possibility of positive, close human relations, good care and education, a safe environment, and by avoiding corporal punishment or exploitation. In doing this, the parents have the right to decide about the care, education, living arrangements and other personal issues concerning the child. In cases where the parents are deceased, these rights and obligations are transfered to the closest kin. However, in Finland, grandparents are not specially mentioned in this context.

The legal mentionings of age illustrated in Table 6.2 provide little information about multi-generational family relations: the age-mentioning paragraphs refer to parent–child relations rather than parent–grandparent or grandparent–child relations. The emphasis on the nuclear family is also evident in the laws dealing with marriage and child protection.

In relation to the adult generations (aged 25+), Table 6.2 illustrates the model of the citizenship life-course in Finland: youth is primarily the time when the opportunity field is gradually widened and old age is the time when it is gradually closed. Adulthood as an age stage (i.e. ages 25–55) is less age-categorised, but it has more duties and rights over the younger age stages than have older age groups (ages 56+). This citizenship model related to legal ages also confirms the thesis of Kohli (1988) about societal generational flow: there exists a contract between the state and its citizens. If a citizen is in paid employment during adulthood, she/he is entitled to expect social security when she/he reaches old age. This contract is not, however, a family generational one: Finnish children do not have any legal obligations to take care of their elderly parents. These obligations were deleted from the Finnish law in 1970, when Finland adopted the Nordic welfare ideology (Karisto et al. 1998: 309).

Resource effects of laws

A resource effect occurs when the law acts as a mechanism to distribute economic and social resources between the generations. This distribution takes place for instance in the marriage code, inheritance and taxation laws, as well as in laws concerning employment, unemployment, and survivor's pensions.

These laws primarily regulate the relations between parents and their children. As pointed out in the previous section, monetary benefits often come directly from the state to parents in order to support their task as child-carers. The parents can also regulate the working and education of their children (especially when they are under 15 years of age), and thus affect the personal economic situation of their children. There is the possibility of children at the age of 15 retaining their own earnings and receiving, under certain circumstances, child allowance money into their own bank account (usually it is paid by the state directly to their parents). The parents are, however, legally required to look after their children's welfare as pointed out above. Thus, although children can legally 'own money', they are still dependent on their parents to use it.

The economic position of children is affected by the financial circumstances of their parents even after children have reached the full citizenship age of 18. Unemployment security of a young person and student support (monetary support for living and housing) are both dependent on the wealth of the parents before the young person reaches the age of 20. If the young person lives at her/his parents' home, she/he can receive only 60 per cent of the total unemployment support until the age of 26. These examples show how parents are supposed to economically support their children even after their full citizenship age.

Finnish inheritance law emphasises the lineage, and secures equality among children. In addition to inheritance, the parent generation can benefit economically from the grandparent generation by, under certain circumstances, getting paid by public authorities and receiving some other benefits from them as caretakers (as 'kin-caretakers') of their parents or parents-in-law. They are also entitled to act as applicants for different kinds of state-subsidised social and welfare services for their elderly parents, in case the latter are too frail to do so themselves. These opportunities to serve as 'kin-caretakers' or as advocates in relation to elderly parents' social and welfare issues, however, also obtain for other kin members or people in close contact with the elderly person. Thus these rights and benefits are not solely related to family membership.

Finnish laws reflect two kinds of generational ideas: first, the parents' generation should mainly act as supporters and advocates of their children and be able to benefit from it financially. However, they have no legal obligations in relation to the older generations. Second, the grandparents do not have any privileged position in relation to their grandchildren compared with the position of other relatives or close friends. Neither do they have any legal obligations to take care of their grandchildren if their parents are deceased.

In Finland, only inheritance law specifically refers to the family lineage, which confirms the continuation of family financial welfare status. Otherwise the three-generational model of the family is largely absent from Finnish laws. The state-centered welfare system has enacted laws to remove any lineage responsibilities from the three-generational family to a situation in which adults in paid employment have normative obligations to the younger and the older societal generations. At the same time, the nuclear family has retained its central role in parent–child generational relations.

The 'generational ideas' behind the law

Another way of looking at the relations between the law and generations is to examine the 'generational ideas' that laws reflect or represent. 'Generational ideas' refer to the ways in which the law interprets generations and their relations. In Finnish law, there is no single generational idea but several. This has resonance with Luhmann's (1986) conception about the law as representing the nature of society, since modern society is a complex system where various ideas concerning specific societal issues coexist. In addition, the legal system is not a coherent system. Various laws have their roots in different time periods, from the nineteenth century onwards, and laws are enacted separately from each other.

In relation to family generations, it is possible to illustrate the generational ideas enshrined within law as representing three different kinds of ideologies: antagonistic, compensative and integrative.

The *antagonistic idea* of family generations is based on the conception that the youngest generation (children and adolescents) are immature, unable and dependent on the older generation. This idea is evident in the greater rights and power of parents over their children. The parents have the legal right to represent the interests of their children, on the assumption that they are operating in the best interests of the child and have the same interests as the child. The starting point is both antagonistic and differentiating: children are seen as very different from adults. Children mature slowly to adulthood and thus to full independence from their parents. This process gives younger family members an opportunity to take on different views and values to those of their parents while they are developing towards adulthood; the legal widening of their opportunity field (the field of rights and obligations) gives them more room to make their own choices according to their own will. This antagonistic idea can be seen quite clearly in the normative content of laws, especially the age-mentioning laws dealing with ages 0–21 (e.g. as shown in Table 6.2).

The *compensative idea* in law is based on a similar conception to the antagonistic idea, in terms of the younger generation being different from the adult generation, but here the younger generation are seen as a burden on the adult generation. These differences are conceptualised as if parents should be compensated by the help of law because of the burden of their children. Typical laws in this category try to reduce these differences between the generations (e.g. in Finland there are special loans for young persons and young families in order to assist them to live as 'ordinary adults'). Some of them, especially when targeted to younger people, have a more or less implicit educational purpose (e.g. housing arrangements for young people up to 28 years of age emphasise training to live independently, both in a social and economic sense).

There are also laws that through compensatory mechanisms seem to increase the differences between societal generations instead of levelling them. These laws try to compensate for an assumed handicap by offering special rights or by relieving from certain obligations (e.g. a law relieving 60-year-old persons from the duty to take part in some communal affairs, due to the legal conception that they are less capable in social activities than younger people). These laws, therefore, reinforce the conception of older people as less able, making age differences socially visible and by supporting or even constructing ideas of older people as not full citizens.

Third, the *integrative idea* of law considers the younger generation as a continuation of the older one, and emphasises the similarities and shared interests of different age groups and generations. Examples of these kinds of laws are the new laws on children's rights (e.g. the right to be heard in divorce cases at as young an age as possible).

Different societal generations and the law

Societal or historical generations can be seen as biographical communities, characterised by shared experiences with similar collective interpretations of these experiences. Within these societal generations there are likely to be similarities in life courses, such that the occurence of comparable life events links people together. The law can reinforce the existence of these societal generations in two ways: first, it can cause similar life events to occur at certain specified chronological ages and through these generate a collective sense of the same experiences; second, the law can be a function of these shared events and experiences, i.e. it subsequently legalises the existing life course ('the normal life-course'). Here, the generational experiences lead to a normative life-course view that is then formalised through law.

In legal studies there has been much discussion about which of these two interpretations of the role of the law is more valid (e.g. Mahkonen 1980). Due to the different historical origins of laws and the variety of arenas with which laws deal, the conclusion is that there always exists several life-course ideas within the law. Since people can adopt non-conforming behaviour in relation to legal rules, laws can at the same time both generate and reflect the shared experiences of societal generations.

The concept of societal generations may also include the collective feeling of belonging together, of being a member of the same generation, which does not actually require people to be the same age. This feeling of belonging together may be produced by an event that arouses similar feelings and from them similar interests, expectations and reactions. What are those events which the law can produce and thus operate to generate shared generational interests? One good example is the retirement and employment pension laws. As pensions in Finland are mainly based on earned salaries, these laws have confirmed and generated differences within the older generation and thus produced conflicting interest groups. There is both a consciousness of belonging to an older generation that is not treated equitably compared with younger generations, and also a consciousness of diversity among all older people, as exemplified by the three different political parties representing pensioners in Finland in the 1970s. Although on a theoretical level there may be unifying effects of similar life events (caused by law), in practice the same life events may have different meanings and importance to people, even when they occur at the same chronological age.

Thus, to clarify the concept of societal generations and in order to understand the mechanism of legal influence, it is useful to consider the generational idea of the life-style (habitus or partial) generations. The habitus generations are formed when people experience similar events and historical changes from different social positions but at approximately the same age. These different social positions may influence the consequences of legal events, and the ways these events are interpreted and reacted to.

The relation between the law and the partial or habitus generations can be twofold. First, the difference between social and chronological age supports the possibility of separating statutory age requirements (that are tied to chronological age) from individual behaviour (the person's own interpretation of her/his age, capacities and opportunities). The law mentions certain

111

ages and gives specific rights and obligations according to them but it does not usually tie personal behaviour solely to these age limits. It often provides the possibility of individual choice. In doing this it allows other factors, such as social background, social networks and the environmental context, the possibility of influencing individual's behaviour. This allows the possible emergence of habitus generations. Second, the law itself may be focused on different groups and handle them differently. In Finland this is especially the case with various retirement and employment pension laws which, while distributing different benefits to different occupational groups, influence the standard of living and welfare of their members in old age. Thus these laws implicitly have a role in constructing and sustaining habitus generations.

Conclusion

To date there has been little research interest in the legal regulation of the generational order within society. The generational order consists of both the family (lineage) and societal (historical) generations: their succession, relations, exchange patterns, normative and economic regulation, cultural meanings and images. The law acts to support the social order by both regulating and patterning the generational order. It also represents and reinforces prevalent cultural ideas.

This chapter has provided examples of how the law influences generational relations. The law is a complex and culturally varying system of codes and is not easy to use as research data. Here, the main interest has been in laws that specifically deal with different ages (referred to as age-mentioning laws). They are laws which both pattern and reflect the 'normal' age-bound life course in society. These age-mentioning laws also have an important role in modelling the relations between family generations, especially between children and their parents. They position the family generations in relation to each other, especially normatively (by distributing rights and obligations according to age) and economically (by distributing economic resources by age). By regulating the timing of central life events (e.g. marriage, education, work and retirement) they can also affect the historical characteristics of successive age cohorts.

In addition to age-mentioning laws, there are several legal areas which are connected with the generational order, e.g. laws on family and marriage, child protection, inheritance, taxation, employment, education, retirement and pensions. These laws provide insights about the generational and age images prevalent in society. This chapter shows that these laws either aim to differentiate or to integrate age cohorts and family generations, or to compensate economically for their assumed differences.

It is accepted that the legal system in society is a tool for social integration, but in addition, it can operate to reduce generational tensions and conflicts when there is the political will to do so.

References

Bengtson, V., Cutler, N.E., Margen, D.J. and Marshall, V.W. (1985) 'Generations, cohorts and relations between age groups', in *Handbook of Aging and Social Sciences*, New York: Van Nostrand Reinhold Co.

Bourdieu, P. (1979) *La distinction – critique sociale du jugement*, Paris: Les Editions de Minuit.

Braungart, R. and Braungart, M. (1986) 'Life-course and generational politics', *Annual Review of Sociology* 12: 205–31.

——(1987) 'Life-course and generational politics', *Journal of Political and Military Sociology* 2: 1–8.

Durkheim, E. (1938) *The Rules of Sociological Methods*, 8th edition, Chicago: The Free Press.

——(1947) *The Division of Labor in Society*, trans. G. Simpson, Glencoe, Ill.: The Free Press.

Esping-Andersen, G. (1990) *The Three Worlds of Welfare Capitalism*, Cambridge: Polity Press.

Gross, A.M. (1991) *New Welfare Mixes in Care for the Elderly*, Israel: Eurosocial Report 40/2.

Hegel, G.W. (1961) 'The civic community', in T. Parsons, E. Shils, K.D. Naegele and J.R. Pitts (eds) *Theories of Society I*, Glencoe, Ill.: The Free Press.

Karisto, A., Takala, P. and Haapala, I. (1998) *Matkalla nykyaikaan. Elintason, elämäntavan ja sosiaalipolitiikan muutos Suomessa*, Porvoo: Werner Söderström Osakeyhtiö.

Kertzer, D.L. (1983) 'Generation as a sociological problem', *Annual Review of Sociology* 9: 125–49.

Kohli, M. (1988) 'Ageing as a challenge for sociological theory', *Ageing and Society* 8 (4): 367–94.

Luhmann, N. (1986) *Soziale Systeme*, Frankfurt a M: Suhrkamp.

Mahkonen, S. (1980) *Avioero. Tutkimus avioliittolain erosäännösten taustasta ja tarkoituksesta*, Suomalaisen lakimiesyhdistyksen julkaisuja, A149, Vammala: Suomalainen lakimiesyhdistys.

Mannheim, K. (1952) 'The problem of generations', in *Essays on the Sociology of Knowledge*, London: Routledge and Kegan Paul.

Marin, M. (1984) 'Laki ja elämänkaari. Osa 1. Lain ja elämänkaaren väliset yleiset yhteydet', *Jyväskylän yliopiston sosiologian laitoksen julkaisuja* 29, Jyväskylä: Jyväskylän yliopisto.

Parsons, T. (1962) 'The law and social control', in W.M.Evan (ed.) *Law and Sociology*, Glencoe, Ill: The Free Press.

Rheinstein, M. (ed.) (1954) *Max Weber on Law in Economy and Society*, Cambridge, Mass: Harvard University Press.

Roos, J.P. (1986) 'Elämäntapateoriat ja suomalainen elämäntapa', in K.Heikkinen (ed.) *Kymmenen esseetä elämäntavasta*, Lahti: Esan kirjapaino.

Sumner, W.G. (1957) 'The mores', in L.A.Coser and B.Rosenberg (eds) *Sociological Theory*, New York: Macmillan Company.

Thomas,W.I. and Znaniecki, F. (1951) 'The Polish peasant in Europe and America', in E.H.Volkart (ed.) *Social Behavior and Personality: Contributions of W.I.Thomas to Theory and Social Research*, USA: Social Science Research Council.

7

DISCONTINUOUS CHANGE
AND GENERATIONAL
CONTRACTS

Henk Becker

Introduction

In the last few years, research on social change has begun to investigate discontinuities between the experiences of successive cohorts, in particular related to social inequality between the experiences of successive cohorts. However, explanatory models are lacking (De Graaf and Ganzeboom 1993). There are two main reasons for this shift from the previous focus on processes of continuous change. First, empirical data on relatively long periods across the life course have become available, even for cohorts born after 1970. In other words, we have data on many cohorts of individuals that have finished their initial education and grown up in periods showing the effects of processes of discontinuous macro-social change.

Second, concern with discontinuous social change has increased because macro-changes have led to social problems. An example is the effects of the 'baby boom' and the 'baby bust' on social equality and social distribution, especially with regard to the costs of the greying of the population. Generational contracts oblige younger generations to support older generations, but the financial costs of these obligations vary for different generations. Generational accounting describes and analyses such generational differences. A second example relates to gender differences. Retirement incomes and other resources show substantial inequality between women and men, for example in Britain (Hutton and Whiteford 1994:199). Some argue that the position of both women and men is changing dramatically – a 'genderquake' – and that inequalities between women and men have to be interpreted mainly as generational differences (Wilkinson 1997:32).

Research on the effects of discontinuous macro-social change on individual behaviour and institutions in most cases takes the form of research on generational differentiation. In this research tradition, attention has focused mainly, but not exclusively, on the emergence and further development of generations, that is, the continuation, decline and ultimately disappearance of distinctive generations. Social problems, especially those related to generational contracts are analysed, and the likely effects of current or proposed policy actions are assessed (Becker 1997b).

This chapter will examine three questions. First, how can we define and identify generations? Second, how can we define generational justice and intergenerational contracts, taking gender differences as our main example? Third, where can we identify (a risk of) generational conflicts and what ought to be done about it?

Emergence and development of generations

My definition of a generation is: 'a category of contemporaries that shows in its behaviour effects of discontinuous macro-change experienced during the formative period of its members' (Becker 1997b: 17). This definition implies that I am focusing on 'historical generations' (Jaeger 1977). It is important to clarify this definition and illustrate how distinct generations arise.

First, we have to examine the kind of effects discontinuous change may have on individuals and institutions. Discontinuous macro-social change influences the opportunities of all individuals that are in their formative years. These contemporaries constitute a 'population at risk', sharing a similar socio-economic climate. This does not imply that each individual reacts to the same circumstances in the same way, since distribution processes can lead to differences in the reactions of individuals. An example of this is an economic crisis, which affects the opportunities of all youngsters that want to leave the educational system and enter the labour market. However, the ability to cope with the effects of an economic crisis will differ according to class background. Children of wealthy parents are more likely to get financial support from home and therefore will not be affected by the crisis in the same way as children with less well-off parents.

Second, the formative period is very important in influencing the characteristics of an historical generation. This period lies between about the age of ten and the age of twenty-five, at least in contemporary Western countries. In their formative years, young people try to master a number of crucial transitions in their life course. For instance, the transition from primary education to secondary education, and for some, to university, from the educational system to the labour market, from the parental home to a home of their own, and from being financially dependent to being financially independent. If one or more of these transitions are not made, or are made at a time in the life course that does not fit into established life-course patterns, the consequences will persist for many years. The formative period is also a phase in the life course that requires the acquisition of important values and norms, which usually stay with an individual for a long time, although they may be modified or reinforced later in life by further societal changes. The formative period is, furthermore, a phase in life in which individuals acquire a lot of skills. Some believe that learning a new language or how to use information technology later on in the life course is relatively difficult (Turner and Helms 1995).

Third, the concept of 'historical generations' relates not only to phenomena in the past, but also to the present and the future. For example, to the extent that the ageing of the population has economic consequences, these will affect generations in the future. The term 'historical generations' is often used interchangeably with 'societal generations' (see earlier chapters).

Fourth, discontinuous macro-social change leads to the emergence not only of 'general generations' but also of 'partial generations' (Jaeger 1977; Becker 1992), which are subdivisions within a generation having a particular experience due to their social position, such as a particular occupational group. Partial generations have also emerged as a consequence of technological macro-change, such as youngsters that have grown up with computers and now assist their parents in handling their PC.

Fifth, it is important to remember that discontinuous change also has an impact on individuals before and after the formative period in their life course. Therefore, social research needs to consider not only the formative period of a generation, but also the childhood of its members and later periods in their life course.

Finally, societal generations sometimes show differences between countries, for example the 'early baby-boom' generation in Britain and in The Netherlands. In Britain, the baby boom after World War II represented a relatively small discontinuous change, whereas in The Netherlands the demographic effect of the war caused a major disruption of society that put substantial stress on the generational contract.

Characteristics of a generation

Research on a generation starts with a social scientists' hunch that a distinct new generation may have emerged. In order to assess whether this is so and to test hypotheses about a generation, a scheme of variables is required. A new generation is specified as: 'a grouping of a number of cohorts characterized by a specific historical setting and characteristics on an individual level (biographical characteristics, values and norms, and behavioural patterns) and a systems level (size and composition of cohorts, generational culture and generational organizations.' (Becker 1992: 23). This set of variables requires some explanation.

The specific historical setting of the cohorts refers to the discontinuous macro-social change that has had effects on individuals and institutions. Examples of macro-social change include the Second World War, the Cultural Revolution of the 1960s and early 1970s, and the economic recession of 1975–85. Each of these macro-changes has to be specified in detail before it can be measured in social research. For instance the Cultural Revolution in the West was composed of a movement towards democratisation, a sexual revolution and a new wave of emancipation of women.

Biographical variables include the individual's year of birth, gender, education of parents, education of the individual himself or herself, occupational career, sexual career, income career and housing career. Values (or value orientations), norms, attitudes and expectations are a category of types of variables which differ substantially from the biographical variables. For instance the level of education in most cases remains constant after the formative period, whereas values may change. The proposed theoretical model will specify the situations in which values will remain constant or will change. Behavioural patterns refer, for example, to voting behaviour, political participation, and behaviour towards health. These patterns may also change over the life course.

On a systems level, variables concerning the size and composition of cohorts indicate demographic trends, such as 'greying' or 'greening' of the population. They may also influence, for example, cost-benefit ratios concerning government provisions, the risk of not receiving health care and the risk of living in a deteriorated environment. Generational culture relates to collective memories and generational style. Generational organisations refer to the interest groups and social networks of that generation. Sometimes organisations explicitly focus on generations, like 'Americans for Generational Equity' (AGE), focusing on the interests of the younger generations. However, in most cases we are dealing with organisations or social networks that treat generations as a sideline activity.

It is not suggested that every historical generation differs significantly on each variable from all other generations, but the above sets of variables include those which are potentially important. Whether variables are relevant in a specific study in generational research depends on the theoretical model. Generational research is not restricted to the effects of discontinuous macro-change on behaviour and institutions, but usually includes the effects of continuous macro-change, for example, the process of modernisation contributes to individualisation.

Towards a theoretical model of generational differentiation

According to the theory of generations, distinct generations emerge as a result of the effects of discontinuous macro-social change on individual behaviour during the formative period of the life course. As soon as a new generation has emerged, the development of its members before and after the formative period can be studied, together with research on institutions related to the new generation (Becker 1992, 1997b).

The emergence of distinct generations can be explained by two hypotheses. The first is the differential cohort socialisation hypothesis, which leads to the prediction that the effects of discontinuous change on values and norms experienced during the formative period lasts for a relatively long time. The second is the hypothesis of relative scarcity, which leads to the prediction that the effects of restrictions on individual behaviour experienced during the formative period last for a relatively long time.

The continuation of generations can also be explained by two hypotheses. First, the hypothesis of reinforcement which leads to the prediction that values and norms acquired during the formative period only last if they are reinforced after the formative period. Second, the hypothesis of lifelong socialisation, which leads to the prediction that values and norms that are not reinforced will be replaced by values and norms adopted by the individual later in life.

The effects of discontinuous change on values and norms can be explored through a number of hypotheses: discontinuous economic change leads to effects on occupational and income careers, and on socio-economic values and norms; discontinuous cultural change leads to effects on participation in cultural activities and on socio-cultural values and norms; discontinuous political and military change often leads to war trauma later in life; and discontinuous demographic change leads to effects on occupational and income careers.

This overview of the theoretical model is restricted to aspects relevant to the argument in this chapter. Elsewhere (Becker 1997b, 2000), more elaborate versions of the theoretical model can be found.

Minimal requirements of a generation

This section discusses minimal requirements for a generation, and argues that a generation has to meet three minimal criteria:

1 The behaviour of individuals in cohorts has to show cohort effects during the formative period and for at least ten years afterwards. The cohort effects have to be related to the theoretical model, for example discontinuous economic change has to result in cohort effects related to occupational and income careers.
2 The behaviour of individuals in cohorts has to show generational differences with regard to earlier and later generations. These differences must be related to variables listed in the theoretical model, such as relationships of dependency between members of different generations. For instance, many members of the Pre-War generation with regard to information technology are dependent on assistance from members of generations much younger than their own.
3 Generations have to show a certain degree of institutionalisation, for example the name of a generation is used frequently in newspapers. Institutionalisation is relevant only if a name of a specific generation is related to the theoretical model, for instance the name 'baby bust generation'.

The three minimal criteria apply to general generations. Partial generations must only meet the first and the second criteria. A partial generation is not required to have a name that is institutionalised on a national scale.

Identification of historical generations

With regard to The Netherlands and a number of other Western countries, a pattern of general generations has been identified (Becker 1992, 1997b). A short discussion of each of these generations is presented.

A first cluster of cohorts consists of individuals that have experienced the economic depression of the 1930s and the Second World War during their formative period. Many male members of this cluster undertook active military service during the war. All members belong to the 'population at risk' with regard to the effects of war trauma. In many countries this cluster of cohorts (born about 1910–29) is called the Pre-War generation.

A second cluster of cohorts comprises individuals who experienced during their formative years the period of reconstruction after the Second World War, followed by a period of rapid economic growth. The war memories of the members of this cluster are less direct than those of the former cluster, because they were children during the war. From the 1990s onwards this cluster, known as the Silent generation (born about 1930–44) joins the Pre-War generation in retirement and are therefore relevant because of their position in the distribution of the costs of the greying of the population.

A third cluster of cohorts consists of the members of the early baby boom (born about 1945–54). The members have been confronted with the Cultural Revolution during their formative period and many of them have participated actively in this cultural movement. Many members have adopted post-materialist values, also called non-bourgeois values (Inglehart 1977, 1990). This generation will start to leave the labour market about 2005–10. Because we are dealing with the early part of the baby boom, the retirement of these cohorts will lead to substantial changes in the labour market. The costs of the greying of this generation will rise early next century. This generation is called the Early Baby Boom generation or the Protest generation.

A fourth cluster of cohorts consists of the members of the late baby boom (born about 1955–69). The members of this generation have experienced the effects of the economic crisis (1975–85) during their formative period. Many members have acquired post-materialist values (Inglehart 1977, 1990). In The Netherlands this generation is the first one with a very unfavourable position regarding the cost-benefit ratio (discussed in the next section) with respect to government provisions (Jansweijer 1996). This cluster can be characterised as the Late Baby Boom generation or the Lost generation. Members of this generation have made the transition to the labour market and to social independence later in life than the preceding generation due to the economic crisis (Becker and Sanders 1993; Sanders and Becker 1994).

A fifth cluster consists of members of cohorts born between about 1970 and 1985. During their formative period economic growth had returned, and the values of the members of these cohorts are relatively pragmatic. The generation is called the Baby Bust generation or the Pragmatic generation. The cost-benefit ratio concerning government provisions is even more negative than in the case of the Lost generation. There is no clear borderline yet between this generation and later cohorts.

The names given to the clusters of cohorts represent a typology of generations. A typology provides a characterisation, abstracting from all details with regard to the behaviour of cohorts and existing social institutions. A typology of generations abstracts also from time delays in the effects of discontinuous macro-change on behaviour and institutions. This implies that hypotheses about generations have to be derived from the theory of generations, not from the typology of generations.

This identification of historical generations focuses on whole generations, not partial ones. The model does not differentiate in a systematic way between countries. For instance, differences between Britain and other Western European countries like The Netherlands and the Scandinavian countries are not discussed (for Britain, see Hutton and Whiteford 1994: 199; Hills 1996: 56; Baldwin and Falkingham 1994; Falkingham and Hills 1995; and for the USA, see Fullerton and Rogers 1993).

Generational justice over time

Among economists, 'generational' relationships began to be discussed with respect to welfare as a result of an article published by Paul Samuelson (1958), which raised concern about the welfare of future generations through cost-benefit analyses. A watershed in the exploration of justice over time was the appearance of *A Theory of Justice* by Rawls (1971). In a section of chapter V entitled 'The Problem of Justice Between Generations', Rawls advocated the doctrine of an implicit social contract between generations. He specified this idea as follows: 'Each generation must not only preserve the gains of culture and civilization, and maintain intact those just institutions that have been established, but it must also put aside in each period of time a suitable amount of real capital accumulation' (p. 285). According to Rawls, justice as fairness contrasts with the utilitarian view: 'The just savings principle can be regarded as an understanding between generations to carry their fair share of the burden of realizing and preserving a just society' (p. 289).

The debate about generational justice concerns how the state provides for the welfare of future generations, including those as yet unborn (Fishkin 1992). According to Goodin (1988) the essence of the welfare state is moral: preventing the dependency and humiliation of members of our society often produced by poverty. When deciding how to use resources, or to protect the environment, or when selecting other policies with long-term consequences, governments and their advisers often use a social discount rate. For example, this can be applied to building a set of windmills to generate clean energy or to building a new harbour to boost the economy of a specific region. Using a social discount rate, possible costs and benefits are expected to be less important if they are assumed to occur further in the future. Such a social discount rate applies not only to the costs and benefits that will affect existing people in the future, but also the effects on the lives of all future generations. An issue is how much we require future generations to contribute, and some authors, such as Cowen and Parfit (1992: 144), are against using any social discount rate. Cowen (1992: 162), examining the consequences of build-now-pay-later policies, advocates a zero rate of intergenerational discount.

Thomson (1992) argues that the interests of generations are in conflict. After World War II, free health and educational services, housing grants, and other benefits were institutionalised in England and a number of other developed countries: 'The effect was to create the first welfare generation, consisting of those reaching adulthood between 1945 and the end of the 1960s – a generation soon in heavy and lasting debt to the collectivity' (p. 222). He argues that the second welfare state consists of the disfavoured generations, obliged to pay the high taxes needed to fund the welfare state of their predecessors. Thomson continues: 'Why should the young adults of the 1990s and beyond feel bound to pay for the welfare state of their predecessors? What bonds, what obligations, what contract requires this of them? What possible moral basis could such an exchange have? Why would they not argue that there now is no contract between generations, because it has been voided by the behaviour of their elders?' (p. 231). At this point the issue of the welfare of future generations confronts the issue of a social contract between generations, although analysts have pointed out that Thomson's scenario of generational inequity, based on New Zealand, does not apply in all welfare states (see for example, Falkingham and Hills 1995).

A social contract between generations

The modern welfare state is commonly said to be founded on a kind of intergenerational contract. According to this contract, during its productive years each generation pays to support those who are dependent on it, assuming that when its own dependent phase comes, it will be supported in turn by successor generations:

> If this kind of intergenerational contract were viable, it would resolve many of the moral relations among generations. Issues of distributive justice and mutual obligations would be viewed as settled by a continuing implicit agreement.
>
> (Laslett 1992: 2)

A strong version of the generational social contract argument would apply if the contract settled, in a determinate manner, the sufficient conditions for obligations among generations. Laslett and Fishkin (1992) are sceptical that any strong version of a social contract argument can apply across generations, first, because benefits and burdens undertaken by the parties cannot reasonably be foreseen, and second, because there are no possibilities of redress among the relevant parties for gross unforeseen inequities. Variations in cohort size (the Baby Boom cohorts, followed by the Baby Bust cohorts) and in political decisions about the character and destination of welfare flows make burdens and benefits unforeseeable. The temporal asymmetry of the parties make redress impossible. This does not mean Laslett and Fishkin argue that there may not be some room for weaker versions of the contract metaphor. The weaker version of the social contract between generations would require that the substantive effects of policies across generations is considered:

> If these arguments are correct, we will have to rethink radically how we assess the consequences for future generations of all public policies, from decisions for capital expenditures for dams and highways to the disposal of nuclear waste.
>
> (Laslett and Fishkin 1992: 5)

Laslett poses the question: 'Is there a generational contract?' (1992: 24). He explores the plausibility of an intergenerational contract, taking past, present and future generations into account. He looks at pressure groups such as 'Americans for Generational Equity', which make use of contractual language when complaining that the retired are taking more than is justly due. He concludes: 'Strictly speaking, the notion of generations that can enter into contracts, or of intercohort trusts that are bounded in time by the temporal limits of generations, are unrealistic constructs, however that notion is formulated.' (p. 46). This conclusion is debatable. In Laslett and Fishkin (1992), no reference is made to human rights or to the jurisprudence available regarding violations of these rights. The European Convention on Human Rights (Jacobs 1975), for example, acknowledges property rights, and rights acquired under a contributory pension scheme are protected. However, the provisions for property rights in the Convention have no application to general social security systems where there is no direct correlation of contribution and benefit.

According to Epstein (1992), the debate on equity between the generations focuses too much on duty, and too little on practice and incentive.

> There is little that coercion and duty can do specifically to ensure that the next generation receives its fair share of human and natural resources. In general if we continue to create sound institutions for

the present, then the problem of future generations will pretty much take care of itself, even if we do not develop overarching policies of taxation or investment that target future generations for special consideration.

(p. 85)

Why, he asks, should anyone want to adopt this leave-bad-enough-alone attitude? 'Because the alternatives are worse' (p. 85). According to Epstein, relations between generations are not regulated by ideas of solidarity but by market mechanisms. He combines his explanatory model with a prescriptive model.

Braybrooke (1992) argues that earlier generations cannot block radical changes in legal rights. For instance, gross inequalities in the distribution of private property pose enormous dangers of oppression – oppression quite as intolerable as that by dictators or monarchs. In a case like this, revision of rights is to be expected. On the other hand, it is clear that in some contracts people in one generation can bind not only themselves but also people in succeeding generations. Braybrooke could have added the example of a huge national debt accumulated by the present generation and passed on to future generations.

It is relevant that each generation's 'inheritance' includes other assets and liabilities which are non-financial. For example, Barry's (1983) article 'Inter-generational Justice in Energy Policy' initiated the debate about generational obligations related to the environment. Since 1983 the interests of 'future generations' and 'intergenerational justice' are standard issues in cost-benefit analyses of projects like dams, reservoirs and related major interventions, both in industrialised and developing countries (see von Amsberg 1992). The report by the World Commission on Environment and Development (1987), commonly called the Brundtland Report, defines *sustainable development* as: 'development that meets the needs of the present without compromising the ability of future generations to meet their own needs'. In 1992, sustainable development was a major issue at the UNCED Earth Summit in Rio de Janeiro. In the Brundtland Report 'generations' is not defined, but the concept is used in a way that places the cohorts concerned in a specific historical setting.

Generational accounting and its consequences

Without doubt, older generations in the West are better off than younger generations with regard to paying taxes to finance pensions and health care for elderly citizens, although for Britain this conclusion has been challenged (Hills 1996). Recently, methods have been developed and applied to quantify generational differences with regard to public finance. Generational accounting is proposed as a meaningful way to evaluate fiscal policy (Kotlikoff 1992;

Auerbach *et al.* 1994), and is even discussed as an alternative to public budgets and deficits (Haveman 1994). In the debate about generational accounting, authors do not question the existence of generations. Although a definition of generations is lacking, publications of economists like Kotlikoff indicate that in generational accounting economists use the term 'generation' to indicate categories of birth cohorts.

Auerbach *et al.* (1994) argue that they have developed generational accounting as a method of assessing generational fiscal burdens independently of the labels and categories used by governments to classify receipts and payments. Generational accounts indicate, in present value, what the typical member of each generation can expect to pay, now and in the future, in net taxes, that is taxes paid net of transfer payments received (Auerbach *et al.* 1994: 75). Generational accounting indicates both what existing generations will pay and what future generations must pay, given current policy and the governments's intertemporal budget constraint. The latter budget constraint requires that those government bills not paid by current generations must ultimately be paid by future generations (Auerbach *et al.* 1994).

Generational accounts comprise a set of monetary values, one for each existing and future generation. Their combined present value adds up to the present value of government consumption less initial government wealth. This principle can be extended to distinguish cohorts of men and women within each generation, and to distinguish groups according to other demographic characteristics, as well as lifetime income levels (Auerbach *et al.* 1994). Since generational accounts reflect only net taxes paid to government (taxes less transfers received), they do not impute to particular generations the value of the government purchases of goods and services made to provide them with, for example, education, highways, national defence, health care and other services. Therefore, they do not show the full financial net benefit or burden that any generation receives from government policy as a whole, although they can show a generation's net benefit from a particular policy change that affects only taxes and transfers.

Using generational accounting, the present value of the future taxes to be paid by the young and middle-aged generations has been estimated in some countries to exceed the present value of the future financial transfers they will receive. For newborn males and females, on the other hand, the present value of the net payment is much smaller, because they will not pay much in taxes for a number of years.

The differences in male and female generational accounts reflect differences in labour force participation, family structure, and mortality. For example, older women are projected to receive a greater present value of health-related transfers because they will live longer, on average. However, it needs to be borne in mind that women have, on average, contributed much more unpaid care to others – within their own, the preceeding and the succeeding generation – compared with men.

As a group, older generations, both male and female, will receive more social security, medical care and other future benefits than they will pay in future taxes. However, it is important to remember that the figures in these calculations show the *remaining* lifetime net payments of particular generations, and do not include the taxes a generation paid or the transfers it received in the past. Males who are now 65, for example, paid considerable taxes when they were younger, and these past taxes are not included in the remaining lifetime net payments shown in their generational accounts. Therefore, the remaining lifetime net payment by one existing generation cannot be directly compared with that of another. Such a comparison requires a different methodology.

Auerbach *et al.* argue that their method of generational accounting does not show a normative bias:

> Generational equity is an ethical concern, and our choice for any particular norm for purpose of illustration is not meant to impose this norm as our preferred ethical judgment. Rather, we simply choose a norm we think is of general interest: namely, that generations born in the future should not pay a higher share of their lifetime income to the government than today's newborns.
>
> (1994: 84)

This chapter will not discuss lifetime tax rates because they do not alter the line of argument of the preceding discussion. However, I agree with Haveman (1994) that generational accounts can serve as a useful supplement to the annual budget, but not as a replacement of it.

Generational accounting has also been introduced in The Netherlands (Jansweijer 1996; Nelissen 1994; Van Kempen 1997), and the analyses of costs and benefits with regard to social security and old-age pensions show the same developments as discussed for the US (Kotlikoff 1992; Auerbach *et al.* 1994).

However, we need more analyses of gender differences originating from early stages in the life-cycle. An example of this kind of difference is changes in the proportion of men and women with university degrees in Western Germany. In the 1916–20 birth cohorts, 3.4 per cent of German women obtained a university degree, compared with only 1.8 per cent of the 1921–25 cohorts and 1.3 per cent of the 1926–30 cohorts. For German men the percentages are 5.1, 5.6 and 5.4 (Blossfeld 1993: 58). Evidently during the harsh struggle for survival after the First World War families primarily invested in university education for boys, not for girls. In situations like this, generational justice would require compensation for the handicap women had suffered or experienced in their formative period.

If we consider health care as part of generational accounting, there is a clear message about the generational contract. Older generations have a right to formal and informal health care as soon as they need help. In many cases people assume that the quality of health care for elderly people should meet the standards of the best years of the welfare state. The years of retrenchments in health care are seen as a temporary setback. Research has shown that health care provision for the elderly will not be able to meet the expectation based on the generational contract in most Western countries. Some economists argue that, first, financial resources do not permit an increase of health care facilities or allow payment of sufficient numbers of professional health care staff, and second, the demand for health care for the elderly has increased substantially (Hollander and Becker 1987).

Decreases in the funding of professional health care may force members of younger cohorts, in particular those born between 1955 and 1970, to increase their contribution to the informal health care of older relatives. Because women traditionally provide more of this kind of informal health care, it is very likely that they will have to carry most of the burden, unless this aspect of their emancipation gets more attention (Becker 1997b).

Risk of generational conflicts

The risks of generational conflicts are assessed in terms of the cost-benefit ratio concerning government provisions relating to state pensions, and the costs of health care. An overview is presented in Figure 7.1 for each of the five ideal types of historical generations identified earlier. In both cases, there is a serious *risk* of conflict between the older generations (born in 1915–29 and 1930–44) and the youngest (born in 1970–85). In most Western countries, generational conflict is not yet evident. This implies that there is still some time for social policy to prevent an outbreak of severe generational conflict.

To this end, more information should be obtained: first, by presenting the outcomes of intergenerational accounting, and, second, through a public debate which will provide individuals with an opportunity to choose between models that differ in their hypotheses. Moreover, collective saving by the Baby Boom generations (born 1945–69) has to increase. The advantages of the economic boom will have to be used not only to please voters in these years, but also to generate funds for government expenses in the next decades. In addition, individual saving and investment has to be stimulated. Where government policies fail, individuals need to be able to fall back on their own resources. Cost-benefit ratios need to be reviewed in relation to government provisions, taking into account that welfare transfers differ substantially between generations in countries like the United States, Scandinavian countries, Germany and The Netherlands. Special attention ought to be paid to young cohorts, for example in The Netherlands the cost-benefit ratio will become negative for cohorts born later than 1985 (Becker 1997b).

Tax reforms will have to contribute to a redistribution of costs and benefits with regard to provisions by government for the costs of the greying of

	PRE-WAR (1915–29)	SILENT (1930–44)	EARLY BABY BOOM (1945–54)	LATE BABY BOOM (1955–69)	BABY BUST (1970–85)
PRE-WAR (1915–29)		COST-BENEFIT GOVERNMENT PROVISIONS 1	COST-BENEFIT GOVERNMENT PROVISIONS 2	COST-BENEFIT GOVERNMENT PROVISIONS 3	COST-BENEFIT GOVERNMENT PROVISIONS 3
SILENT (1930–44)	HEALTH CARE 1		COST-BENEFIT GOVERNMENT PROVISIONS 2	COST-BENEFIT GOVERNMENT PROVISIONS 2	COST-BENEFIT GOVERNMENT PROVISIONS 3
EARLY BABY BOOM (1945–54)	HEALTH CARE 2	HEALTH CARE 2		COST-BENEFIT GOVERNMENT PROVISIONS 1	COST-BENEFIT GOVERNMENT PROVISIONS 2
LATE BABY BOOM (1955–69)	HEALTH CARE 3	HEALTH CARE 3	HEALTH CARE 1		COST-BENEFIT GOVERNMENT PROVISIONS 2
BABY BUST (1970–85)	HEALTH CARE 3	HEALTH CARE 3	HEALTH CARE 3	HEALTH CARE 2	

Figure 7.1 Generational differences and risks of generational conflicts.

the population. Schemes for flexible retirement are needed to increase the size of the labour force, although the benefit will be limited unless more jobs are available. Part-time early retirement may become more common in most Western countries. On the other hand, part-time participation of elderly workers in the labour force is urgently needed, so that organisations can also profit from the experience of such workers. Furthermore, in-service training of employees aged over thirty requires attention. The human capital of members of the late baby boom (born 1955–69), with a high level of initial education, can still be enhanced substantially by post-experience education (Becker 1997b).

Last but not least, social inequality related to gender and generational differences has to be taken into account. Susan MacManus has speculated on the generational combat in the 21st century, taking Florida as an example. She predicts that age will become a more important factor (1996: 23), while gender roles will change substantially for both women and men. She notes the different political implications of ageing for men and women:

> Older women are less politically active than older men, for several reasons: marital status, the nature of their infirmities, and the time period in which they became politically socialized. First, fewer older women live with their spouses (women generally outlive men and, as widows, tend to live alone), and previous studies have found that older women remain more politically active when living with their spouses. Second, older women have a higher incidence of infirmities that limit mobility. Finally, many of today's older women grew up in a time when politics was regarded as a male domain – when sexual stereotypes prevailed.
>
> (p. 34)

With regard to gender and voter turnout she identifies a generational shift:

> For example, in the past, models anticipated finding a negative relationship between the size of the female voting population and voter turnout rates. Now, however, the reverse is true. Today, more women than men vote because of gains they have made in education, income, and employment opportunities, as well as the removal of stereotypes about 'appropriate' female electoral behaviour. The more the gap narrows between men and women on these dimensions, the less powerful gender will be as a predictor of voter turnout.
>
> (MacManus 1996: 42)

MacManus advocates bridging the generational gap by educational programmes, community programmes and a rethinking of what it means to be old. The argument of MacManus has much in common with Helen

Wilkinson's notion of the 'genderquake', taking place in combination with generational change (Wilkinson 1997: 32). According to Wilkinson the emancipation of women has resulted in substantial changes in the roles and behaviour of both men and women. This new situation can no longer be described as an emancipation of women only. Research on these developments is ongoing, focusing primarily on political preferences and political behaviour.

Conclusions and discussion

The first question was: how can we define and identify generations? In this chapter a definition has been presented that tries to keep close to everyday language but nevertheless is precise enough to be useful in empirical research. An explanatory theory and a scheme of variables have been elaborated, as well as minimal requirements for characterising a number of birth cohorts as a generation. The identification of generations leads to results that in many cases differ both between and within countries. For example, Germany did not have a baby boom shortly after the Second World War, but the term 'early baby boom' has been institutionalised in Western countries to such an extent that even in Germany the term 'baby boom' is understood and applied. In this chapter, five generations have been identified that are relevant for the discussion about generational contracts and conflicts.

The second issue examined was: how can we define generational justice and intergenerational contracts? This question was answered by taking into account discussions in moral philosophy. In the juridical sense, speaking about a generational contract is not possible. Yet in a wider sense, the idea of a generational contract is applicable; for example, referring to financial relationships between generations in terms of pensions and health care, to non-financial legacies such as the environment, and to the nurturance and care provided in the informal sector of the economy by women (see Chapter 8 by Ginn and Arber, this volume).

The third question was: where can we identify (a risk of) generational conflicts and what ought be done about it? Generational accounting provides an overview of the costs and benefits individuals derive from government with regard to social security, old age pensions, health care, etc. At first sight differences in the cost-benefit ratio do not look alarming. However, differences do become alarming if we consider individuals with different levels of income, since those in lower income brackets are unlikely to be able to cope with a severe reduction in their income. The differences also become substantial when we look at gender and at the fate of younger cohorts, for instance those born since 1985 in countries like The Netherlands.

The term 'generation' is frequently used in everyday language. It has a number of meanings, but in most cases the context indicates what is meant by the term. To generational research it is an advantage that the term is widely known, facilitating communication between social researchers and the public in general. However, this situation is also a handicap, because popular meanings of the term 'generation' are often mistaken for definitions formulated in scientific analyses, and vice versa. Generations that are identified in typologies are often used in everyday language. Non-specialists may try to interpret situations and developments in social reality by drawing conclusions directly from a typology of generations.

Research on discontinuous social change will increase in the years to come, primarily because more long-term data on these developments will become available. Research is needed to elucidate the circumstances in which the changing nature of generational contracts leads to social inequality, and sometimes to social conflict.

References

Amsberg, J. von (1992) 'The sustainable supply rule for the economic evaluation of natural capital depletion', in R. Goodland (ed.) *Industrial and Third World Environmental Assessment: the Urgent Transition to Sustainability*, Washington: The World Bank.

Auerbach, A.J., Gokhale, J. and Kotlikoff, L.J. (1994) 'Generational accounting: a meaningful way to evaluate fiscal policy', *Journal of Economic Perspectives* 8 (1): 73–94.

Baldwin, S. and. Falkingham, J. (eds) (1994) *Social Security and Social Change. New Challenges to the Beveridge Model*, Hemel Hempstead: Harvester Wheatsheaf.

Barry, B. (1983) 'Intergenerational justice in energy policy', in D. Maclean and P.G. Brown (eds) *Energy and the Future*, Totowa, New Jersey: Rowman and Littlefield.

Becker, H.A. (1992) 'A pattern of generations and its consequences', in H.A. Becker (ed.) *Dynamics of Cohort and Generations Research*, Amsterdam: Thesis Publishers.

——(1997a) *Social Impact Assessment*, London: UCL Press.

——(1997b) *De toekomst van de Verloren Generatie*, Amsterdam: Meulenhoff.

——(2000) *Risiko Generation*, München: Deutscher Taschenbuch Verlag.

Becker, H.A. and Sanders, K. (1993) 'Explaining generational behaviour, the case of the transition from education to work', in H.A. Becker and P.L.J. Hermkens (eds) *Solidarity of Generations*, Amsterdam: Thesis Publishers.

Blossfeld, H.-P. (1993) 'Changes in educational opportunities in the Federal Republic of Germany: a longitudinal study of cohorts born between 1916 and 1965', in Y. Shavit and H.-P. Blossfeld (eds) *Persistent Inequality. Changing Educational Attainment in Thirteen Countries*, Boulder/Oxford: Westview Press.

Braybrooke, D. (1992) 'The social contract and property rights across the generations', in P. Laslett and J.A. Fishkin, J.A. (eds) *Justice between Age Groups and Generations*, New Haven, Conn.: Yale University Press.

Cowen, T. (1992) 'Consequentialism implies a zero rate of intergenerational discount', in P. Laslett and J.A. Fishkin (eds) *Justice between Age Groups and Generations*, New Haven, Conn.: Yale University Press.

Cowen, T. and Parfit, D. (1992) 'Against the social discount rate', in P. Laslett and J.A. Fishkin (eds) *Justice between Age Groups and Generations*, New Haven, Conn.: Yale University Press.

Epstein, R.A. (1992) 'Justice across the generations', in P. Laslett and J.S. Fishkin (eds) *Justice between Age Groups and Generations*, New York, Conn.: Yale University Press.

Falkingham, J. and Hills, J. (eds) (1995) *The Dynamic of Welfare: Social Policy and the Life-Cycle*, Hemel Hempstead: Harvester Wheatsheaf.

Fishkin, J.S. (1992) 'The limits of intergenerational justice' in P. Laslett and J.A. Fishkin (eds) *Justice between Age Groups and Generations*, New Haven, Conn.: Yale University Press.

Fullerton, D. and Rogers, D.L. (1993) *Who Bears the Lifetime Tax Burden?*, Washington: The Brookings Institution.

Goodin, R. (1988) 'Reasons for welfare: economic, sociological and political – but ultimately moral', in E.D. Moon (ed.) *Responsibility, Rights and Welfare*, Boulder: Westview Press.

Graaf, P. M. De and Ganzeboom, H.B.G. (1993). 'Family background and educational attainment in the netherlands for the 1891–1960 birth cohorts', in Y. Shavit and H.P. Blossfeld (eds) *Persistent Inequality: Changing Educational Attainment in Thirteen Countries*, Boulder/Oxford: Westview Press.

Haveman, R. (1994) 'Should generational accounts replace public budgets and deficits?', *Journal of Economic Perspectives* 8 (1): 95–111.

Hills, J. (1996) 'Does Britain have a welfare generation?' in A. Walker (ed.) *The New Generational Contract. Intergenerational Relations, Old Age and Welfare*, London: UCL Press.

Hollander, C.F. and Becker, H.A. (eds) (1987) *Growing Old in the Future, Scenarios on Health and Ageing 1984–2000*, The Hague: Martinus Nijhoff Publishers.

Hutton, S. and Whiteford, P. (1994) 'Gender and retirement incomes: a comparative analysis', in S. Baldwin and J. Falkingham (eds) *Social Security and Social Change. New Challenges to the Beveridge Model*, Hemel Hemstead: Harvester Wheatsheaf.

Inglehart, R. (1977) *The Silent Revolution, Changing Values and Political Styles Among Western Publics*, Princeton: Princeton University Press.

——(1990) *Culture Shift in Advanced Industrial Society*, Princeton: Princeton University Press.

Jacobs, F.G. (1975) *The European Convention on Human Rights*, Oxford: Clarendon Press.

Jaeger, H. (1977) 'Generationen in der Geschichte, Ueberlegungen zu einer umstrittenen Konzeption', *Geschichte und Gesellschaft* 3 (4): 429–52.

Jansweijer, R.M.A. (1996) *Gouden bergen, diepe dalen: de inkomensgevolgen van een betaalbare oudedagsvoorziening*, The Hague: Government Printing Office.

Kempen, E.J. van (1997) 'Betaalt de baby de 'boom'?', *Economisch-Statistische Berichten* 4(9): 724–28 (Dutch only).

Kotlikoff, J.K. (1992), *Generational Accounting – Knowing Who Pays, and When, for What we Spend*, New York: Free Press.

Laslett, P. (1992) 'Is there a generational contract?' in P.Laslett and J.S. Fishkin (eds) *Justice between Age Groups and Generations*, New Haven, Conn.: Yale University Press.

Laslett, P. and Fishkin, J.S. (1992) 'Processional justice', in P. Laslett and J.S. Fishkin (eds) *Justice between Age Groups and Generations*, New Haven, Conn.: Yale University Press.

MacManus, S. A. with Turner, P.A. (1996) *Young v. Old. Generational Combat in the 21st Century*, Boulder/Oxford: Westview Press.

Nelissen, J.H.M. (1994) *The Redistributive Impact of Social Security Schemes on Lifetime Labour Income*, Tilburg: TISSER.

Rawls, J. (1971) *A Theory of Justice*, Cambridge: Harvard University Press.

Samuelson, J.P. (1958) 'An exact consumption-loan model of interest, with or without the social contrivance of money', *Journal of Political Economy* 66: 467–82.

Sanders, K. and Becker, H.A. (1994) 'The transition from education to work and social independence: a comparison between the United States, The Netherlands, West Germany, and the United Kingdom', *European Sociological Review* 10: 383–92.

Thomson, D. (1992) 'Generations, justice, and the future of collective action', in P. Laslett and J.S. Fishkin (eds) *Justice between Age Groups and Generations*, New Haven, Conn.: Yale University Press.

Turner, F.S. and Helms, D.B. (1995) *Lifespan Development*, 6th ed., Fort Worth: Harcourt Brace College Publishers.

Wilkinson, H. (1997) 'No turning back. Generations and the genderquake', in G. Mulgan (ed.) *Life after Politics. New Thinking For the Twenty-First Century*, London: Fontana Press.

World Commission on Environment and Development (1987), *Our Common Future* (Brundtland Report), Oxford: Oxford University Press.

8

GENDER,
THE GENERATIONAL
CONTRACT AND PENSION
PRIVATISATION

Jay Ginn and Sara Arber

The implications of population ageing, combined with high levels of un-employment and earlier exit from the labour market, have fuelled concerns in developed societies about the sustainability of public pensions and whether welfare transfers between generations are equitable. In particular, as the ratio of employed people to pensioners declines, it has been argued that public pension levels can only be maintained by the working population paying more in some form or other, leading to intergenerational conflict over resources (Johnson *et al.* 1989). Generational accounting, in which net financial trans-fers of cohorts are compared, has been used to help to legitimate cuts in public pension provision. Yet this technique ignores the non-financial inputs made by women, as part of the normative gender contract, on which the viability of pension systems, and society as a whole, depend.

The issue of intergenerational equity has become entangled with arguments about the relative merits of public Pay-As-You-Go (PAYG) pension schemes compared with private funded pension schemes. In the former, contributions by employed people are used to pay pensions to the older population – a 'generational contract' in that each generation relies in retirement on succeeding generations continuing the arrangement. Funded pension schemes are usually private and include both both occupational and individually arranged pension schemes. In funded schemes, contributions are invested and the accumulated funds used to pay pensions at retirement. Although funded schemes appear to entail no generational contract, the demographic and em-ployment trends thought to undermine the viability of state pensions may have similar or worse effects on funded pensions, especially if the private sector of pension provision is expanded (Mabbett 1997; Toporowski 1998).

The thesis that, in the context of an ageing population, welfare states create inequity between generations has been examined by generational accounting techniques (see Becker's chapter). These measure (or project) each cohort's financial inputs to the welfare state, in taxes and social insurance contributions, and receipts from it in terms of state welfare (Kotlikoff 1992). Although such methods may be useful in demonstrating how net transfers of resources in the welfare state have differed among a series of birth cohorts, we argue that they are flawed as measures of intergenerational equity for several reasons.

First, the idea of a generation as a distinct self-contained entity is questionable. Phillipson (1996) has pointed out that two views of generation can be distinguished – the economic one envisaged in the accounts referred to above – and a sociological one which is more complex, recognising that each generation is linked through family ties with individuals in other generations and that inequities by class, ethnicity and gender outweigh those between generations. Moreover, the blurring of life stages, as employment in mid-life becomes increasingly insecure, challenges the generational labels of 'worker' or 'pensioner' (Phillipson 1996). Second, measuring generational differences in total taxes paid and welfare benefits received ignores variations over time in the proportion of taxes used for non-welfare purposes such as military spending, space research and subsidies to industry. Third, the quality of life is profoundly affected by such factors as war, technological innovation and environmental change which are 'bequeathed' by each generation to its successors. Fourth, generational accounts neglect all the family financial transfers which flow up and down between generations (see Chapters 2–5). Finally, no account is taken of the unpaid work performed by members of one generation (mainly women) for another. Physical reproduction and nurturing of the younger generation, as well as provision of informal care to the parental generation, are vital forms of transferred resources between generations and incur substantial costs for the carer; yet such care is socially constructed as non-work (Grace 1998) and finds no place in generational accounts.

The kinds of intergenerational transfer omitted from generational accounting are likely to vary between cohorts. Therefore, assessing intergenerational equity solely in terms of financial transfers through the welfare state fails to capture the complexity of the relative net contributions of different generations. The selective character of generational accounts is important since the claim of intergenerational inequity has been used for political purposes (Guillemard 1996). In the US, for example, analysts have used generational accounting to support the argument that pension provision should be privatised and public pension provision reduced (Kotlikoff and Sachs 1997).

In this chapter, we focus on the implications of women's unpaid work for intergenerational transfers of resources. In the first part, we consider the ways in which the gender and generational contracts are intertwined. We review the arguments for shifting the balance of pension provision further towards the private sector in response to the alleged 'old-age crisis' (World Bank 1994). In the second part, we argue that the impact of the gender contract on women's retirement income depends on the structure of pension systems and show how, in Britain, privatisation of pensions is set to exacerbate the feminisation of poverty in later life.

The gender contract: dividing paid and unpaid work

The gender contract, a term which encompasses the norms concerning the division of paid and unpaid work between men and women, achieves an accommodation between the immediate demands of a market economy and the longer-term survival of society. While the gender division of domestic labour facilitates men's unfettered participation in paid employment, the employment participation of married and cohabiting women is constrained, especially if they have children, with adverse effects on their pensions. The ideal typical gender contract is exemplified in the male breadwinner/dependent wife family model: non-employed married women provide domestic services, childcare and parent/-in-law care in return for an unspecified and uncertain amount of 'free' accommodation and other goods from their employed husband. Although such an arrangement is claimed by rational-choice theorists to be efficient and advantageous to both partners (Becker 1991), Folbre (1994) suggests that rational economic man is cared for by altruistic woman, while others have pointed out that a woman's part in the contract is 'compulsory altruism' (Land and Rose 1985).

Few families in contemporary Western societies conform to the ideal type of gender contract, the majority of men and women combining varying amounts of unpaid responsibilities with paid employment over the life course. Women who have children generally pursue a combination career, adjusting their employment to fit evolving family needs, with interruptions to employment, periods of part-time employment and downward occupational mobility (Dex 1987; Ginn and Arber 1996; Jacobs 1997). The pivotal role of childcare responsibilities (rather than choice) is confirmed by the close association of women's employment with the provision of publicly provided childcare (Joshi and Davies 1992).

Support for the ideal typical gender contract, where the separation of roles is complete, is declining, but change is slow and varies with age, birth cohort, country and gender. For example, the proportion of women in the US who agreed or were indifferent to the statement that the husband should be the breadwinner and the wife should stay at home was a third in 1982 but only a quarter in 1993; the corresponding figures were 28 and 21 per cent in Britain and 16 and 13 per cent in Sweden (Hakim 1996).

In terms of behaviour, change in the gender division of domestic labour is slower than would be expected from the shift in attitudes (Gershuny 1997a). In Britain the gender division of domestic labour is gradually becoming more equal, although women's share of the total time spent on domestic work is still nearly two-thirds (Jackson et al. 1997). The decline over time in women's domestic work means that, on average, women who are over 65 have invested more time in domestic work than their daughters. Figure 8.1 compares, for 1961 to 1995, the time spent by British men and women on four components of domestic work: cooking and washing up, housework (including cleaning and laundry), childcare and odd jobs (including do-it-yourself activities and car maintenance). Women's time spent on cooking/washing up and house-work had fallen over the 34 years, largely compensated by men's greater contribution to these tasks. However, it is significant that women's time spent on childcare has not diminished.

A recent British time use survey, in which adults of all ages were included, found that women spent twice as much time as men on unpaid work but 60 per cent as much time in paid employment; significantly, men's total work time (paid and unpaid) was only 87 per cent of women's (Murgatroyd and Neuberger 1997). Men's contribution to child-rearing, in particular, is substantially less than women's and is rarely at the expense of their employ-ment and earnings. As Gershuny (1997b) points out, women who do unpaid caring and servicing work lose out doubly in the competitive career stakes; they have less time and energy for their paid jobs, prejudicing their occupa-tional advancement, while men who have wives to do these things for them appear more dedicated to their jobs and can make correspondingly better career progress.

The way in which men and women negotiate domestic roles is often pre-sented as a private matter within the family; women's unpaid work is seen as a voluntary labour which benefits individual men by allowing them to participate unfettered in the labour market. Yet women's domestic labour, especially their reproductive work, is crucial to the survival of society, a point which is obvious but is rarely discussed in economics or sociology (van Krieken 1997). However, the value of unpaid domestic labour to the economy is gaining recognition in the European Union, with plans to measure and record unpaid work in national statistics. In Britain, there are plans to record and monetise domestic activity as a satellite account; a recent estimate of the value of unpaid domestic work amounted to between £341bn (56 per cent of GDP) or £739bn (122 per cent of GDP) depending on the notional rate of pay, with women contributing the bulk of the work (Murgatroyd and Neuberger 1997). The unsatisfactory nature of the GDP as a measure is in-creasingly recognised, partly because it counts as a 'gain' all the activities required to deal with crime, natural disasters and man-made blunders but also because it excludes unpaid work.

In assessing the value of women's contribution to society as mothers, we need to consider what happens when women withdraw from this fundamental aspect of the gender contract, either failing to care for their children or choosing childlessness, as an increasing proportion of women do (McAllister and Clarke 1998). Falling fertility rates can be seen throughout Europe due to childlessness, later child-bearing and smaller families. The average total

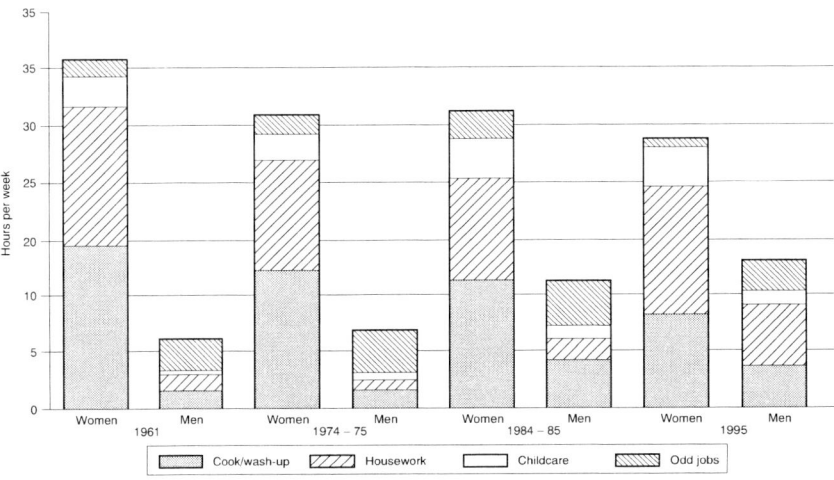

Figure 8.1 Hours per week spent on each component of domestic work. Women and men, Britain 1961–95.

Source: Jackson *et al.* (1997).

fertility rate in the fifteen EU countries has nearly halved in thirty-three years, falling from 2.7 in 1960 to 1.4 in 1993 (Eurostat 1995). Low fertility is the major reason for the rising ratio of pensioners to the working-age population, outweighing the effect of increased longevity (Ermisch 1990). Thus, declining fertility, although partly compensated by increasing productivity and possibly by immigration as well, adversely affects the viability of both state Pay-As-You-Go and private funded pension schemes, because pensions schemes rely on each generation producing no less resources than the preceding one.

The kin-keeping, caring and supportive roles performed mainly by women facilitate bonds between generations, while adequate parenting promotes the physical health, emotional stability and creativity of each generation. Rossi warns that an employment-dominated society threatens not only fertility but also the quality of life:

> Nor is it in the interest of the nation, or the well-being of individual men and women, to diminish the time and energy invested in parenting; or to crowd out of their lives the time available to enjoy

137

marital intimacy and quiet self-reflection, as so often demanded by busy work lives, with the result of stressed marriages, psychological depression, or cardiovascular disease.

(Rossi 1993: 208)

British sociologists have echoed these concerns. For example, some have linked the demise of authoritarian patriarchy and growth in women's employment to an increase in anti-social behaviour and in the numbers of unhappy and disruptive children, although the question of causality is recognised as contentious (Coward 1997). Morgan (1997), from a conservative, right-leaning perspective, has no doubts that mothers' employment, especially if full-time while children are pre-school, leads to stress and fatigue in the women and to emotional impairment and educational disadvantage in the children; she argues that the benefits to the economy of maternal employment must be balanced against the value of their parental role: 'Children are the generators of future wealth, whose productivity depends to no small extent upon the investment made by parents in their upbringing' (1997: 74).

These considerations are mentioned not as arguments against women's employment but as a reminder of the value to society of domestic and civic work and of the need for social institutions and employment practices which assist men and women to combine home life and paid employment successfully (Brannen et al. 1994; Ginn and Sandell 1996).

Societal changes relating to the gender contract, in which women's paid work increases at the expense of unpaid, tend to inflate the GDP and to influence state welfare transfers. Although most women work the 'double shift' of paid and unpaid work, often bearing a very heavy total workload, the time spent in domestic work tends to decline as employed hours increase. When women provide only minimal care for their children, in order to maximise their earnings, either the state or private carers must replace their caring role, at least partially, and the costs of caring labour escalate (Folbre 1994). Similarly, if informal care provided by working-age women for frail older parents/-in-law were withdrawn, it would have to be replaced at much greater cost by employing care staff, generally women. Thus the trend towards greater employment of women increases the demand for women's labour in the personal services occupations; previously invisible and uncounted labour in the domestic sphere then becomes visible as part of the formal economy and accessible to generational accounting techniques. As women's labour shifts across the private–public boundary, from unpaid to paid, the tax base is broadened and social insurance revenue increases. This mitigates the effects of population ageing, by increasing the public resources available to pay pensions and health care costs.

Falkingham and Hills' (1995) examination of financial inputs to and receipts from the British welfare state shows that although women pay less tax and receive more in state benefits than men, they have average lifetime living standards 10 per cent lower than men, even when equal sharing between couples is assumed. Women who conform most closely to the ideal typical gender contract, by following a domestic career, tend to have the lowest personal income from pensions in later life, while those employed full-time and continuously for most of their working life have the highest (Ginn and Arber 1996). In Britain, where there is little public provision of day care, Joshi (1996) has estimated the earnings cost of motherhood for a British 'Mrs Typical' with two children as £230,000 over her lifetime; she receives only 45 per cent of her childless sister's lifetime earnings, substantially reducing her income from private pensions. Only an elite minority of highly qualified and well-paid women can avoid the adverse impact of motherhood on employment, earnings and pensions (Glover and Arber 1995; Jacobs 1997). For the majority of British women, motherhood results in low income in later life.

However, the structure of a country's pension system influences the severity of the pension penalty of motherhood (Ginn and Arber 1992). Whereas public pension schemes tend to be universal and to compensate in various ways for the effects of caring responsibilities, private pensions are selective in coverage and provide poorer value for money for those without full-time continuous employment (Luckhaus 1997). We next examine the claim that public pensions necessarily create intergenerational inequity and render the generational contract unsustainable.

Generational accounting, intergenerational equity and gender

Some have argued that certain birth cohorts (a 'welfare generation') have secured for themselves larger state pensions than they have paid for, placing an unfair burden on younger generations whose taxes and social security contributions fund welfare spending (Thomson 1989). Although this may be the case in some countries, Hills (1995) found no evidence of a privileged generation in Britain. On the contrary, analysis of redistribution between generations, in which past and projected lifetime financial inputs (tax and National Insurance contributions) and benefits (including state pensions) were calculated for 5-year cohorts, showed the welfare state to be well balanced, with most cohorts roughly breaking even over their lifetime (Hills 1995).

Thomson (1991) claims the generational contract embedded in the welfare state is unsustainable, using the analogy of a chain letter game, in which the numbers involved multiply at each stage. Hills (1995) suggests that a more accurate analogy for the dynamic of British welfare is a line of people (representing generations) each of which gives a box of chocolates to the next person and later receives one. In this analogy, only the first recipients of welfare (born between 1901 and 1921) are net gainers and subsequently intergenerational equity will be ensured provided the game continues indefinitely. If, on the other hand, one person (generation) panics and stops the process or changes the rules, they, or the following generation, which bears the full effect of the changes, will be the only losers (Hills 1995: 61). Thus breaching the generational contract by reducing public Pay-As-You-Go (PAYG) pensions would have the perverse result of creating intergenerational inequity. Hills' findings have been questioned by other analysts; but his neat analogy of a balanced PAYG welfare system draws attention to the need for continuity in welfare and to the likely adverse effect on those of working age and younger of eroding public provision.

Although such generational financial accounting is important and illuminating, Hills (1995: 61) acknowledges that 'intergenerational equity is not just about the welfare state', nor confined to monetary transfers. Generation-specific misfortunes such as living through the Depression of the 1930s or being required to fight wars are hard to value in monetary terms but are nevertheless relevant to consideration of fairness between generations. Gender is also 'a significant axis in intergenerational relations' (Rossi 1993: 192). If we ignore the gender division of labour, we fail to take account of the variation between different cohorts of women in their contribution to other generations' welfare. The unpaid caring services which women have always provided (as mothers or as daughters/-in-law) are increasingly combined with paid employment, in which tax and social insurance are paid. Yet later cohorts of women raise fewer children than earlier cohorts. Thus the nature of women's contribution to the welfare of other generations has been changing over the 20th century, as the balance of their workload shifts away from the domestic economy and towards the formal, monetary economy. The claim of inter-generational inequity is thus based on a flawed and partial measure. In the next section, we consider the merits of the argument that public pension retrenchment is necessary.

Pension privatisation: driven by demography or ideology?

Population ageing and the issue of pension reform have been the subject of much debate since the 1980s (Johnson *et al.* 1989; World Bank 1994; Disney 1996; Kotlikoff and Sachs 1997). Many recent papers have assessed the possible macroeconomic consequences of population ageing in OECD countries (for example, Roseveare *et al.* 1996; Chand and Jaeger 1996; Daykin 1996; European Commission 1996). An ascendant creed has developed among economists that private funded pensions are preferable to public PAYG pensions: privatisation, it is argued, will avoid intergenerational inequity and will also limit the non-wage costs of labour, boost the level of savings and stimulate economic growth (Field 1995).

A sense of crisis has pervaded much of this writing. For example, a World Bank report predicts 'a looming old age crisis that threatens not only the old but also their children and grandchildren, who must shoulder, directly or indirectly, much of the increasingly heavy burden of providing for the aged'

(World Bank 1994: iii). In the World Bank scenario, public pension systems will face unmanageable liabilities and must either reduce benefits or extract unacceptably high contributions or taxes from future generations of workers (World Bank 1994). A neo-liberal reform package is recommended for both industrial and developing countries, including a modest basic pension with mandatory private funded pensions (on the Chilean model) and voluntary additional private pensions. An emotive theme has been the supposed withdrawal of funds from child welfare. Yet there is no evidence of an inverse relationship between the amount of spending on older people and on children (also shown in Chapters 2 and 3). International comparison of the balance of state spending on young and old, in which indices of spending on pensions and family allowances were constructed, suggests that, among Sweden, the UK, Canada, Japan, Belgium, France and Germany from 1959–86, only Germany's spending was biased towards older people (McDaniel 1997).

The World Bank report employs 'resource base' arguments about the impact of demographic change on public pension systems but at the same time appeals to political economy arguments – about how the claims of pensioners and others on resources are defined and exercised, and the possibility of intergenerational conflict over this.

The 'resource base' arguments for switching to private funded pensions have been challenged by numerous writers (for example, Mabbett 1997; Toporowski 1998; Myles and Street 1995; Hills 1995; Lloyd-Sherlock and Johnson 1996; Quadagno 1996). A major problem is that, as indicated by Hills (1995), the generation affected by such a transition has to pay twice: once for its own future private pensions and again for the existing public pension scheme until its last liabilities are fulfilled. Mabbett (1997) finds that the case for funding based on its potential to increase the rate of saving is weak, while the double burden of taxation during the transitional period is likely to reduce economic performance. She points out that while population ageing lowers the rate of return in PAYG schemes, it will also tend to reduce interest rates, bringing a diminishing return on capital. As new private pensions mature, they will depress equity prices and international diversification provides no escape if similar conditions prevail in other economies. Toporowski (1998) points out that in a financial market dominated by pension funds, their synchronous maturation will require a corresponding influx of new contributors so that the 'chain letter scenario' may be more applicable to private than to public pension schemes. For the Chilean pension funds started in 1980 and acclaimed as a successful model by other governments, the sustainability of rates of return has been questioned (Barrientos 1996). Indeed, there has been a substantial fall in annual rates of return since the 1980s, accelerating since 1994 (Barrientos, 1998). It is unclear whether these private funds will be able to honour their pension promises, as the ratio of entitled pensioners to contributors rises over time.

A recent report by the European Federation for Retirement Provision estimates that providing private funded pensions (at 25 per cent of previous earnings) to 60 per cent of employed people in the EU would expand the European pension fund asset base ninefold to ECU10,200 billion by 2020, twice the size of the US pension fund (cited in Griffin 1996). The eagerness of the British finance industry to expand into Europe is in no doubt; one pro-EMU writer stresses that 'With London as Europe's leading financial centre, the British financial services industry will be able to penetrate the fast-growing private pensions markets of continental Europe' (Griffin 1996: 6). But Toporowski's (1998) analysis suggests this strategy is driven not only by a desire for increased profit; it also follows the logic of 'Ponzi finance' (pyramid-selling or chain letters), in which funded pension schemes can only remain viable if they have an expanding contribution base. Because private pension schemes must generate additional income to cover large administration costs and profits, they would seem to be more prone to the chain letter scenario than public schemes.

> The battle to wean German and Italian workers from their state pensions is not just a struggle for sound government finance. Even more importantly, it is a struggle to save the soundness of the capital markets of the US, the UK and Japan and the solvency of their funded pension schemes.
>
> (Toporowski 1998: 25)

Many commentators have pointed out that the challenge of a skewed worker/pensioner ratio is not solved by funded pensions since pensions in the future will have to be paid from economic output at the time; funded pensions, at best, merely shift the problem from the public to the private sector.

Political economy arguments for a switch to funded pensions stress the desirability of linking pension benefits more closely to contributions, claiming that the redistributional elements of public pensions may lead to a breakdown of the generational contract. These arguments have also been questioned (Walker 1993, 1996; Phillipson 1996). Walker (1993) notes the continuing high level of support by people of all ages for ensuring a decent standard of living for older people, indicating no evidence of a desire to renege on the generational contract (also shown in Chapters 2–5). The fact that those countries which most radically changed their pensions systems in the 1980s were those with neo-liberal governments suggests that: 'concern about population ageing has been artificially amplified as an economic-demographic imperative intended primarily to legitimate policies aimed at restructuring the welfare state' (Walker 1993: 41).

In the debates over intergenerational equity and privatisation of pensions, little attention has been paid to existing gender inequality of pension income and to the likely impact of state welfare retrenchment on older women in the future. This omission is particularly serious since women constitute the majority of older people, especially among those aged over 75, and since older women are already more vulnerable to poverty than older men in most countries of the European Union (Walker *et al.* 1993; Walker and Maltby 1997; Dooghe and Appleton 1995).

Reforms to curb the cost of public PAYG pensions and to encourage increased private funded pension provision have been implemented or are planned in most Western countries (OECD 1992; Gillion 1991; Lloyd-Sherlock and Johnson 1996; Street 1996) and in the transitional economies of Central and Eastern Europe (Gotting 1994). In the next section, we consider the gender impact of pension retrenchment, focusing on Britain.

Gender impact of pension retrenchment

Women's financial disadvantage in retirement can be traced to their earlier working lives, lower lifetime earnings being reflected in a lower pension income. However, such an explanation is an oversimplification, insofar as it fails to account for variation over time or across countries. With rising female employment rates, women's independent entitlement to state pensions in Western countries is growing, especially where the state pension scheme allows contribution credits for periods of caring. However, this advance for women will be negated if public pensions are reduced and the balance of pension provision shifted towards the private sector.

Evans and Falkingham's (1997) comparative analysis of six countries – Australia, Chile, Italy, Poland, Sweden and Britain – shows how the effect of women's constrained employment on their pension income depends on the structure of the pension system. The performance of each country's mandatory pension system was measured in terms of the amount of (simulated) pension at retirement as a proportion of average gross male earnings, computing the value of this 'relative income' for seven hypothetical employment histories. For part-time, low-paid work with childcare gaps, relative income was about 50 per cent in Sweden and Poland, 37 per cent in Italy, 23 per cent in Britain and Australia, but only 11 per cent in Chile, where the major pension scheme is a funded, defined contribution scheme. The authors conclude that the latter type of pension scheme (versions of which are being promoted as private pensions in Britain and elsewhere) widens income inequality in retirement, disadvantages women whose employment was restricted by raising children, and will lead to expansion of means-tested assistance in old age. In contrast, a universal pension well above the level of assistance safety nets protects the vulnerable and provides an incentive for additional voluntary provision. For example, Denmark's tax-funded social pension, which is more generous than the British basic pension, has minimised gender inequality of income in later life (Ginn and Arber 1998; Walker and Maltby 1997).

Pension retrenchment has been defined as: 'purposive policy decisions to cut either current or future direct public expenditure for pensions, through ideologically consistent changes that permanently restructure pension regimes to increase needs-testing, privatisation or both, and that alter the future political environment of pension policy-making' (Street 1996). Britain provides a good example of this process: ideological objectives and a concern to minimise the social wage played a major role, while the switching of resources from the public to the private sector of pension provision has been more radical in Britain than elsewhere (Pierson 1994).

The relationship between state and private pensions appears to be a reciprocal one, as argued by Tamburi and Mouton (1986), an increase in one being associated with a decrease in the other. Government policy contributes to this zero-sum relationship, influencing both the economic and political viability of the two sectors. In the privatisation process, first, cuts in state pensions release resources which can be used as incentives for private pensions, generally in the form of tax reliefs on contributions and investment returns; second, demand is fuelled, especially among higher earners, for additional insurance against income loss in retirement as state pension promises are eroded; and third, as the middle-class stake in state pensions diminishes, political support for state pension provision may be undermined. Thus a vicious circle operates to further erode state pensions.

It is instructive to examine the gender impact of the privatisation process in Britain since its privatisation programme has been the most extensive among EU countries, and may indicate the effect on women if other countries were to adopt the World Bank's (1994) recommendations.

In spite of having one of the smallest projected rises in the elderly dependency ratio among twenty OECD countries (Roseveare et al. 1996: Figure 1), the British Conservative government from 1979 to 1997 implemented neo-liberal pension reforms, placing increased emphasis on individuals' responsibility to provide for themselves in retirement through private pensions, while ignoring structured inequality in the ability to do so. As has been shown elsewhere, occupational pensions discriminate against women, mainly through penalising early leavers (Groves 1987; Ginn and Arber 1991, 1993; Arber and Ginn 1991), while the more portable personal pensions are unsuitable for most women, as outlined below. Thus women rely more than men do on state pensions for their income in later life.

Three major reductions in British state pensions have been set in motion since a Conservative government was elected in 1979. First, indexing the basic state pension according to prices instead of national average earnings has eroded its value since 1980 from 20 to 16 per cent of average male earnings by 1990 and to 12 per cent (projected) in 2010 (Johnson and Falkingham 1992). One result has been that, by 1994, a third of pensioners, predominantly women, required means-tested benefits to top up their income (Johnson 1994). Because the basic pension is below the level of Income Support (IS), a small additional pension brings no financial advantage, merely disqualifying the recipient from IS and associated benefits. As the basic pension falls further below the IS level, increasing numbers of pensioners, mainly women with small amounts of other income, will be caught in the pensions poverty trap.

Second, the value of the State Earnings Related Pension Scheme (SERPS) was substantially reduced from its 1975 formulation by the 1986 Social Security Act. The accrual rate was cut and, most serious for women, the pension is now based on revalued earnings over the whole working life instead of the best twenty years. This change has removed what in 1975 (under a Labour government) promised to be a new deal for women, in which years of family care or part-time employment would have been disregarded in calculation of their SERPS. The survivors' pension was cut to half from the year 2000, affecting mainly women since, among those aged over 65, nearly half (47 per cent) of women are widows, whereas only 17 per cent of men are widowers (ONS 1997).

Third, for women born after 1950, raising the state pension age from 60 to 65 will further reduce the amount of both basic and SERPS pensions by lengthening the required contribution period (Hutton *et al.* 1995; Ginn and Arber, 1995). Although raising the pension age for women appears to promote gender equality, it will only benefit women in the unlikely event that they are able to continue in full-time employment from age 60 to 65.

The most significant reform by the Conservative government was the promotion of personal pensions in the Social Security Act 1986. Personal pensions are individually arranged, defined contribution schemes, to which employers rarely contribute, apart from the minimum required to replace the employer's SERPS contribution. All British employees must contribute either to SERPS, to a 'contracted out' occupational pension scheme or to an 'approved' personal pension (APP) fulfilling minimal benefit requirements. Financial incentives to employees to opt out of SERPS were paid for from the National Insurance Fund, thus robbing the state sector to pay the private. Personal pensions provide less generous benefits than occupational, because of the lack of employer contributions and the higher cost of administration and sales commissions (Davies and Ward 1992). The pension amount is unpredictable, depending on the fund's investment performance and on the fees charged. The latter can absorb 20 or even 30 per cent of the fund.

Although any pension based on lifetime earnings places women at a disadvantage, personal pensions offer women a particularly poor deal (Davies and Ward 1992), especially if they have children. For those with interrupted employment, increased charges are incurred, so that a higher proportion of the fund is forfeit (Ward 1996: 43–4). The effect of charges is more serious for women than for men because of women's lower average earnings combined with flat rate charges. A further disadvantage for women is that the same fund buys a smaller annuity than for men, due to the use of sex-based actuarial tables.

Table 8.1 shows the change in private pension membership of working-age men and women in Britain between 1987 and 1994. Among all adults aged 20–59, occupational pension scheme membership had declined from 34 per cent to 32 per cent over the seven years, although this obscures a rise in women's membership from 22 to 25 per cent and a fall in men's from 46 to 40 per cent. Men were more likely than women to be contributing to a personal pension (APP) in 1993–4, 13 compared with 9 per cent. Among employees, occupational pension scheme coverage remained stable at 51 per cent, although women's membership rate increased from 36 to 42 per cent while men's declined slightly from 64 to 61 per cent. Coverage by occupational pensions was strongly associated with full-time employment and with an advantaged position in the labour market. Employees without access to an occupational pension scheme tend to be low-paid, part-time employed, to have lower socio-economic status and to have worked for a shorter time for their employer. Among employees, 17 per cent were contributing to a personal pension (APP), a fifth of men and 14 per cent of women.

Occupational pension scheme membership among women is strongly associated with childlessness and with relative freedom from responsibility for childcare (see Figure 8.2). Among women aged 40–59, over 40 per cent of those who had never had a child belonged to an occupational pension scheme in 1988–90. The membership rate was just over a quarter among women with no children still living at home, just over a fifth among women with only adult children (over 16) at home and 18 per cent among women with at least

Table 8.1 Occupational and personal pension (APP) coverage among British adults aged 20–59, 1987 and 1993–4

Percentage with pensions	Employees			All adults		
	All	Men	Women	All	Men	Women
Occupational pensions:						
1987	51	64	36	34	46	22
1993–4	51	61	42	32	40	25
Full-timers 1993–4	60	62	56			
Part-timers 1993–4	22	23	22			
Managers/professionals 1993–4		78	71			
Unskilled manual 1993–4		42	13			
10+ yrs with employer 1993–4		85	66			
1–2 yrs with employer 1993–4		35	22			
Personal pensions (APP):						
1993–4	17	20	14	11	13	9

Sources: General Household Surveys 1993–4 (authors' analysis) Ginn and Arber 1993.

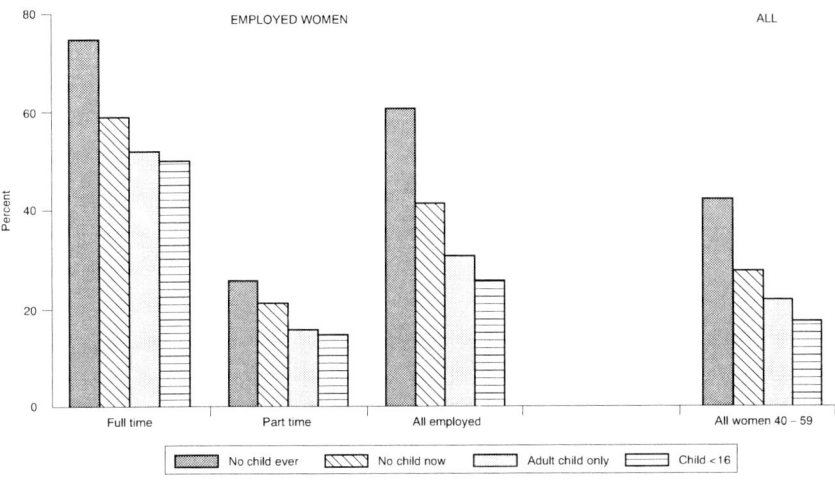

Figure 8.2 Percentage contributing to an occupational pension. Women aged 40–59 by parental and employment status.

Source: General Household Surveys 1988–90 (author's analysis).

one child under 16 at home. A similar, but stronger, membership gradient by parental status was evident among employed women. Even when hours of work were controlled, the effect of parental responsibility was clear: Among women employed full-time, three-quarters of childless women belonged to an occupational pension scheme, compared with half of women with a child under 16. It is clear that women's role in raising the next generation incurs a heavy cost in lost opportunities to accumulate an occupational pension.

The rationale for the introduction of personal pensions was to allow employees without access to an occupational pension an opportunity to build a better pension than provided by the much-reduced SERPS. However, many of those who lacked access to an occupational pension scheme and opted for a personal pension plan are likely to find themselves worse off in retirement than if they had remained in SERPS (Ginn and Arber forthcoming).

Researchers have questioned whether the British Conservative government's pension reforms were justified. Hutton *et al.* (1995: 15) point out that 'the UK pension system is currently one of the "cheapest" of all the OECD countries', costing less than 7 per cent of GDP, and that state pensions provide the lowest earnings replacement rate in the EU, with the exception of Ireland. As noted above, the idea that the British welfare state is in financial

147

crisis has been challenged by Hills (1993). The provision of large and growing subsidies to private pensions in the form of tax reliefs and incentives has led Sinfield (1993) to point out that the government, despite its stated intention to target benefits on the poorest, has been using public funds to target benefits on the well-off. Pensioners' organisations have put these arguments to the Labour government and urged that state social insurance should be revitalised in order to lift all pensioners off means-tested benefits (National Pensioners Convention 1998), but without success. Walker's (1993) thesis – that pensions policy has reflected political priorities (to capture middle-class votes and appease business interests) rather than demographic imperatives – seems to be borne out.

Public subsidies to private pensions diminish the ability of the state to provide adequate retirement income in three main ways. First, large and increasing tax relief for private pension provision reduces the funds available for state pensions. Second, tax reliefs create divisions among citizens, especially between high earners who benefit from private pensions and low earners who depend on state pensions. Third, subsidy of private pensions preserves the illusion that private pensions are the result of entirely market transactions and acts of individual responsibility; this heightens the perception of private pension income as an appropriate market wage and undermines the legitimacy of public sector pension receipts by portraying them as unhealthy dependence on the state (Myles and Street 1995; Street 1996). In all these ways, private pensions imperil the state provision which is vital to those with low lifetime earnings, mainly women.

The British pension reforms of the 1980s have most adversely affected those women who have conformed to the gender contract, giving priority to their family roles. The Labour government elected in 1997, despite having criticised the Conservatives' pension reforms, has not reversed them. Instead, new private funded 'Stakeholder Pensions' (in effect, personal pensions with lower charges and more flexibility) are proposed (Labour Party 1997). These will do nothing to prevent the pension penalties suffered by those whose lifetime earnings are reduced by their caring responsibilities.

Conclusions

The contract between generations cannot be fully understood in isolation from the gender contract. Women's role in physical reproduction maintains the numerical balance between generations, while nurturing and socialising children underpins the next generation's productivity, supporting the viability of pension provision. Yet capitalist economic systems tend to encourage individualism, opposing the logic of family life; 'the ultimate market society is a childless society' (Beck 1992: 116).

In Britain, the signs are that women's employment will continue to increase, although much of it will be part-time. The Conservative government in the 1980s was riven by competing ideologies: the conservative pro-family lobby saw women as mothers, their place firmly in the home, while the neo-liberal view saw women primarily as (low-) paid workers. The latter view prevailed in Thatcherism and is also ascendant in the Labour government elected in 1997, as shown by its measures to persuade lone mothers of young children to take jobs. As women increasingly behave as though motivated by economic rationality, maximising their employment and earnings, the traditional gender contract erodes and fertility declines.

The dilemma, then, is that the generational contract and the welfare of society depend on unpaid work which disadvantages women in the labour market and hence in private pension schemes. The further privatisation of pensions, whether necessary to avert an 'old-age crisis' or promoted because of an ideological hostility to collective welfare, will sharpen the pension penalties women incur when they restrict their earning capacity in order to care for others.

State pensions, in contrast, can reduce the pension costs of caring. Western European countries facing more severe demographic pressure and public pension liabilities than Britain have so far rejected a radical dismantling of state welfare, their modest reforms reflecting solidaristic cultural traditions and the fierce resistance of organisations of workers and pensioners. However, in Chile and in Britain alarmist accounts of population ageing and intergenerational inequity have been used to legitimate public pension retrenchment, shifting the balance of pension provision from state to private and tightening the link between lifetime earnings and pension income. Yet because the proportion of productive activity carried out in the domestic and the formal economy changes over time, claims of intergenerational inequity based on time trends in financial transfers are misleading.

Pension retrenchment in Britain has been driven by political rather than economic concerns and has benefited the private pensions and insurance sector more than workers or pensioners. The individualistic ideology on which pension privatisation is based may lead to a society in which no one can afford to care for others.

Acknowledgements

We are grateful to the Office of National Statistics for permission to use the General Household Survey data and to the ESRC Data Archive and Manchester Computing Centre for access to the data. The research is part of a project funded by The Leverhulme Trust, grant number F/242/4.

References

Arber, S. and Ginn, J. (1991) *Gender and Later Life: A Sociological Analysis of Resources and Constraints*, London: Sage.

Barrientos, A. (1996) 'Ageing and personal pensions in Chile', chapter 5 in P. Lloyd-Sherlock and P. Johnson (eds) *Ageing and Social Policy. Global comparisons*, London: Suntory-Toyota International Centre for Economics and Related Disciplines.
——(1998) *Pension Reform in Latin America*, Aldershot: Ashgate Publishing.
Beck, U. (1992) *Risk Society*, London: Sage.
Becker, G. (1991) *A Treatise on the Family*, London: Harvard University Press.
Brannen, J., Meszaros, G., Moss, P. and Poland, G. (1994) *Employment and Family Life*, London: Employment Department.
Chand, S. and Jaeger, A. (1996) *Aging Populations and Public Pension Schemes*, Occasional Paper 147, London: International Monetary Fund.
Coward, R. (1997) 'Was feminism wrong about the family?' in G. Dench (ed.) *Rewriting the Sexual Contract*, London: Institute of Community Studies.
Davies, B. and Ward, S. (1992) *Women and Personal Pensions*, Manchester: Equal Opportunities Commission.
Daykin, C. (1996) 'Developments in social security and pensions worldwide', *British Actuarial Journal* 2: 207–26.
Dex, S. (1987) *Women's Occupational Mobility: A Lifetime Perspective*, Basingstoke: Macmillan.
Disney, R. (1996) *Can We Afford to Grow Older?*, Massachusetts: MIT.
Dooghe, G. and Appleton, N. (1995) *Elderly Women in Europe: Choices and Challenges*, London: Anchor Housing.
Ermisch, J. (1990) *Fewer Babies, Longer Lives*, York: Joseph Rowntree Foundation.
European Commission (1996) *European Economy No. 3. Ageing and Pension Expenditure Prospects*, Luxembourg: European Commission.
Eurostat (1995) *Demographic Statistics 1995*, Luxembourg: Eurostat.
Evans, M. and Falkingham, J. (1997) *Minimum Pensions and Safety Nets in Old Age: A Comparative Analysis*, WSP/131, London: Suntory-Toyota International Centre for Economics and Related Disciplines.
Falkingham, J. and Hills, J. (eds) (1995) *The Dynamic of Welfare. Social Policy and the Life Cycle*, Hemel Hempstead: Harvester Wheatsheaf.
Field, F. (1995) *Making Welfare Work*, London: Institute of Community Studies.
Folbre, N. (1994) *Who Pays for the Kids? Gender and the Structures of Constraint*, London: Routledge.
Gershuny, J. (1997a) 'Sexual divisions and the distribution of work in the household', in G. Dench (ed.) *Rewriting the Sexual Contract*, London: Institute of Community Studies.
——(1997b) 'Time for the family', *Prospects*, January: 56–7.
Gillion, C. (1991) 'Ageing populations: spreading the costs', *Journal of European Social Policy* 1(2): 107–28.
Ginn, J. and Arber, S. (1991) 'Gender, class and income inequalities in later life', *British Journal of Sociology* 42(3): 369–96.
——(1992) 'Towards women's independence: pension systems in three contrasting European welfare states', *Journal of European Social Policy* 2(4): 255–77.
——(1993) 'Pension penalties: the gendered division of occupational welfare', *Work Employment and Society* 7(1): 47–70.
——(1995) 'Moving the goalposts: the impact on British women of raising their state pension age to 65', in R. Page and J. Baldock (eds) *Social Policy Review No. 7*, London: Social Policy Association.
——(1996) 'Patterns of employment, pensions and gender: the effect of work history on older women's non-state pensions', *Work Employment and Society* 10(3): 469–90.

——(1998) 'How does part time work lead to low pensions?', chapter 8 in J. O'Reilly and C. Fagan (eds), *Part Time Prospects*, London: Routledge.

——(forthcoming) 'Who took the bait? Personal pension take-up in the 1990s', *Journal of Social Policy*.

Ginn, J. and Sandell, J. (1996) 'Balancing home and employment: stress reported by social services staff', *Work Employment and Society* 11(3): 413–34.

Glover, J. and Arber, S. (1995) 'Polarisation in mothers' employment', *Gender, Work and Organisation* 2(4): 165–79.

Gotting, U. (1994) 'Destruction, adjustment and innovation: social policy transformation in eastern and central Europe', *Journal of European Social Policy* 4(3): 181–200.

Grace, M. (1998) 'The work of caring for young children: priceless or worthless?', *Women's Studies International Forum* 21(4): 401–13.

Griffin, A. (1996) *No Panic on Pensions*, London: Action Centre for Europe.

Groves, D. (1987) 'Occupational pension provision and women's poverty in old age', in C. Glendinning and J. Millar (eds) *Women and Poverty in Britain*, Brighton: Wheatsheaf.

Guillemard, A-M. (1996) 'Equity between generations in aging societies: the problem of assessing public policies', in T. Hareven (ed.) *Aging and Generational Relations: Lifecourse and Cross-cultural Perspectives*, Berlin: de Gruyter.

Hakim, C. (1996) 'The sexual division of labour and women's heterogeneity', *British Journal of Sociology* 47(1): 178–88.

Hills, J. (1993) *The Future of Welfare. A Guide to the Debate*, York: Joseph Rowntree Foundation.

——(1995) 'The welfare state and redistribution between generations', in J. Falkingham and J. Hills (eds) *The Dynamic of Welfare. Social Policy and the Life Cycle*, Hemel Hempstead: Harvester Wheatsheaf.

Hutton, S., Kennedy, S. and Whiteford, P. (1995) *Equalisation of State Pension Ages: The Gender Impact*, Manchester: Equal Opportunities Commission.

Jackson, T., Marks, N., Ralls, J. and Stymne, S. (1997) *Sustainable Economic Welfare in the UK 1950–1996*, London: New Economics Foundation.

Jacobs, S. (1997) 'Employment changes over childbirth: a retrospective view, *Sociology* 31(3): 577–90.

Johnson, P. (1994) *The Pensions Dilemma*, London: Institute for Public Policy Research.

Johnson, P. and Falkingham, J. (1992) *Ageing and Economic Welfare*, London: Sage.

Johnson, P., Conrad, C. and Thomson, D. (eds) (1989) *Workers versus Pensioners: Intergenerational Conflict in an Ageing World*, Manchester: Manchester University Press.

Joshi, H. (1996) *The Tale of Mrs. Typical*, London: Family Policy Studies Centre.

Joshi, H. and Davies, H. (1992) 'Daycare in Europe and mothers' foregone earnings', *International Labour Review* 131(6): 561–79.

Kotlikoff, L. (1992) *Generational Accounting: Knowing Who Pays and When for What we Spend*, New York: Free Press.

Kotlikoff, L. and Sachs, J. (1997) 'Privatising social security: its high time to privatise', *Brookings Review* 15(3): 16–19.

Labour Party (1997) *Security in Retirement*, London: The Labour Party.

Land, H. and Rose, H. (1985) 'Compulsory altruism or an altruistic society for all?', in P. Bean, J. Ferris and D. Whynes (eds), *In Defence of Welfare*, London: Tavistock.

Lloyd-Sherlock, P. and Johnson, P. (1996) *Ageing and Social Policy. Global Comparisons*, London: Suntory-Toyota International Centre for Economics and Related Disciplines.

Luckhaus, L. (1997) 'Privatisation and pensions: some pitfalls for women?' *European Law Journal* 3(1): 83–100.

Mabbett, D. (1997) *Pension Funding: Economic Imperative or Political Strategy?*, Uxbridge: Brunel University.

McAllister, F. and Clarke, L. (1998) *Choosing Childessness*, London: Family Policy Study Centre.

McDaniel, S. (1997) 'Intergenerational transfers, social solidarity and social policy: unanswered questions and policy challenges', *Canadian Journal on Aging/Canadian Public Policy*, Supplement, Spring: 1–21.

Morgan, P. (1997) 'Evaluating the effects on children of mother's employment', in G. Dench (ed.) *Rewriting the Sexual Contract*, London: Institute of Community Studies.

Murgatroyd, L. and Neuberger, H. (1997) 'A household satellite account for the UK', *Economic Trends* no. 527: 63–71.

Myles, J. and Street, D. (1995) 'Should the economic life course be redesigned?' *Canadian Journal on Aging* 14(2): 335–59.

National Pensioners Convention (1998) *Pensions Not Poor Relief*, London: NPC.

OECD (1992) *Private Pensions and Public Policy*, Paris: OECD.

Office of National Statistics (ONS) (1997) *Living in Britain*, London: The Stationery Office.

Phillipson, C. (1996) 'Intergenerational conflict and the welfare state: American and British perspectives', in A. Walker (ed.), *The New Generational Contract*, London: UCL Press.

Pierson, P. (1994) *Dismantling the Welfare State? Reagan, Thatcher and the Politics of Retrenchment*, Cambridge: Cambridge University Press.

Quadagno, J. (1996) 'Social security and the myth of the entitlement crisis', *The Gerontologist* 36: 391–99.

Roseveare, D., Leibfritz, W., Fore, D. and Wurzel, E. (1996) *Ageing Populations, Pension Systems and Government Budgets: Simulations for 20 OECD Countries*, Paris: OECD.

Rossi, A. (1993) 'Intergenerational relations: Gender, norms and behaviour', in V. Bengtson and A. Achenbaum (eds) *The Changing Contract Across Generations*, New York: Aldine de Gruyter.

Sinfield, A. (1993) 'Reverse targeting and upside down benefits – how perverse policies perpetuate poverty', in A. Sinfield (ed.) *Poverty, Inequality and Justice*, Edinburgh: Edinburgh University Press.

Street, D. (1996) 'The politics of pensions in Canada, Great Britain and the United States, 1975–1995', Ph.D. dissertation, Tallahassee: The Florida State University.

Tamburi, G. and Mouton, P. (1986) 'The uncertain frontier between private and public pension schemes', *International Labour Review* 125 (2): 127–40.

Thomson, D. (1989) 'The welfare state and generation conflict: winners and losers', pp. 35–56 in P. Johnson *et al.* (eds) *Workers versus Pensioners: Intergenerational Conflict in an Ageing World*, Manchester: Manchester University Press.

——(1991) *Selfish Generations: The Ageing of New Zealand's Welfare State*, Wellington: Bridget Williams Books.

Toporowski, J. (1998) 'Ponzi finance and pension fund capitalism', paper presented to the Association for Social Economics meeting, Chicago, January 5th.

van Krieken, R. (1997) 'Sociology and the reproductive self: demographic transitions and modernity', *Sociology* 31(3): 445–71.

Waine, B. (1995) 'A disaster foretold? The case of the personal pension', *Social Policy and Administration* 29(4): 317–34.

Walker, A. (1993) 'Whither the social contract? Intergenerational solidarity in income and employment', in D. Hobman (ed.) *Uniting Generations*, London: Age Concern England.
——(ed.) (1996) *The New Generational Contract*, London: UCL Press.
Walker, A., Alber, J. and Guillemard, A.-M. (1993) *Older People in the EU: Social and Economic Policies*, Brussels: CEC.
Walker, A. and Maltby, T. (1997) *Ageing Europe*, Buckingham: Open University Press.
Ward, P. (1996) *The Great British Pensions Robbery*, Preston: Waterfall Books.
World Bank (1994) *Averting the Old Age Crisis*, New York: Oxford University Press.

9

TRAIL-BLAZERS
AND PATH-FOLLOWERS

Social reproduction
and geographical mobility
in youth

Gill Jones

Families are often described as the primary social units, the 'building blocks' of society. The processes by which members of each generation achieve social status in their own right, therefore, begin in the everyday life of the family of origin, and continue through the education system, the labour market and other social institutions. Family members may be involved in the inter-generational transmission not only of wealth, but also of social and cultural capital in the form of skills, social networks, aspirations and values (Bertaux and Thompson 1997). Young people as they grow up may draw heavily on family resources such as these, if they can, to help them become established in the adult world. If the concept of a 'generational contract' exists at all outside its construction in social science, then perhaps one clause in the contract is that parents should not only 'want the best' for their children, but that they should contribute to this end. This contribution could be seen as an instrumental act: an investment which pays dividends when the parents become older and need care themselves. The 'generational contract' is potentially reciprocal over time.

Intergenerational transmission of social and cultural capital is thus a mechanism for social reproduction, including the reproduction of social in-equality from one generation to the next. The process is, however, complex and with changing social and economic structures may be becoming more so. First, other inequalities and conflicts within families may interfere with class reproduction processes. Second, when social change is so rapid, the parent generation may not possess social and cultural capital which has value for the younger generation, and the structures in which family transfers could once flourish may now be threatened. This is not to suggest that we are moving towards a more equal society, only that social divisions, and the mechanisms for maintaining them, change.

Intra-household inequalities

Studies of intergenerational social mobility tend to be quantitative (Goldthorpe 1980), exploring inter-household differences on the basis of the occupational class of the head of the household. Stratification research can gain from a combination of quantitative and qualitative methods (as Bertaux and Thompson 1997, argue). The former indicating the extent and nature of social class movement, the latter offering insights into the micro-processes which may act as aids or as barriers to social reproduction. The family household has an internal structure of inequality (age, gender and, perhaps, also social class), which may interfere with the role of 'the family' – where this is viewed as an entity – in ensuring the transmission of social class and status from one generation to the next. intergenerational occupational class transmission tends, for example, to be gendered – from father to son, or to a lesser extent from mother to daughter (Jones 1987, 1992). Age inequalities in the household may affect the younger generation's attitudes to receiving advice and help and the older generation's willingness to offer them (Jones 1995).

Social change

The transmission of social and cultural capital may help to maintain or enhance the class location of the next generation. One reason inequality persists is because some parents have knowledge and skills which they can pass on to their children, while others do not, which is one of the reasons why educational achievement tends to be clustered in some families, while unemployment is in others. However, it has been argued that the stability previously associated with institutions, such as the labour market and the family, has ceased to exist in conditions of post-modernity (Lash and Urry 1987; Bauman 1995) or 'reflexive modernity' (Giddens 1991; Beck 1992). A flexible labour market (Bagguley 1991; Lash and Urry 1987) and the increase in marital breakdown (Kiernan *et al.* 1998) result in the individualisation of biographies which in turn involve greater uncertainty and risk. Beck (1992) refers to the increased 'fragility' of family support, as more marriages end in divorce. Equally, the changes in the transition from school to work, with extended education and training, with a shift from manufacturing to service industry, involving fewer full-time jobs, mean that the experience of young people entering the labour market now is very different from that of their parents' generation. The ability of parents to offer up-to-date guidance to their adult children, for example to provide job information, becomes more limited.

Parents are once again de-skilled and 'replaced' by professionals (in this case careers teachers and guidance staff). In these circumstances, parents are less able to transmit cultural capital and complete their side of the 'generational contract'.

Geographical mobility as a case study

One of the expectations of present-day life is that people should be prepared to move geographically to where there are jobs. Migration is likely to increase, affecting a wider group, as a means of escaping the lack of jobs in specific local areas. Urry (1995) stresses that in conditions of post-modernity, cultural capital needs to be transferable. Geographical mobility has long been associated with upward social mobility and thus with the middle class, with the result that middle-class families in particular have geographically spread kinship networks (Bell 1968; Finch 1989a). Grieco (1987) demonstrated that 'chain migration' could occur, resulting in the establishment of supportive kinship networks in the new location. Young people in rural areas may migrate to 'get on' and avoid downward mobility, if they are middle class, or to achieve upward mobility, if they are working-class (MacDonald 1988; Jones 1992). Elliott (1997) suggests that where downward social mobility is threatened or upward mobility blocked, a family's cultural capital may be mobilised. He argues that youth migration can form part of a 'family mobility project', involving the mobilisation of family resources. Entry into the job market is a time when young people may need to mobilise many forms of support, including knowledge and guidance.

The ability of the family to play a continuing role in social reproduction must therefore be investigated afresh. The question of whether cultural capital can be transferred in the face of migration provides an interesting case study. This chapter, based on a study of youth in rural Scotland, examines some of the ways in which rural parents may transfer cultural capital to their migrating children and some circumstances in which they may fail to do so. It is informed by earlier research on the poverty faced by young people who cannot access family economic support (Jones 1995). Here, qualitative evidence will suggest that migration does not in itself inhibit the transmission of social class from generation to generation, because a 'culture of migration' forms part of the cultural capital of some families, along with appropriate and up-to-date knowledge of education and the labour market. Young people with access to these forms of cultural capital appear more able to achieve upward mobility through migration than those who lack it. While some young migrants can be described as 'path-followers', following an established pattern of migration and social class, others must be seen more as 'trailblazers', pioneers who have no family precedent to guide them and who have to map out and follow transition paths of their own making, in true postmodernist style.

The study

This chapter examines qualitative data from an ESRC-funded research project on migration behaviour and decision-making among young people in rural Scotland,[1] in which, apart from revisiting previous research which found that the more educationally gifted tended to migrate away in order to get on, we also wanted to explore why others, including some with educational ability, stayed in the area. The data reported here come from follow-up personal interviews in 1995 with forty-five young people, all originally from the same school year cohort and all aged approximately 23 years. All were in the final compulsory school year in secondary schools in the Scottish Borders in 1988: seven years later, some were still in the area and some had migrated away.

The research drew on the Scottish Young People's Survey (SYPS) 1989/91, a longitudinal study based on a 10 per cent sample of young people in their final compulsory year at secondary school in Scotland, surveyed in 1989 at around 16¾ years and again in 1991 at around 19¼ years of age. All survey respondents who had attended school in the Borders Region in 1988 were extracted as a subset. From this, 50 per cent of respondents to both survey sweeps, plus all respondents to one or other sweep (a non-systematic way to reduce bias by weighting non-response) were targeted (n = 84), 69 per cent were traced and 54 per cent interviewed in 1995. We stopped tracing and seeking interviews once our target of forty-five cases had been reached. In this chapter, quotations from the interview transcripts are anonymised and local colloquialisms have been 'translated' for clarity.

Some definitions are needed. We defined 'migrants' as those young people who had left the Borders Region, even if they had only moved a short distance, comparing them with 'stayers', who had not migrated away, and 'returners' who had migrated and returned to the area again. 'Incomer' families were defined as where both parents had migrated into the Borders Region; 'Local' families were where one parent or both were of local origin. Social class of origin was based on father's current or last occupation, where data were available, otherwise it was assessed from other family characteristics.

The Borders Region of southern Scotland (now the Scottish Borders, following local government reorganisation in 1996) was chosen for the research as a rural area subject to strain because of its proximity to the more populated Central Belt of Scotland, which includes Edinburgh and Glasgow. Its population of around 100,000 people lives in scattered communities and small towns, the largest of which is Hawick (population: 16,500). Woollen-mills and knitwear factories have been the main local employers for over a century, but this industry is now in decline. Local agriculture is no longer a major employer. There is some tourism, and light engineering and electronics factories are scattered through the area, representing a minor development of new industry. There is a shortage of non-manual and 'career jobs' locally, and wages are often low: the region has the highest proportion of low-paid workers in Scotland, 40.5 per cent earning under £220 per week in 1996 according to the New Earnings Survey (ONS 1997). According to the SYPS, 19-year-olds living in the Scottish Borders had lower opinions of local job opportunities than those in any other part of Scotland, while 42 per cent had experienced unemployment since leaving school (the highest proportion of any Scottish region) (Jones and Jamieson 1997). It is perhaps unsurprising that youth out-migration is high. The SYPS analysis showed that, after the remote rural areas of the Scottish highlands and islands, the Borders Region was the area where 19-year-olds were most likely to have left their parental homes (49 per cent of males and 60 per cent of females, compared with national figures of 34 per cent of males and 43 per cent of females), and most likely to have combined leaving home with migrating away (Jones and Jamieson 1997).

Reasons for migrating or staying

The lack of local opportunities provided a strong structural reason for young people to migrate away. Furthermore, economic migration seems to 'work': when we compared the stayers and migrants with similar qualifications at the age of sixteen, we found that, by the age of twenty-three, migrants tended to be in jobs which were more secure, better paid, and more likely to involve training and a career structure (Jamieson 1999). However, there were also less obvious factors affecting migration behaviour. Communities appeared to push some people out and to hold others in. Those feeling most 'pushed out' were the children of incomers, thus encouraging a continuing family history of migration. In contrast, those who stayed on tended to be locally 'born and bred'. In exploring the ways in which young people developed socio-spatial identities as they became adult, we found that some had or developed a close attachment to their local communities while others did not, and that family history played an important part in this process (Jones 1999).

Though it is mainly the children from middle-class families who migrate from the area, a family history of migration has an effect which is greater than that of social class of origin (Table 9.1). Those staying on are mainly locals and of working-class origin, and returning migrants were all the children of locals. The study showed several young migrants to have retained a high degree of attachment to their local communities, but these were mainly from local families. Migration is also associated with educational achievement, but it is not simply the case that the more academically gifted leave the area while the lower achievers stay. The children of locals are more likely to stay in the area even when they have educational qualifications, possibly lowering their sights in the face of limited local job opportunities (see Jamieson 1999).

Young migrants mainly left home for education or employment reasons. The only exception was Morag, a local who 'migrated' over the border from the area when she left home to live with a partner. Fifteen migrants had left

Table 9.1 Migration by social class and migration history of parents

Respondent	Middle-class parents		Working-class parents	
	Incomers	Locals	Incomers	Locals
Migrant (n = 21)	Peter	Helen	Hugh	Linda
	Tim	Malcolm	Alasdair	Morag
	Stephen	Cathy		Sean
	Calum	Theresa		Carol?
	Stewart	Mary		
	Jill	Laura		
	Chris	Shona		
	Alison			
Returner (n = 5)		Tracy	Keith	
		David	Karen	
		Francine		
Stayer (n = 19)	Ian	Andrew	Gordon	Kate
		Ewan	Richard?	Paula
		Lorna	John	Caroline
		Nicky		Brenda
		Moira		Iona
		Hilary		Graham
				Jackie
				Jean
				Pat?
Total (n = 45)	9	16	5	15

to go on a course and nine to take up a job (in two cases with training involved). It was the children of middle-class incomers who predominantly left home to go on educational courses, while the children of locals (mainly middle class) left to take up jobs. Some migrants now had partners. The five returners to the area had originally left for work reasons and were all single. Stayers had experienced job instability, and were usually unable to get training in transferable skills. This left some feeling 'trapped' in the local labour (Jamieson 1999). For stayers, leaving the parental home was associated with family formation (n = 8) or family conflict (n = 3); eight stayers, mainly women, had never left their parents' homes.

Since young people apparently have to get out in order to get on, the remainder of this chapter will focus on the twenty-six migrants and returners, and explore the extent to which they were able to draw on their families for cultural and social capital.

Geographical mobility

Working-class migrants tended to stay either nearby or in the Central Belt of Scotland. Middle-class migrants split between the children of incomers, who tended to move further away, and the children of locals, most of whom moved only to neighbouring areas. Out of sixteen migrants from local families, most did not move far: six to Edinburgh, and three just over the border into nearby towns. The two most notable exceptions both took up jobs with accommodation provided: Shona working in Brussels as a nanny, and David based in the Midlands with the armed forces.

In other cases, however, we find the advantage of a family culture of migration, where young people are following established paths. In some cases we see 'chain migration' (Grieco 1987), with young people following kin – mainly older siblings – to the same new location (Tim and Stephen to southern England, Stewart, Jill and Laura to the Central Belt of Scotland); another pattern was the reversal of the parents' migration: thus some (like Alison to Durham, Alasdair to Glasgow, and Malcolm to southern England) moved to the areas that their parents had left, and sometimes reunited with kin. Alison is a 'return migrant' who had always wanted to live near Durham, while Tim is a 'chain migrant'.

Alison: I think it's because most of my family are here [Durham area] and I know a lot of people, so I think I always wanted to come back down.

Tim: My older brother was at Newcastle and I'd actually been out to see him, visit him, and I liked the place, liked the people and it was the only place, other than Edinburgh, that I had actually been to the place, to actually have a look round. So yeah, I was quite happy to go to Newcastle. [And later he says] I think it's always nice when you go somewhere not to be thrown in at the deep end and not knowing anybody. [...] I mean, I didn't really spend that much time with him. It was just nice to know that he was there if I needed anybody.

In most cases where migration followed a previously defined trail, the young people were the children of middle-class incomers (Malcolm and Laura both had one incomer parent). When migrating, they may thus have several advantages over the children of locals, including the availability of informed advice, and the potential for using geographically distributed kinship networks. Indeed, many migrants drew on kinship support when they migrated, living with kin such as siblings and grandparents, or staying temporarily with more distant kin. There are thus 'migrant families' – mainly middle class – with a history, a structure and a culture which support geographical mobility in the next generation.

Social mobility

In order to identify social mobility among migrants, we need to define the social class not only of the parents but also of their children. The latter is complex, because young people are moving from ascribed class (based on family of origin) to a situation where they have achieved their own social class positions, through a combination of intergenerational and intra-generational processes of mobility (Jones 1987). In the following analysis, definitions of social class are approximate, as many of the respondents were only beginning to embark on occupational careers. Table 9.2 shows whether migrants at age 23 were in a similar class position to that of their family of origin, and suggests that the migrant children of incomers were tending to replicate their class of origin, while the migrant children of locals were more likely to be upwardly mobile. Migration away from rural disadvantage thus allows both reproduction of the middle class, and upward mobility from the working-class.

Transfering cultural capital

We now explore the extent to which parents are able to pass on relevant knowledge to young people who may be socially as well as geographically mobile. As with other forms of parental support (including the transfer of economic capital), this involves the willingness and ability both on the part of parents to give and on the part of children to receive (Jones 1995). Even where young people have a need for help and parents may possess the required capital, the question of willingness is still a problem, which stems from the internal age inequalities within families. According to Parsons (1956), a principal function of parents is to facilitate the eventual emancipation of children within the family (and thus redress the inequalities associated with age), but there is likely to be ambivalence among both parents and children about the latter's move to independence. Finch (1989b) stressed the difficulty of achieving the 'desired blend of dependence and independence'

Table 9.2 Social mobility among migrants

Social mobility of respondent	Middle-class parents		Working-class parents	
	Incomers	*Locals*	*Incomers*	*Locals*
Same social class as parents	Peter Tim Stephen Calum Stewart Jill Chris	Cathy Shona David Francine	Alasdair	Morag Sean Karen
Upwardly mobile		Helen Malcolm Laura Mary	Hugh	Linda Carol
Downwardly mobile	Alison	Theresa Tracy		Keith

in determining the appropriate level of parental support. These tensions may inhibit the transfer of cultural capital from parents to their children, and thus interfere with the function of the family in social reproduction.

Ambivalence on both sides

Laura and Carol both commented on the ambivalence of their parents, faced with the prospect that their daughter would have to leave the area in order to get on in life.

Laura: My mum was very opinionated that I was going to sort of get a good job and good qualifications, but at the same time she didn't want me to leave home, so I could never fathom that out!

Carol: They didn't – they wanted me to do whatever I wanted to do. That's what they said. I don't think my mum or dad really wanted me to move away, because I was their little girl, and because I had been the first person to move out of the family, I think they were a bit wary, but they knew that I wanted to go to college, and they wouldn't have stopped me.

Young people described parallel ambivalence about accepting parental help, and some were keen to indicate that they had made their own decisions. This may have led them to downplay their parents' influence. Sons of middle-class incomers in particular talked about this. For example, Calum, who described himself as 'not very close' to his family, stressed that it was his choice what he did in career terms, while Tim, who said that his parents 'expected' him to go to university, managed to convey a convenient convergence between his parents' aspirations and his own:

Calum: It was a choice. I mean, I think we did discuss it and I said that I wanted to go to university and they had no objections to that. I mean, it's what they would want me to do. So they weren't trying to influence me in that way.

Tim: Well, I was quite happy with the idea of going to university, and they wanted me to. That's as far as it went.

Finding the balance

Young people who are attempting to define themselves as adult and assert their independence may see encouragement as pressure to be resisted. Finding an acceptable balance between encouragement and pressure was clearly a difficulty, and some felt that they had been put under either too much or too little pressure by their parents. Too much pressure could adversely affect motivation. Stewart, for example, had just started a degree course, after a spell working in the local mill and a supermarket. He wished that he had been more motivated when younger, and put responsibility for his lack of motivation on 'maybe initially too much pressure from my parents'. Too much pressure was seen to stifle independence: Laura avoided career discussions with her parents because her mother was so 'opinionated'.

Laura: Up until I left home – this sounds really bad – I never really had much of a chance to make decisions, because my mother was very opinionated, and I would do what my mother said, when she said it. That's why I was so keen to leave home, because I was like 'locked up' on the farm.

Without parental pressure or guidance, the young people were left to their own devices. Shona, now a nanny in Brussels, discussed her job plans with friends rather than her parents: 'Ma mum and dad they just let me go on'. Theresa's parents appear to have respected her need for independence, and she appreciated the lack of pressure.

Theresa: I was always pretty much independent of my parents. I was allowed to do whatever I wanted, just as long as I was responsible and looked after myself, you know what I mean. I was sort of given that trust really early on, so I never felt really pressurised then.

Too little guidance and encouragement could, however, be problematic. Alasdair's parents were 'quite happy' with his plans, but after a bakery course, he had several sales jobs and some unemployment. Chris finished his degree but still has no clear career plans. His parents appear to have taken a liberal view though they broadly encouraged migration away:

Chris: They basically said 'Go off and do your own thing'. They pointed me in a direction and said 'There's a lot more to living than living in this sort of area for the rest of your life'.

Morag, who moved away to live with a partner, works for the council and is currently on a course in administration. She too says that her parents were easy-going about her career:

GJ: Did your parents have any ideas about what they wanted you to do in the future?
Morag: No, they never pushed me or anything like that.
GJ: Did you ever discuss what you should do, with them?
Morag: Aye, aye.
GJ: But did you have disagreements at that time, this is going back.
Morag: Mhmm, no they were easy going, compared to some people's anyway.

Given the paucity of good jobs in the area, young people needed to leave the area if they were going to do well. Middle-class parents could not remain inactive if they were to prevent downward mobility in their children. However, as we have seen, while several children (mainly sons) of middle-class parents felt under pressure from their parents to succeed, this was not the case for working-class migrants, whose parents were less likely to intervene. Following Elliot's (1997) observation, one might expect there to be little parental dynamism involved in the social reproduction of the working-class. Social reproduction would be guaranteed perhaps by parents not doing anything, rather than through their intervention.

Supporting upward mobility?

Upward intergenerational mobility can be difficult for both generations. Some parental effort went into trying to encourage upward mobility in the next generation, but the effectiveness of this varied. As a result, upward mobility could be an individual, rather than family, achievement. Parents who had themselves been migrants, and undergone higher education, or worked in the relevant sector of the labour market, were better equipped to offer advice. Two daughters of farming families (Linda and Helen) were upwardly mobile in relation to their parents: one became a vet and the other an architect, but there were differences in parental support. Helen's family are tenant farmers, and encouraged her to raise her aspirations. Both her parents had been to university and it was 'always just assumed' that she would. She hated school in the fifth year and wanted to do Youth Training in agriculture (this would have allowed her to leave school earlier) and then work on the family farm, but her parents wanted her to study veterinary medicine:

Helen: My mum and dad were quite sort of – 'you can get into vet so you may as well go for it'. [...] So they were quite sort of, not pushing me but encouraging me to stay on at school another year and get into vet school. [...] I'm so glad my dad didn't let me [do farming], but at the time I was – 'parents, they're just trying to run my life for me'. I had quite a lot of arguments with them.

Helen decided that being a vet would be 'the next best thing' to farming and is now about to start work as a vet in England, though she still intends to return to the farm in time.

Others, like Linda, had to find their own mobility paths. Several commented on the inability of parents to offer appropriate guidance; this appears to be a problem experienced particularly by those who were on upward mobility paths (Laura, Malcolm, Hugh, Carol and Linda). Linda's father was a shepherd, but she will soon be an architect. Her family seems not to have been able to offer her informed advice, although they were trying to support her.

Linda: My father wanted me to be a teacher, which I was never, ever interested in because that was what he wanted me to do.

GJ: Was that because that's what women do, sort of thing?

Linda: No. My dad was obsessed with being at college. He thought it was the ideal life!

GJ: And what did your mother want you to do?

Linda: I don't think she had any fixed ideas. [Later she says] I think she was always quite happy for me. She always encouraged me that I was good with my hands. Every time I suggested doing something with my hands, she always said architecture's a good idea.

More parental guidance and encouragement might have been helpful to Mary and Carol. Mary has a senior nursing post, but her mother appears to have been undermining her confidence rather than supporting her in her career. She did not talk with her parents, she says, until she had already decided what she wanted to do, 'and then it was just the practicalities of moving and things like that'.

Mary: I think they always thought I would go away and do something, but it surprised them that I did nursing. Nobody thought I would go into nursing.

GJ: What did they think you would do?

Mary: I think they thought I would do something with History. I don't know. It was a really – I didn't have any interest in that until the end of sixth year.

GJ: So did you have any discussions and disagreements with your parents at all at this time?

Mary: Not really. I always remember my mum going 'Oh, I'd be very surprised if you stick it out when you get on the wards' and that was it, really. But I did and really enjoyed it, but we didn't really have any discussions.

Carol is another example of upward mobility without support. She has now obtained a degree in Business Studies through a combination of sandwich courses. She had little guidance or pressure from her parents, and despite encouragement from her schoolteacher seems to have lacked confidence in her own ability. Nevertheless she has persevered.

Carol: I didn't want to go for the degree at that time, because I was a bit worried – I thought only intelligent, really intelligent people go for degrees, but then you realise when you get to college that you are capable of it. But at that time, all the people that I saw as being more intelligent than me in my class, were going on to do degrees, and I suppose I didn't have that much confidence in myself.

When young people are upwardly mobile, they are on yet another untrodden path. Parents who are keen to help, may be unable to do so appropriately. Where they are apparently pushing in the right direction, their sons and daughters may resist the apparent interference: thus Helen resented at first what she saw as pressure. Resistance can also be a positive response to negative interference though: thus Mary was determined to do nursing despite the lack of encouragement from her mother. Upward mobility can be a lonely business.

Preventing downward mobility?

If upward social mobility is sometimes unsupported, or inadequately supported, can young migrants be protected from downward mobility through the mobilisation of their family's cultural capital, as Elliott (1997) argued? Some parents actively discouraged their children from risking downward mobility. We have seen how Helen's father stopped her from doing a Youth Training scheme in farming. Sean's father discouraged him from going into agricultural labouring when he saw there was no future in it, and Sean is now a contract fencer instead.

On occasion, though, some daughters were resistant to parental aspirations. Alison and Tracy might have gone on to do non-manual work and enter more typical women's occupations, but Alison is a groom at a stables, while Tracy is a contract shepherd. Their parents did not approve, but let them have their way. Tracy has worked on her parents' small-holding since she was young:

Tracy: Oh aye, they were quite happy to let me do that, but all my sisters – my two sisters before me – had helped on the farm. It's just the way my mum and dad were brought up, that your children helped you if you needed a hand, sort of thing. [...] But then when I decided that I wanted to do it for a career that was a different sort of story. [...] Ach, they weren't that keen at first, but once they realised that's what I really wanted, that's what they went for.

LJ: So why were they not keen?

Tracy: Just a lassie into farming, basically what they were frightened of.

Alison: I wanted to leave school in the fourth year before I sat my Highers, and it was a bit of a drama then because they thought I should stay on and everything, so yeah. But apart from that, they've been behind me wherever I've gone.

Theresa received contradictory messages from parents who were in differing class positions, and was downwardly mobile in relation to her mother. Her mother wanted Theresa to do a degree, but she took a vocational course in communications instead: 'Well, my dad never said anything, but my mum was a bit annoyed that I wasn't doing a degree.' Though other factors may have been involved (her mother was said to suffer from manic depression), it seems that the rest of the family did not rate educational success among women very highly.

Theresa: Like my family – my mum would be the first woman in the family to be professionally qualified. And she's quite high up in her job, and nobody in the family really took her very seriously, you know what I mean, and just that sort of attitude prevails quite a bit in the area.

The data suggest some ambivalence in parental aspirations for migrant daughters in particular: in the cases described, manual work was discouraged, but there was little support for academic achievement either. The evidence may indicate parents' reluctance to let their daughters' migrate rather than concerns about their intended careers.

Parental competence

Parents may draw on their own experience in guiding their children, but the world has changed since they were young. Cathy indicated that (despite some evidence of gender stereotyping described below), her parents' own experience of upward social mobility had influenced her, steering her away from mill work towards a middle-class career (she obtained a degree and is now in a management job):

Cathy: My mum and dad started off working in the mills when they were my age, like about twenty and that, in Hawick, but then they chose to get out of it and my dad got into the family business, so I suppose it depends on how you're brought up and what your parents did, that influences you.

The accounts indicate that parental competence may vary. Some parents (like the 'opinionated' mother of Laura) were unable to offer guidance in an acceptable way, some (like Sean's father and Theresa's mother) were handicapped by illness, some (like the parents of Linda, Hugh, Malcolm and Stewart) lacked access to appropriate information. Young people needed confidence in their parents' ability to pass on good advice. Stewart had talked to his parents, because 'they've got a more balanced outlook on things', but later questions his own (and their) judgement on this: 'I mean, maybe I'm completely wrong, they're maybe in fact not and that's been a mistake.' Illness affected the ability of some parents to help, though Theresa's mother's 'manic depression' may have been an excuse for not taking her seriously.

When Sean was in need of advice, his family was instead preoccupied with his father's health:

Sean: Yeah, aye, because the whole family was pretty preoccupied with that, you know. He had his first heart attack when I was in second year. [...] A year later he had a pace-maker and that put in, so like all the time there was like something going on with him, you know. I wouldn't say I was out of the thingy, ken, and they weren't wanting anything – but I couldn't really – I didn't really want to discuss my worries and problems and all that when he had that to think about.

Linda (the architect), clearly academically very gifted, was undecided about what to do – fashion was also an option, and she applied to thirteen university courses and was accepted by them all, but her parents were unable to advise her:

Linda: It was beyond all them, really. My father kept saying 'Well, if you want to do it, yeah'.
GJ: If you want to do which?
Linda: Anything!

One of the problems for parents supporting upward mobility, as Linda has already indicated, is their competence to give appropriate advice and support. Hugh, who studied computing and now works for a cable TV company, says that his parents were not able to help much in an area which was unfamiliar to them: 'They never really – they just let me decide and they would help me out in any way they could.' When Malcolm was thinking what to do, he says there was no discussion: 'They were fine whatever I did'; while Laura is equally uncertain of the competence of parents to help in career guidance.

Malcolm: I did consult them, but only to keep them up to speed really, rather than asking them for much advice, because I don't think they had that much experience of what I was going into.

Laura: Maybe saying what they experienced when they were that age is maybe not quite just it, because times have changed, but they might be able to say 'Well, go and see such and such' and set you in the right direction.

A problem emerging from these accounts is the ability of fathers to offer guidance to their daughters. Theresa has suggested that educational achievement among women was not valued locally. Some parents may be unaware that there are wider opportunities for women now than when they were young, and retain a very gendered view of labour opportunities, based on their experience of local labour markets. Despite the fact that both Tracy and Cathy had worked in family businesses as children, their parents held gender stereotypes which influenced their advice. Thus, Tracy's parents were 'frightened' of the idea of 'a lassie into farming'. Cathy's father had a newsagent's shop. Asked whether she had thought about joining the business, she said:

Cathy: Not really. It was a sort of a joke. Well not a joke really, but Dad always said – 'do you not fancy doing it', and it just wasn't something that appealed to me. I mean I worked there when I was at school, during the holidays and at weekends and stuff, before I, you know, started to get into the hotel industry. But that was all I really wanted to do. I didn't want to take it over.

LJ: But he was kind of encouraging you?

Cathy: Not really, no. I think, well I haven't got any brothers or anything, so I think he sort of knew that when he gave it up, that would be it. He didn't expect us to take it over. Because it's not traditionally a women's business, it's more a man's work, you know.

Jobs may be less gendered than some suggest, but gender stereotypes persist. Farming provides two examples. Apart from Tracy, who is a shepherd, Laura's sister works on the family farm and according to Laura is likely to take it over eventually. Helen thought that her father was thwarting her plans to do farming because she was a woman. She says she 'had a chip on her shoulder' about this for some time, thinking that her brother was being favoured, but later realised that her father did not want either of the children to go into farming, and thought they could do better. This suggests that though parental expectations may be gendered, so may be their daughters' responses. Thus, Helen's response can be seen as resistance on gender lines, another layer on the problem of accepting advice and support while at the same time asserting independence.

Formal guidance

In the wider context, governments are increasingly stressing the need for parents to take responsibility for they children, but there are times when impartial guidance is needed. Where parents were chronically ill or ill-informed, where young people were moving into new territory, where young people were too keen to assert their independence from their parents, formal guidance away from home may fill a deficit. Career guidance was provided in all the schools, and the accounts suggest that some young people were more in need of it that others. The data suggest, however, that guidance provision was patchy across the area, and inadequate in many cases. Its impartiality is questioned by Tim and David, according to whom it caters for the needs of the system rather than the individual.

Tim: I think the careers advice is geared either from the school's point of view, just getting people to go away to university, or from the local job centre point of view, of getting people jobs in the local area and keeping them there, rather than actually necessarily helping them or giving them advice into looking further afield.

In consequence, some people are given college prospectuses, while others are told about the local jobs. This was acceptable to some, but not others. Stewart for example says 'it was pretty shoddily organised', but Cathy said her school was 'good in that way' and 'they didn't just leave you, like wandering about'. Some respondents indicate that the initiative rested with them unless they had been identified as a 'problem': thus, Mary stresses the importance of individual motivation, 'You had to sort of seek out yourself what you wanted to do and find out'; Linda on the other hand says, 'If I had went and said I didn't know what to do, I wasn't interested in anything, I would have got good guidance'.

Guidance intended to encourage young people to raise their aspirations was not necessarily well received. As with parental advice, young people could perceive guidance as something to be resisted:

Shona: There was a careers officer at school, but I don't think she was that much good really. I remember one of them telling me that I shouldn't go into nannying, I could do much better for myself than that. But that was what I wanted to be, so I was going to do it, sort of style. But she told me not to do it.

GJ: What did that do for you?

Shona: Well, it made me even more determined to do it!

David: The careers interview was a joke, basically. A lady came and said 'What do you want to be?' 'I want to be in the Air Force.' 'Oh well, you'll never be that. It's far too difficult. You'll have to look at something different. How about going to university?' and throwing you a whole lot of prospectuses down and that was it. I thought, oh well, I'll show you.

When a young person is upwardly mobile, formal sources of guidance become crucial. Neither Helen, the vet, nor Linda, the architect, received formal guidance they perceived as helpful at the time. Linda was once again left to her own devices:

Linda: I didn't get enough guidance. I had always had my idea of what I was going to be doing, but guidance staff never homed in on me, and then I was left to make out application forms and I ended up making – I made fifteen applications for thirteen courses, and they were in seven different subjects. Which I don't think they ever really picked up on, and at the end of the day I was left, I got no guidance on what I should say yes or no to.

In a locality which many young people will inevitably leave for jobs or courses, one might expect there to be some preparation for migrating away. As Hugh points out, 'they have to give you good advice'. Since most migrants are the children of incomers, there may be some help and preparation in the family, as indicated. There are, however, some children of locals who will leave the only area they know, and this can be a frightening experience:

Linda: I mean you had grown up with people and you knew everyone from the age of five up, and you knew all their families, so you knew people all round town, whereas actually discovering you're in a place where you don't know anyone, it's very different.

None of our sample had received any preparation in their schools for a life away from the area, though some said that guidance may since have improved. Even if such information were available, young people may not want to accept it. As in their relationship with their parents, they may prefer to make their own decisions. David says, 'You can never get enough advice, but you tend to not take it in when you're young. You think "this is not going to affect me"'; but he thinks that the information should still be available at school. Although Chris says he did not need formal guidance because his parents were 'very clued up', this is not always the case, and some young people have to rely on formal sources of guidance, or otherwise cope alone.

Discussion

The question explored here has been whether, in conditions of post-modernity, patterns of social reproduction involving the family as an institution can prevail. The research on youth out-migration from rural Scotland provided a case study. It is an advantage to young migrants if they can access appropriate informal support from their families, when formal guidance and support appear so inadequate. It is therefore an advantage to come from a family where there is a history of migration, and which can provide networks and knowledge, and from a middle-class family which may also (though this has not been explored here) be more able to provide financial support.

This chapter has examined whether young migrants have access to cultural capital, and has found that access can be difficult. While, structurally, those who are both middle class and the children of migrants are in a better position to benefit from the cultural capital of their families, in practice the process is often complex even for these young people. In part, the problem is at individual level, in the health of parents, perhaps. However, in part it is the consequence of the problematics posed at the start of this chapter. Internal inequalities in the family of origin affect the intergenerational transmission of capital, including cultural capital. Age inequalities in the parent–child relationship are revealed in the ambivalence about giving and accepting help; gender inequalities in the gendered aspirations which fathers may still have for their daughters. In addition, wider social and economic changes affect parents' access to up-to-date and appropriate knowledge. Thus, even when parents are keen to offer guidance and their children keen to accept it, the competence of parents to comment on changing education and employment structures is called into question. Parents have been de-skilled.

While some young people may be able to follow in the footsteps of their kin and especially their siblings, others have to rely on apparently inadequate guidance from formal sources. This is the case particularly for young migrants whose rural families have no recent experience of migration, and whose knowledge of non-local labour markets and housing markets may be limited. In consequence, many young people are forced to become 'trail-blazers', navigating individualised biographies by default rather than choice. Whether these paths lead to 'success' or 'failure' may depend not only on individual ability or external structures of opportunity, but also on factors such as motivation and confidence, both as we have seen affected by the parent–child relationship. One of the new social divisions is between young people who have supportive families and those who do not, a division which widens when state policies place increasing responsibility on parents. Over and above parents' resources for the transfer of cultural capital, their ability to pave the way for their children depends, like other aspects of the implementation of the 'generational contract', on the quality of relationships. Laura makes the point that ultimately, it is relationships rather than rules that count:

Laura: It all depends on what kind of relationship you've got with your parents. It's not really a thing you can lay down a thing for.

Notes

1 The project was supported by the ESRC (R000235394). Lynn Jamieson was both co-applicant and co-investigator and I am indebted to her for her collaboration, and to Karen Brannen and Chris Martin for their contribution to the research. The Scottish Young People's Survey was conducted by the Centre for Educational Sociology at the University of Edinburgh, and was funded by the Scottish Office and the Employment Department. Particular thanks to our respondents who have been so generous with their thoughts and their time. The views expressed here are the author's alone.

References

Bagguley, P. (1991) 'Post-Fordism and the enterprise culture' in N. Abercrombie and R. Keat (eds) *Enterprise Culture*, London: Routledge.
Bauman, Z. (1995) *Life in Fragments: Essays in Postmodern Morality*, Oxford: Blackwell.

Beck, U. (1992) *Risk Society: Towards a New Modernity* (trans. M. Ritter), London: Sage.

Bell, C. (1968) *Middle Class Families: Social and Geographical Mobility*, London: Routledge and Kegan Paul.

Bertaux, D. and Thompson, P. (eds) (1997) *Pathways to Social Class: A Qualitative Approach to Social Mobility*, Oxford: Oxford University Press.

Elliott, B. (1997) 'Scottish migrants in Canada', in D. Bertaux and P. Thompson (eds) *Pathways to Social Class: A Qualitative Approach to Social Mobility*, Oxford: Oxford University Press.

Finch, J. (1989a) *Family Obligations and Social Change*, Cambridge: Polity Press.

——(1989b) 'Policy assumptions about family support and their implications for social security', paper presented at the International Seminar The Sociology of Social Security, Edinburgh, July.

Giddens, A. (1991) *Modernity and Self-Identity: Self and Society in the Late Modern Age*, Cambridge: Polity Press.

Goldthorpe, J. (1980) *Social Mobility and Class Structure in Modern Britain*, Oxford: Clarendon Press.

Grieco, M. (1987) *Keeping it in the Family: Social Networks and Employment Change*, London: Tavistock.

Jamieson, L. (1999, forthcoming). 'Loss of youth: leaving and staying in the Scottish Borders', *The Sociological Review*.

Jones, G. (1987) 'Young workers in the class structure', *Work, Employment and Society* 1, 4: 486–507.

——(1992) 'Leaving home in rural Scotland: choice, constraint and strategy', *Youth and Policy* 39: 34–43.

——(1995) *Leaving Home*, Buckingham: Open University Press.

——(1999) 'The same people in the same places? Constructing socio-spatial identities in youth', *Sociology* 33(1): pp. 1–22.

Jones, G. and Jamieson, L. (1997) 'Migrating or staying on: decision-making and behaviour among young people in rural Scotland', end-of-award report, R000235394, Economic and Social Research Council.

Kiernan, K., Land, H. and Lewis, J. (1998) *Lone Motherhood in Twentieth-Century Britain*, Oxford: Clarendon Press.

Lash, S. and Urry, J. (1987) *The End of Organised Capitalism*, Cambridge: Polity Press.

MacDonald, R. (1988) 'Out of town, out of work: research on the post-16 experience in two rural areas', in B. Coles (ed.) *Young Careers*, Milton Keynes: Open University Press.

Office of National Statistics (1997) *New Earnings Survey 1996*, London: The Stationery Office.

Parsons, T. (1956) *Family: Socialization and Interaction Process*, London: Routledge and Kegan Paul.

Urry, J. (1995) *Consuming Places*, London: Routledge.

10

THE TRANSMISSION
OF LIFE STORIES FROM
ETHNIC MINORITY FATHERS
TO THEIR CHILDREN

A personal resource to promote
social integration

Catherine Delcroix

Introduction

In France today, many families stand just short of the outer margins of society: the homeless and other destitute persons (Castel 1995). Individuals in these families experience unstable patterns of employment as well as precarious relations with their employers. The nature of their work is often associated with health risks and their income is generally low. Such families are mostly housed in large public housing with all the accompanying features that expose young children and adolescents to danger. These children are at risk of becoming disconnected from family and social life through a process which Castel describes as 'a specific fracture of the social ties', that is a situation of destitution which can be seen as resulting from 'the interaction of two vectors: the axis of integration–non-integration through paid employment, and the axis of insertion–non-insertion through family socialisation' (Castel 1995: 138–9).

From time to time these suburbs (where it would be possible to live comfortably in times of full employment) make known their problems through the actions of discontented youth. Stolen cars are set on fire in central squares which are given the nickname 'barbecued car square' and nocturnal joyrides often end tragically. Such images of a foreign and alienated world are often portrayed by the media.

But these young adults are not aliens, they are for the most part French citizens. However, their parents often originate from other countries, particularly from one of the three countries known as the Mahgreb (Morocco,

Tunisia and Algeria). Moreover, the problems that these young adults face are not linked to their origins. Their parents have proved through many years of hard and honest work, that integration is possible. It is mostly due to their labour in creating the infrastructure of roads, railways and airports, the office buildings of La Defence (Paris), and the production of cars and lorries, that the modernisation of France has been made possible. As their parents before them, children from ethnic minority families represent the majority of the population in poor suburbs. These children are increasingly confronted by the crises of unemployment where they have the double handicap of being the children of ethnic minority workers and being unemployed.

Research on these families from the Mahgreb living on a large housing estate in Toulouse is the subject of this chapter.[1] The aim of this research is to understand the ways in which vulnerable families cope with their insecurity. The methodology consisted of interviews undertaken with members of families (fathers, mothers and children aged 16–25 years old) and interviews with civil servants in charge of social, economic and urban issues. Thirty families have been interviewed, of whom twenty were from the Mahgreb.

One common representation of vulnerable families put out by the media (also by some social workers and some sociologists) is that of the dysfunctional family, where the father, if he is still present, is unemployed and retains little responsibility. Similarly, the mother is represented as semi-illiterate and therefore not capable of adequately parenting her children. Thus the children are left to fend for themselves. From the long interviews with parents and their children that were undertaken (sometimes with everybody sitting around the dinner table but more often individually) these stereotypes were shown to be false. On the contrary, from these interviews it is possible to determine the point at which families mobilise to reduce the risks that consistently threaten their weak equilibrium, and how this mobilisation takes place when family stability is threatened.

The chapter will examine what these families have to do to mobilise against external threats. They have no capital, little economic resources, no qualifications and few social relations (network capital) other than neighbours. What else is there left to mobilise? The constant worry of what will become of the children, which was the central theme of the parents, is in itself not sufficient to resolve their problems. What other practical resources are there that can be helpful for these young adults at the end of their education? The only resource these parents have is of a *subjective* nature, composed of physical, psychological and moral energy together with their knowledge of social relations and sociability (what Bertaux (1997) has called 'the biographical capital of experience'), which they have accumulated throughout the life course.

Research shows that despite the fact that all ethnic minority families in the face of hardship mobilise in one way or another, some of them succeed better than others in encouraging their children to continue with their education and to find work – a significant achievement considering that the current

175

unemployment rate for young ethnic minority adults is at, or above, 50 per cent (Aubert *et al.* 1997: 170–1). These parents consider themselves to have succeeded whatever the nature of employment for their children.[2] Thus the following question is raised: what is it that makes this difference?

It would appear that there are four characteristics which explain the different success rates of ethnic minority families in achieving their most desired goal, the integration of their children despite the constraints of the host society which rejects them.

Two of these characteristics are to be expected. The first is the father's level of education. Despite the fact that all of the fathers in the research were obliged to work in manual trades for all or most of their working lives, small differences in levels of education made a large impact on the development of their children. The second is the social class background of the mother. Some mothers who came from urban lower-middle-class families in their country of origin had married men from lower social classes in order to be able to live in France, and therefore they found themselves among the lowest social classes in France. Such women seek to re-establish their social class position through their children and they are often active in voluntary organisations and become advocates on behalf of other families (Delcroix *et al.* 1996). In such cases, the concept of the 'biographical capital' of experience is particularly relevant.

The other two characteristics are less well known. The first is what Gilbert Delapierre (1993) has called 'social power'. Social power refers to the ability of the head of the family to become part of the community or other wider networks (as for example through trade unions), to become aware of information which will be relevant for their children, and to transform this information into strategies for action. The importance of this notion of social power, as it was developed by Gilbert Delapierre in the field at Vaulx-en-Velin (a city located near Lyon), is emphasised by the findings of the housing estate research in Toulouse. But it is, above all, the fourth characteristic which will be the focus of this chapter. From studying the families where children succeed in overcoming the barriers they face throughout their childhood (first at school and then later in finding employment), it would appear that the *transmission of the father's own life story to their children* was a central factor. Such a 'variable' would seem at first sight to be of little importance and moreover to be orientated in psychological rather than sociological explanations. However, the main theme of this chapter will be concerned with this 'variable' which, of course, deals with a subjective and non-material resource, but one which is crucial for those parents who do not possess any material capital.

By taking into account the transmission of the father's life story to his children, several theoretical lines of inquiry, either related or unrelated, can be pursued. These include Robert Castel's (1995) notion of the fracture of social ties; Abdel-Malek Sayad's (1991) work on the importance of the original reasons for emigration in determining the future of children from ethnic minority families; and the work of Pierre Legendre (1988), the historian of law and Lacanian psychoanalyst, on family transmissions and relations.

First, some of the observations that have led to the formulation of this notion of the transmission of the father's experiences to his children (Bertaux and Delcroix 1990) will be reported, followed by an initial attempt to explain them in terms of the parent–child dyad. If it is acknowledged that factors leading towards social exclusion are at the origin of the fracture of social ties (Castel 1995), then it holds true that those factors which prevent marginalisation will also be linked to strong social ties. Moreover, such ties, both at symbolic and material levels, are built up and even founded upon the family in general and filial ties in particular.

Since the subject of this chapter is the intergenerational transmission of collective family experiences among families from the Mahgreb living in France, it is necessary to take into account the history of emigration from these countries. This collective history forms not only the backdrop of microlevel phenomena, but also the macro-level phenomena that constitute the context within which these transmissions take place. The brief historical account which follows is centred upon the following question: how is it that a whole category of people, that of 'immigrant workers' (for whom the term 'ethnic' is no longer appropriate for their children), has been able to pass without notice from being an integral feature of the labour force to, what some commentators see as being exactly the opposite, a surplus population who are a drain on resources? In order to address this question it is necessary to take account of the underlying position (both symbolic and practical) of these families and their current behaviour in contemporary society.

A brief historical account

'We invited foreign workers here and we are aware today that they are also human beings', wrote the Chicago sociologist Robert Park (1950: 251) in the 1920s. The same process of becoming aware of the impact of immigration started only some ten years ago in France.

France has historically been, like the United States, a country with a very low rate of emigration and a high rate of immigration. France differs from the USA, however, in that it has hardly thought about and still resists the idea that it is above all a country characterised by immigration (Noiriel 1988). It is in France, rather than in the USA, that the melting-pot syndrome has worked effectively, obscuring the ethnic origins of immigrants.

Under pressure from industrial managers, the French government that signed the Evian agreement, which gave rise to the end of the war between France and Algeria together with independence for Algeria, included a clause whereby the Algerian government would allow several hundred thousand future Algerian workers to come to France. This clause, however, remained confidential. In 1967, Pierre Mendès-France, representing the Left, spoke out against the policy of immigration dictated by the needs of industry. His argument was that a growing number of immigrant workers would eventually compete with French workers for jobs and that, as a result, salaries would decrease. However, at the time it appeared that there was work for everybody. Algerians, Moroccans and Tunisians accepted without complaint the hardest and most dangerous jobs, together with salaries which were (relatively) very low.[3] They worked down the mines, in factories, building public roads and buildings, and in all sectors of industry which were expanding. Over time, every immigrant managed to get a job.

When circumstances began to turn around (at the end of 1973), the policy of immigration for workers ended at the European level in 1974. However, France continued to allow family members to join these immigrant workers until 1976, and many young women, often accompanied by their first children, arrived from the Mahgreb to join their husbands. Other children were born and grew up in France. Unlike Portuguese immigrants, there were few who returned to their country of origin.

However, unemployment continued to grow. From this time onwards the ideological position of holding immigrant workers responsible for the rise in unemployment became possible as they became political scapegoats in the classic way. Le Pen, leader of the extreme right-wing party the National Front, was influential in this process, and his party has subsequently made some notable electoral gains. The idea that there are 'too many of these people' and perhaps too many of their children as well (despite the fact that they were born in France and have never lived in another country), began to be accepted even among those who were not part of the National Front. Those who made negative remarks about ethnic minorities did not realise that only perhaps a tiny fraction of the French population can claim complete French ancestry. The work of Abdel-Malek Sayad (1991), which remains under-acknowledged, shows that 'immigrants' are first and foremost 'emigrants' who bring with them their own history and culture. Sayad's work contrasts starkly with the vague discourse that considers such individuals and their families only as a surplus population which has never done anything of benefit for the host country. Such a view is orchestrated almost daily, even in so-called respectable newspapers such as Le Figaro (one has only to look at the letters on page 2 of Le Figaro, where the section on 'free opinions' and readers' letters are carefully chosen by the editors to promote this discourse). It also appears no less in those areas which should now be free of discrimination, such as in employment (Bataille 1997). Failure to acknowledge discrimination within enterprises is now recognised as a reality.

Thus for many ethnic minority families there is a vicious circle. Children of immigrants born in the 1970s, who are today aged between 18 and 25 years or older, are unable to find work, especially if they do not have qualifications but even if they have gone on to receive higher education. These young people instead become part of a surplus population, achieving a self-fulfilling prophecy. Moreover, they are aware of what they have become. Caught between despair and anger as anyone would be in their position, some of these young people, and often the most conscientious and energetic, show their discontent by outbursts of aggression, which are constantly picked up by the media. Each time this occurs, their position worsens and they become further entwined in the spiral of exclusion ('*exclusion*' in the sense of a process which is directed towards marginalisation), a fact which is naturally seized on by the National Front.

Although the discourse is in terms of a surplus population, everybody is well aware that France is under-populated. The situation hardly resembles England at the time of the Industrial Revolution, when a young and brilliant clergyman called Malthus elaborated his ideas from the somewhat simplistic stance of the dialectic between arithmetic and linear population growth and the wealth of nations:

> A person who is born in an already inhabited world, if they cannot be nurtured by their parents, and if society does not need them to work, has no right to demand even the smallest amount of food, but too many do so. At the dinner table of Nature, there is no place for them. Nature requires them to depart, and takes care of the leaving herself if the person in question is unable to find sustenance from those more fortunate than themselves.
>
> Quoted by Bertaux (1977; 195) from a French translation of Malthus's *Essay on the Principle of Population* (1798)

Exactly two centuries later, however, the economic discourse (in its ultra liberal version) has been superimposed on this old form of naturalism. This discourse has become a religion in a world without religion, with its own dogmas (for example, that labour is only a cost of production and nothing else, a belief contrary to the reality whereby, as Keynes demonstrated, wages form also a part of demand. Keynes' theory has since been regularly applied to modern economic conditions and several Keynsian economists have received the Nobel prize for economics).

Although the context within which these views are held changes, as for example in overt racism and ethnic cleansing, the discourse within demography and economics remains the same. To label someone as being 'something other than', as is the case for a surplus population, changes nothing.

A new hypothesis emerging from fieldwork

Whilst working on an earlier action research project (1991–3), undertaken on a large housing estate in north Nantes, I realised the importance for the children of emigrants from the Mahgreb of knowing the history (or its misrepresentation) of the experiences of their fathers.

At the time, I was working with an agency for the development of inter-cultural relations (ADRI). Part of the training sessions for social workers (both students and those already practising) that I ran, contained modules on the history of immigration in France and Arab-Islamic culture, together with qualitative research methods. Previously I had focused on the role of fathers. With this background, the social workers asked me to help them design a specific piece of research. Juvenile delinquency in the areas where they worked was reaching alarming proportions, and the social workers did not understand why the fathers of these youths seemed not to be interested, or at least were not seen to be active in deterring their children.

I suggested to the social workers that they should try to interview these families and focus upon reconstructing the family history (a method developed by D. Bertaux in the course of life-history work). Small discussion groups containing several fathers met where the central theme was the educative role of fathers and their parental authority. To the surprise of the social workers, the fathers were very concerned about the behaviour of their children and in particular with their sons. Once they had discovered potential allies in the social workers, the fathers began to organise themselves. Moreover, the children began to realise that, for once, people were taking their fathers seriously and that French society (perhaps for the first time) recognised the parental authority that their fathers possessed. For the first time also, the practical demands of the fathers, which had hitherto been ignored (such as the provision of a prayer room), were being met.

What happened during the course of this quasi-social experiment? Following the initiatives taken by the social workers and the fathers, communication between fathers and their children was re-established and intensified (APS and Delcroix 1995). Fathers, in re-establishing the bonds with their sons (who, contrary to the image that social workers had previously held, had never ceased to hold their elders in high esteem), quite simply talked about their own experiences. Observing this process, I was able to form the following hypotheses:

1   Young adults (whether boys or girls from the same precarious socio-economic background) who succeed in moving towards a position of social inclusion are those whose father (and, without doubt, whose mother) has passed on to them the family history in general and their own history in particular. The minds of these children are thereby enriched in a significant way. Having heard their fathers' life stories they become aware of their experiences and, above all, of the present situation in which their fathers find themselves. Thus children are able to use this information to grow into mature and responsible adults.

2   The degree of social influence held by a father has a direct effect upon the behaviour of his children.

At the end of my time in the north of Nantes, two voluntary organisations for the prevention of delinquency in a suburb of Toulouse asked me to undertake some similar research. However, none of the local workers wanted to become actively involved in the research, as they had done in the north of Nantes. The research would never have got off the ground if I had not received, following a grant application to MIRE, funding to study the way in which vulnerable families cope with their situation. The brief of this new research was much larger but it included the theme developed in the north of Nantes together with the same method of data collection, notably interviews with key informants and interviews with several members of the same family.

After interviewing 30 families in this way, including more than 100 hours of personal interviews (Delcroix 1995), I believe that the hypothesis which arose from the Nantes research can be confirmed. Several examples from the Toulouse research will be presented in this chapter.

Presentaton of examples from the Toulouse research

First, it is necessary to briefly describe Bagatelle, the suburb of Toulouse where the research took place. Bagatelle comprises 10,000 inhabitants, of which 6,000 are housed in HLMs (subsidised housing schemes). The suburb has a very negative image and is often the scene of joyriding which ends tragically. Burnt-out cars can often be seen in the streets. These scenes are regularly reported in the local press. In other words, it has a bad reputation.

The 1990 Census shows that Bagatelle has a high rate of unemployment: 30 per cent compared with 12 per cent for Toulouse as a whole (Masero 1997: 115–32). One third of the unemployed are long term unemployed (more than 2 years). 33 per cent of the inhabitants are aged less than 20 years, compared with 20 per cent for Toulouse. 30 per cent of the heads of household are manual workers compared with 14 per cent for Toulouse (the research shows that they work in the construction, road transport and industrial and office cleaning industries). In 1990, the suburb contained only 2 per cent of middle managers or their equivalent and above, 7 per cent of lower professional workers, 12 per cent of administrative employees, and 16 per cent of other inactive categories who received the equivalent of Income Support. 24 per cent of the population of Bagatelle were from the ethnic minorities compared with 8 per cent for Toulouse. Furthermore, these figures on ethnic minorities only take account of persons who do not hold French citizenship. In reality, a majority of the residents of Bagatelle come from Algeria, Morocco or Tunisia, and many of them have acquired French citizenship through birth or naturalisation. Among the 25 families that were interviewed, 18 came from the Mahgreb.

One of the major risks confronting these families is the failure of their children to be integrated and their tendency to drift away from mainstream society. Because of these risks, I examined the educational programmes put in place by parents. Through interviews with fathers, mothers, and young people themselves (one can imagine the problems of gaining their confidence) the hypothesis of the importance of the transmission of the father's own experiences to their children re-emerged. Three contrasting case studies show clearly this process.

The first case concerns interviews with a father and his two eldest daughters, aged 19 and 16 years. Mr Kamel comes from Tunisia, is the driver of a heavy goods vehicle and has six children (the first four are girls). He has taken each of his daughters, from the age of 8 years upwards, with him as he drives around France. In this way, the girls get to go with their father several times a year and are able to discover the towns and historical monuments of France. Here is how the girls describe these treasured moments:

The daughter aged 19 years:

> I go with him to see the towns and places of interest in France. We often stop off on the way. He tells me about the history of these places and I compare one town with another. I often make comparisons with Toulouse but also with Tunis, his home town. He tells me the pros and cons of each place we visit. I think that he has given me an inquisitive mind and that as a result I have taken up learning foreign languages.

This young woman is now in her second year at university studying German and English. The daughter aged 16 years is equally perceptive but in other ways:

> We travel up and down the roads together. He has shown me how to drive and repair a heavy goods vehicle. I watch when he puts on the handbrake. I would love to drive and get my licence. I would also like to take a BEP Services, Transport and Communications course. I would like to take a social and economic baccalaureate course and then start up my own transport business – not here but in Tunisia. I love Tunisia, even if I also feel at home here in France.

The comments of these two girls show how Mr Kamel has opened the door to future career options for his daughters. They also show how he has been able to give them an idea of the world through his own experiences of migration and work, and to enable them to be critical. The children are thus exposed to diverse cultural and social worlds. Moreover, their father, Mr Kamel, is able to build up with each of his daughters a modern and relaxed form of relationship. In this family, these two girls have a good knowledge of the childhood past of their father. They know why he emigrated and what his plans were.

The family which Mr Kamel has created (seen from its educational life-style perspective) is similar in many ways to the ideal type of the open family. It is open to outside influences whilst at the same time being able to retain control over what it assimilates. Some of the other families in the research were also of this type.

At the opposite end of the spectrum are those families which are inward looking, and these families I have called '*closed families*'. Here is a typical example, where the father categorically refused to discuss his own experiences with his children. Mr Mohammed is the father of four children. He has just taken retirement from working for a small servicing company that forms part of the French railways (SNCF). For Mr Mohammed, the most important task is to protect his children from the external world which he sees as threatening. His son aged 16 years describes him in this way:

> My parents, my father: they don't trust me to go ... even now to Wilson Square ... (the centre of town). He has never been to the cinema with me – in fact, I have never been to the cinema at all. During the holidays I do nothing with my parents, with my father [...]. My parents are worried about me; I can't go skiing because my mother doesn't want me to go because of accidents and those things.

Mr Mohammed did not wish to be interviewed and his wife explained his reticence in this way:

> My children don't go to their friends' house. My daughter doesn't have any friends. My son is friendly with the neighbours but because he is not very good at school I don't let him go out ... As far as money is concerned, they are always asking 'why can't we have this' and 'why can't we have that?' The youngest daughter is very close to me and she understands. The others say to me: 'why haven't we ever moved house?'
>
> The most important thing is to pay the rent first. My husband has just been forced to retire and I don't work. He leaves the house in the morning to go for walks and comes back in the evening. He prepares breakfast in the morning and wakes the children up. He hasn't had a close friend since he was married. He is a solitary person, like myself.

This inward-looking attitude came about as the result of several negative experiences, as Mrs Mohammed went on to describe:

> When I first came to France, the social worker wanted to send us back to Algeria. She said that the room we were living in was too small. But it was our choice to live in another country, although in coming here we are not free. In France, we are constantly checked by the authorities. It's not easy for us [...]. Wherever they go, my children are seen as foreigners.

I sometimes feel that we have made a big mistake. You are Arabs, you are foreigners, you are immigrants .... You go into an office and they make you aware of it all the time. Even my little girl of 6 understands. However, some things are better here than over there: freedom, free speech, and trustworthy persons; but we are still strangers .... It's difficult for their father. He never says anything and he doesn't know Algeria. At the same time, he doesn't want to change his nationality and he could never live with other Algerians.

Behind the silence of this father is a personal history. He never knew his father, and therefore had no experience of the father–child relationship. His life history, which, according to his wife, was characterised by a great deal of courage in the face of adversity, had never been told to anyone. His two eldest children, aged 19 and 16 years, were failing at school.

The third case is more complex. This is an Algerian bricklayer (Mr Lilla) who talked about work in an almost courageous sort of way, demonstrating how it has helped him to survive in diverse situations:

I have worked since the age of twelve. If I don't find any work here then I search elsewhere. I leave the house at six in the morning and I come back at six in the evening, and my children are proud of me.

Mr Lilla has endlessly warned his son of the need to study (Algerians are, of course, well known, even in Algeria, for having assimilated the dominant French cultural model, and they are acutely aware of the need for good schooling and further education, more so than, for example, the Portuguese).[4] He had told his son that there was no point in becoming a bricklayer, because such work 'breaks a man'. However, his son told me that:

School wasn't for me. I didn't think much about the future, only about passing the time. I left school at 16 and did one short course after another. We had two weeks of training and then two weeks on the job. At first, I did coachbuilding but that didn't work out. After that I worked in a shop and then became a butcher.

After that, I changed jobs completely, and took a job in the construction industry. My father was reluctant at first and said to me 'if you had stayed on at school it wouldn't have come to this'. I said to myself, 'here we go, he's started again'.

I took this job because actually I didn't have much choice. Why have I chosen the construction industry to make a career? Because I succeeded, and worked hard from the moment that I was taken on. Now I am going to try for some qualifications. I am going to take the CAP, where you do some physics, maths, French and technical studies.

For this young man, even though he has a manual job, what is important in French society is to have an educational qualification. Having a qualification is the way to get on and obtain a secure job. However, he would still like to see some instant results:

> Yes, I do want to have a permanent contract or something like that with my employers. It would be much better if they took me on permanently ... if they gave me a 6-month contract then they would see how I can work and would take me on full time.

Rather than asking his father for help, this young man preferred to rely upon word of mouth to find a secure job: 'I don't want to work with my father as I would really feel uncomfortable about it.'

By drawing upon his father's own experience, he tried to show that he had finally understood not only the message that his father had been giving him, but also that the situation had changed in the course of a generation:

> [With reference to himself] My father thought: 'he must get on with it, like I did myself when I first came to France. He must do the same'. But where am I now, I have got nowhere. It's true that he came to France with only a suitcase and that he managed to overcome many obstacles. It was difficult for him and he wasn't married. He would have had to have worked very hard like everyone else in his position. But equally, at this time there was more work about, and there wasn't as much racism because people were only just arriving. People were more open then. There was more going on then, but now there's nothing, it's finished.

This same young man added:

> Look, our parents, they gave us the gift of life, it was they who created you and made you what you are today. It is our parents who have shown us what you must do and what you must not do, and it is from them that everything else develops.

The observations of this young man can been seen from within a framework of what Anne Muxel calls 'reflexivity', one of the functions of a collective family memory. By reflexivity, Muxel refers to the use of memory to draw conclusions about the links between the self and other family members – 'the individual repositions herself in relation to the past in order to confront more constructively not only her social identity, but also her affective personal identity' (Muxel 1996: 15–26).

These three cases were chosen to illustrate this process, but other similar cases could equally have been represented. The first two were chosen to show the range of the continuum that forms the two poles of active transmission and an absence of transmission. The third case illustrates the complexity within each individual case. In this last example one can see how the efforts of transmitting life experiences from father to son can be a long and complex process. Many other cases could have been chosen, with each one showing a specific context.

Nothing has been said so far about the place and role of mothers, which is evidently also very important. The mother's role is most notable as advocates between their community and the social services (Delcroix *et al.* 1996). However, the first example shows how the effects of the transmission of life experiences and history from parents to children (and especially that of the father, who was generally the first to emigrate) also affects girls. These families, however, come from societies where gender divisions are very strong and the status of women is completely different from that in French society (Delcroix 1986). It is not surprising, therefore, that when looking for role models as they enter the world of paid work, and in the absence of any role model from their mother other than that of housewife, daughters turn to their fathers, even though these men are often working in the exclusively masculine environment of over-worked manual labourers.

To return to the hypothesis that developed from this field work. The logic of ethnosociological research is that hypotheses which are generated from observations in the field only become tenable after they are subjected to a rigorous theoretical analysis. Such a process is therefore attempted in the following section.

The importance of subjective resources

First, it should be noted that the task of interpreting meaning (in the Weberian sense) from within different social milieux is a difficult one. Modern European societies are characterised by social worlds that are rich in material and objective resources, the 'capital' which Bourdieu (1979) has helped to identify. However, if 'reproduction' is conceptualised in this way, then one is forced into a position which sees families with very few material resources as lacking in 'capital'. Subjective resources are also not taken into account. It is precisely the use of these resources that is examined here. In the context of families that lack objective 'capital', subjective resources take on a significant importance.

By focusing on the subjective resources of families, it is possible to see how individual members assume the status of personal subjects, revealing how they are able to mobilise around the central issues in situations of vulnerability. These subjective resources concern the motivation of children by their parents so that they do not fail at school and enter the downward spiral of unemployment, delinquency, stigmatisation and exclusion within which the so-called 'surplus populations' are to be found.

Robert Castel (1991) has emphasised the enormous risks that are associated with the various types of social fragmentation. Using Castel's framework, the efforts of fathers to pass on their experiences to their children can be seen as an attempt to consolidate the process of social integration. By informing children of their 'initial project' (Sayad 1991), fathers are attempting to place children firmly within the family lineage and to give meaning to the despair that many of their children experience.

This process can also be understood with reference to the work of Pierre Legendre (1988), the lawyer and legal historian. Using the work of Freud and Lacan, Legendre evokes the notion of the genealogical principle: 'if an individual is not aware of their genealogical history, then life cannot be fully lived' (pp. 66–7). Similarly, Legendre remarks that 'it is not enough to produce simple physical human beings; they must be endowed with all the attributes of the *biological*, the *social* and the *unconscious*' (underlined in the text; the term 'unconscious' was replaced in a later edition (1992: 32–3) by 'the individual element or the subjective').

The object of transmission, according to Legendre, is to transmit. Beyond the obvious tautology of this statement lies the fact that it is the act of transmission itself that is important over and above the content. In families with few or no resources, where there is no objective 'capital' to transmit, there are still the non-tangible assets of moral values and love which, together with the family history, can give meaning to the current situation (however absurd it might appear to youth who are labelled as being part of a 'surplus population' without ever having been given the chance to prove themselves). Communicating family history can therefore enrich the minds of young people, whilst at the same time giving them an identity which is other than that associated with their rejection by schools, the labour market and by the way in which society in general shapes its discourse on ethnic minority youths.

If these conclusions can be verified from further observations of specific categories of families, the hypothesis could have a wider application.

One of the common characteristics of families in difficulty is the inability of the elders to transmit their own life history to their children. This history will have been shaped by a twofold series of humiliating experiences: first, and common to everybody, irrespective of whether they were born in France or have emigrated, is the experience of having occupied the lowest posts in society; second, and specific to immigrants, is the racism that they have experienced. In common with everyone from the southern shores of the Mediterranean, Arabs and Berbers are a proud and noble people, who are prone to silence when it comes to admitting what they have been through. But this silence is also a collective phenomenon, and the media plays a large part in contributing to it – as they also do in ignoring the history of the French working-classes when compared with the rural history of the population, which has been more comprehensively reported and forms part of the national identity. On this point it is worth mentioning that following the research conducted in the north of Nantes mentioned earlier, French working-class families whose origins were French also expressed interest in seeking help with passing on their family histories to their children.

It is only very recently, with films such as 'Memories of Immigrants' or or 'Le Gône de Chaâba', that the taboo has begun to be lifted. I did not find any hint of pride expressed by the men who participated in the construction of Toulouse airport or other large-scale projects. On the contrary, in answer to the question 'Who built the airport?', if they had not been prompted to reply otherwise beforehand, they would have said 'Monsieur Bouygues' (President and founder of the Bouygues group, one of the largest construction companies in France). Such a reply would be the only legitimate response possible for these men. Perhaps this example illustrates the extent of the ideological oppression to which they have been subjected during their life, an oppression which itself leads to silence and the inability to communicate their life history to their children.

Acknowledgements

This chapter has benefited from the numerous helpful comments of Daniel Bertaux.

Notes

1 This study forms part of the Mission de Recherche et et Expérimentation (MIRE) project of the French government on 'Précarités, trajectoires et projets de vie'.
2 'Mobilization at school was one of the most frequent responses of families concerning the high risk of an unemployed child' (Vallet 1997: 78–9).
3 'Working extra hours increases the basic incomes of an isolated population who send their savings home and hope only to remain in France temporarily, but at great risk to their health ... the number of accidents at work demonstrates the vulnerability of immigrant workers. In 1966, foreigners accounted for 18.2 per cent of the population of BTP workers, but 39.1 per cent of the victims of industrial accidents. These figures represent respectively 10.6 per cent and 20.2 per cent of the population in metallurgical industries, 7.9 per cent and 21.5 per cent in chemical industries, and 4.9 per cent and 18.7 per cent in textile industries. In 1973, they accounted for 9.4 per cent of the active population and 22.3 per cent of serious accidents'. These figures represent what Mercier went on to call an 'intensified usury of the immigrant labour force' (Mercier 1977: 236–41, quoted in Tripier 1990: 80–1).
4 For example, Dubet states 'The diverse patterns (in employment of the children of immigrants) do however differ substantially from one group to another; thus for example from 1962 to 1982, the percentage of qualified workers rose 5.4 per cent among the Portuguese and 28.3 per cent among the Algerians' (1989: 85–6).

References

Aubert, F., Tripier, M. and Vourc'h, F. (eds) (1997) *Jeunes Issus de l'Immigration, de l'école à l'Emploi*, Paris: CIEMI, L'Harmattan.

APS (Association de Prévention Spécialisée de Nantes) and Delcroix, C. (1995) *Une nouvelle approche de la prévention de la délinquance des jeunes maghrébins : le rôle social des pères*, Paris: ADRI, collection Savoirs et Perspectives.

Bataille, P. (1997) *Le Racisme au Travail*, Paris: La Découverte.

Bertaux, D. (1977) *Destins Personnels et Structure de Classe*, Paris: PUF.

——(1997) *Les Récits de Vie. Perspective éthnosociologique*, Paris: Nathan.

Bertaux, D. and Delcroix, C. (1990) *La fragilisation du rapport père-enfant après le divorce*, Paris: Caisse nationale des Allocations familiales.

Bourdieu, P. (1979) *La Distinction, Critique Sociale du Jugement*, Paris: Edition de Minuit.

Castel, R. (1991) 'De l'indigence à l'exclusion, la désaffiliation', in J. Donzelot (sous la direction) *Face à l'exclusion*, Paris: Edition Esprit.

——(1995) *Les Métamorphoses de la Question Sociale, Une Chronique du Salariat*, Paris: Fayard.

Delcroix, C. (1986) *Espoirs et Réalités de la Femme Arabe, Algérie, Egypte*, Paris: L'Harmattan.

——(1995) 'Des récits de vie croisés aux histoires de famille', *Current Sociology* 43, 2/3, pp 61–67.

Delcroix, C. et al. (1996) *Médiatrices dans les Quartiers Fragilisés: le Lien*, Paris: La Documentation française.

Delapierre, G. (1993) 'La puissance sociale des pères, Lyon', *Bulletin de la Société lyonnaise pour l'enfance et l'adolescence*, special issue.

Dubet, F. (1989) *Immigration, qu'en savons-nous? Un bilan des connaissances*, Paris: La Documentation française n° 4887

Legendre, P. (1988) *L'inestimable objet de la transmission. Etude sur le principe généalogique en Occident*, Paris: Fayard.

——(1992) *Les Enfants du Texte. Étude sur la Fonction Parentale des états*, Paris: Fayard.

Masero, J. (1997) 'Le Grand Mirail: une réalité plus riche que son image, *En marge de la ville: ces quartiers dont on parle*, Paris: Aube.

Mercier, C. (1977) *Les Déracinés du Capital*, Lyon: Presses Universitaires de Lyon.

Muxel, A. (1996) 'La mémoire familiale', *Sciences humaines*, Paris, hors série n° 15.

Noiriel, G. (1988) *Le Creuset Français, Histoire de l'Immigration* XIX–XXe *Siècle*, Paris: Seuil.

Park, R. (1950) *Race and Culture*, London: Macmillan.

Sayad, A.M. (1991) *L'Immigration ou les Paradoxes de l'Altérité*, Bruxelles: De Boeck.

Tripier, M. (1990) *L'Immigration dans la Classe Ouvrière en France*, Paris: L'Harmattan.

Vallett, (1997) 'Les élèves étrangers ou issus de l'immigration: les résultats du panel français dans une perspectives comparative', in F. Aubert, M. Tripier and F. Vourc'h (eds) *Jeunes Issus de l'Immigration, de l'école à l'Emploi*, Paris: CIEMI, L'Harmattan.

11

REINVENTING THE GENERATIONAL CONTRACT

Anticipated care-giving responsibilities of younger Germans and Turkish migrants

Dagmar Lorenz-Meyer and Angela Grotheer

Generational contracts and crises

The cohesion between generations in Western societies is assumed to be based on a contract of solidarity between generations. This uncodified generational contract encompasses, first, the so-called 'welfare contract' (Johnson *et al.* 1989; Laslett 1992), institutionalised primarily in the public pension system, and in Germany legally enforced in the principle of subsidiarity. The subsidiary function of societal or state activity vis-à-vis the initiative of individuals and families is derived from the nineteenth-century political economy of social Catholicism which was developed in opposition to state centralism and collectivism. The underlying promotion of self-help is also the official aim of the compulsory long-term care insurance, introduced in 1995 as the 'fifth pillar' of the German social insurance system. It provides social services or a substantially reduced care allowance to those who need long-term assistance in at least two routine activities of daily life, explicitly giving priority to prevention and rehabilitation over care provision and to home care over institutional care (Mager 1997). Second, the generational contract includes what Laslett critically calls the 'procreative contract' (1992: 27): parents care for their dependent children, who in turn are obliged to support them in old age. Yet, long-term care insurance is not discussed in terms of reinforcing the generational contract.

Feminist scholars have long pointed to the gendered character of intergenerational caring work. In the Scandinavian context the term 'caring contract' (Silius 1992) was coined to explicate a central part of the gender contract, namely the tacit agreement whereby women pursue paid work but only under the condition that they also maintain full responsibility within the family. Whereas the state-supported 'welfare contract' historically

190

contributed to an increase in intra-familial independence, the gendered politics of the 'caring contract', institutionalised in the family, the labour market and welfare legislation, bound women in a net of both supportive and obligatory intergenerational relationships which invisibly complemented or substituted for public welfare.

Despite this inherent tension, the generational contract in Germany has been a synonym for solidarity and mutual responsibility. Only in the context of the recent political reassessment of the limits of the welfare state, in the light of demographic change and economic decline, has the generational contract been denounced by some writers as 'immoral' (Dinkel 1997). Discourses of burden centre around the supposedly unbearable costs of the health and pension system, increasingly scapegoating 'the old' (Lorenz-Meyer 1996). At the same time, the prognosis of an erosion of the 'welfare contract' revives fears of a withering of the support relationships within families.

Allegations that younger women will not be willing or able to uphold the 'caring contract' have emerged in conjunction with the theory of individualisation according to which post-modern life-styles are no longer embedded in traditions and regulated by prior obligations. Instead, they are considered to be structured by requirements of the welfare state, notably of the labour market but also, for example, of the care insurance system, which draw on *and* create individual agency and strategic planning (Beck and Beck-Gernsheim 1993). Given this framework of agency, principles of choice and negotiation are argued to finally have penetrated the 'social backwater' of the family and intergenerational relationships are said to have shifted from the obligatory to the voluntary (Hess and Waring 1983).

The prognosis of an erosion of family solidarity is empirically derived from recent demographic trends and changes in family structure. As a result of a decrease in fertility, fewer children will be available as potential care-givers for parents who themselves have increased life expectancy. It is assumed that the rise in one-parent families, cohabitation and reconstituted families following divorce and remarriage further undermines long-term family obligations. With reference to the fact that more women than men file for divorce, their lower remarriage rate and their increased participation in the labour market, responsibility for the alleged decline of family solidarity is assigned predominantly to women (Schunter-Kleemann 1991).

This alleged 'detraditionalisation of family bonds' (Kaufmann 1993: 107) is also hypothesised to affect migrants in Western societies, in Germany specifically labour migrants from Turkey. Although they did not plan their stay as a permanent immigration, Turkish first-generation migrants have now to a large extent settled in Germany or commute between their country of origin and the country where they have spent most of their adult lives. Central aspects of commuting are the residence of their children in Germany, which is bound up with expectations of support and their German health insurance, on the one hand, and their assets and greater spending power in

Turkey, on the other (Potts and Grotheer 1997). Given their relatively low pension entitlements, exacerbated by the high rate of early retirement on medical grounds, the absence of ethnically specific social services, language barriers and limited information about service availability and access, plans for and the practice of living in two countries is rarely seen as an expansion of life chances and opportunities (Krüger 1995).

Recently emerging fears that ageing migrants from Turkey will become a burden on the German welfare state are backed up with social demographic data, which shows that the divorce rate of second-generation migrant women, as well as their labour market participation, has increased (Wilpert 1993). Continuing structural inequality, such as the marginalisation of this group in the labour market (resulting in a lack of material resources), is expected to exacerbate an impending care crisis. Furthermore, discriminatory laws relating to non-EU migrants mean that they are still considered 'foreign' even for those of the third generation. Dual citizenship having been denied, Turkish nationals risk losing their resident status if they leave Germany for more than six months or apply for social assistance (Dietzel-Papakyriakou 1993).[1]

Against this background, our chapter will explore the hypothesis that as a result of socio-structural conditions in the host country, second-generation migrants from Turkey, like their German counterparts, will 'coercively and one-sidedly terminate the (generational) contract' (Nauck 1990: 117) and not care for their parents in old age. The chapter aims to analyse *models of parental care* developed by younger men and women of different ethnicity and socio-economic status in Germany. Norms of filial responsibility are considered as constituting a cultural resource with which to justify plans and anticipate behaviour but are not necessarily constitutive of future behaviour. Studies from North America of adult children's anticipation of care-giving to their elderly parents have focused on personal factors, such as closeness and health of parents and children, often used all-female samples and largely ignored the impacts of ethnicity, gender and socio-economic status, as well as the existence of family traditions and the availability of institutional support (Sörensen and Zarit 1996; Conway-Turner and Karasik 1993; Hansson *et al.* 1990).

Our study therefore examines the following questions: To what extent is parental care-giving part of reflexive life-planning and openly negotiated in families of younger Germans and second-generation migrants as the term generational 'contract' and the theory of individualisation suggest? Have traditional norms of filial responsibility changed and what repertoires do younger Germans and Turkish migrants draw on to justify their expectations? How do their plans build on previous relationships with their parents and to what extent are they affected by family traditions and social institutions?

On the basis of the substantial care-giving experiences of older German women (Born *et al.* 1996), we expected that previous experience of intra-familial caring traditions would have a decisive impact on the models of parental care held by younger Germans. Our assumption was that those who had previously experienced the demanding nature of co-residential care would be less inclined to provide it themselves. First-generation migrants, on the other hand, had not provided long-term personal care for their parents in Turkey and had often left their children with family members in their country of origin. In the absence of an intra-familial tradition of personal care-giving and painful childhood experiences of separation, we assumed that adult migrant children would be less inclined to 'repay' their parents by providing care in their parents' old age. We thus hypothesised that the over-riding impact of a 'negative' model in the case of the majority of Germans and the absence of a 'positive' model in the case of the majority of migrants would weaken feelings of obligations for both men and women across ethnic and socio-economic differences. This assumption was strengthened by the *de facto* expansion of welfare services for the German group. In the case of the migrants, we expected that even though there are fewer (ethnically specific) services available, members of the second generation would have the ability to facilitate service accessibility for their parents.

Research design

The chapter examines two broadly comparable subsamples. First, a sample of forty-nine Germans aged 30–40, and second, a sample of second-generation Turkish migrants aged 25–35. The sample of younger Germans is a theoreti-cally drawn subsample of a life course survey of 149 adult children whose mothers had undergone skilled training after World War II. The mothers were surveyed and interviewed about their work and family lives.[2] On the basis of these research findings and survey data on the children's education, employment and family biography, sampling criteria were chosen to reflect both the heterogeneity of the younger generation and the nature of the relationship to their parents. Apart from selecting the sample on the basis of age, gender, employment and family status (see Table 11.1), additional selec-tion criteria included *familial caring experiences of mothers* (twenty-nine children had mothers who had provided personal care to older relatives and twenty came from families without caring experiences) and *siblings of different gender* (twenty-four respondents were pairs of brothers and sisters, each of whom were interviewed along with three sisters and twenty-two respondents who were unrelated).

The sample of second-generation migrants builds on two previous studies in which the life courses and biographical interpretations of older migrants from Turkey were analysed.[3] The main selection criterion was that fathers and/or mothers came to Germany as *labour migrants* in the 1960s and 1970s; the other sampling criteria are shown in Table 11.1. The vast majority of the sample of younger migrants were born in Turkey. They came to Germany aged between 2 months and 18 years and were separated from their parent(s) for between one and sixteen years. The majority had Turkish nationality with an unlimited residential status in Germany and had their parents living in residential proximity. Table 11.1 gives an overview of the composition of the two subsamples.

Semi-structured interviews were conducted with both subsamples, covering an in-depth exploration of aspects of the perceived life-style of their parents, their own life course transitions and a comparison between the two. To ensure comparable information, an identical topic guide was used to explore thoughts and plans around the potential parental need for care, including the perception of past caring experiences in the family, knowledge about institutions and services, and concrete planning with parents/-in-law, siblings and partners. A theme-centred analysis of the interview transcripts focused on a range of emerging themes including the respondents' ways of talking and approaching the issue of care in old age, and the ways in which dominant discourses provide images, vocabularies and symbols which shape thinking on what is desirable and possible. Patterns of interpretation were investigated for their correlation with socio-structural variables like marital or employment status.

Care anticipations of younger Germans

Nearly all the younger German interviewees had thought about what they would want to do if their parents were in need of care, confirming that the anticipation of this event has become normative (Conway-Turner and Karasik 1993). The interviews show that respondents are less threatened by frailty and the eventual death of their parent(s) than worried about the extent of help that they might be called on to provide. Their concern appears to focus on two extremes: to put them in an 'Anstalt' (institution), a word that connotes confinement and constraint, or to provide care themselves in their own home and thereby sacrifice their own freedom.

> Yes, of course I thought about it. And either I've repressed it, or I've come to the conclusion that there is no – no satisfactory solution. Well, what I actually wouldn't like to do would be to move back home, because my parents needed care. Because that would mean a change of job, that would mean changing your whole life.
>
> (m508b, 1 sister, univ, cohab, empl, 0 child)[4]

In the light of these options, which often entail what Circirelli (1988) has termed 'filial anxiety', some interviewees proceed to argue that there is no need to think about concrete care arrangements until infirmity actually occurs. Men in particular deploy this argument as a strategy to avoid specifying the scope and limits of their own possible commitment. Although the respondents often know from previous family experiences that the

194

Table 11.1 Characteristics of sample of younger Germans and second-generation Turkish migrants

	Germans (age 30–40)	Turkish migrants (age 25–35)
Gender		
Men	21	15
Women	28	15
Level of occupational qualification		
Skilled	24	13
University degree	24	7
None	1	10
Current employment status		
Employed or self-employed	38	15
Housewife/maternity leave	8	5
Student	1	7
Unemployed	2	3
Family status		
Married	33	21
Cohabiting	13	2
Single	4	7
With children	32	17
n =	(49)	(30)

unpredictability of a decline in health requires communication and timely planning, discussion of the subject is avoided, both in interactions with parents and with siblings.

Resp: We had the case that my grandfather needed nursing, 3 years ago [...]. And that was a horrible time, although it had to do with the fact that in this family many things have gone wrong for thirty years. Which means things, important things weren't talked about, which was catastrophic in this situation. But I think, if there is more communication from the beginning it doesn't have to get that bad. But the subject actually gives me stomach aches because I have the feeling that I'm stuck with it.

Int: So you probably haven't talked about this with your brother?

Resp: Yes, sure, I have, um attempted, or let's say, I let him know my worries.

(w707a, 1 brother, univ, cohab, empl, 0 child)

The absence of communication and preparation inevitably increases pressure on those who feel that they are the first line of resort: adult daughters. Daughters articulate their felt burden, results from the expected unshared care-giving responsibilities, often in terms of physical unease. For adult sons, conversely, the availability of a sister relieves the pressure on their part, whether or not the sister anticipates care-giving.

> With the caring, I think that it will most likely amount to my sister doing it. That doesn't mean that I somehow exclude myself, but merely because – because of the relationship which we have. My sister is there much more often. [...] It's mostly like that. And I have to say too that my sister would basically be the most sensible, because she has the best relationship with my mother.
>
> (m816, 1 sister, univ, mar, student, 0 child)

Fears of raising the issue of parental care needs and committing oneself to provide this care, as well as the felt burden of care provision, reflect the underlying dilemma that in anticipating the care of elderly parents the well-being of one family member is perceived as maintainable only at the expense of the well-being of another. Although siblings have detailed and congruent memories of past familial caring experiences, the models that they develop on this basis can differ fundamentally according to current employment status and gender, with sisters feeling burdened and brothers expressing relief from caring responsibilities.

Models of parental care and their justification in previous caring experiences

In the German sample, four alternative models of care emerge. First, the *'sister model'*, in which a sister is expected to take over primary care-giving responsibility. Second, the *'co-residential care model'* where, in contrast, the research participants themselves expect to provide day-to-day care in a shared household. Third, the *'domiciliary care model'* where the social services are assumed to provide care in the parents' home and respondents give complementary practical and emotional support. Lastly, the *'residential care model'* where parents are expected to move into a nursing home.

The 'sister model'

The sister model is not necessarily evidence of a reliance on gendered care-giving responsibilities. Factors which make women consider their sister as a primary carer are not so much personal as structural, such as the sister's residential proximity and the fact that the mother/parents look after the sister's children. The following woman defines such an arrangement of mutual help from which future care will 'naturally' evolve as a generational contract.

> In our case my mother has moved to my sister's and it's, if you want, a generational contract in this respect. My oldest sister is a teacher [...] and if she wants to teach she needs somebody to take care of the kids. And if you do something for me, I do something for you. Well,

in any case that's how it's meant, right, that my mother while she's still fit looks after the kids for her. And I think it's natural, that she stays there.

(w857a, 4 siblings, sk, mar, housewife, 3 child)

If men develop an alternative to the sister option, it is the social service provision. Women, on the other hand, even if they think that their sister will take primary responsibility, expect to take responsibility as well, independently of the nature of their relationship with their parents. If this relationship has been problematic in a number of cases, the husband of the interviewee tries to prevent his wife from taking major caring responsibilities, which highlights the different interests of men as brothers and husbands.

The 'co-residential care model'

Accommodating one's parents, or moving back to live with them, and giving up paid work to provide personal care is only anticipated by women in the German sample as an alternative to residential care. None of the women who expected to provide co-resident care had a university degree, and this option was expressed mainly by the housewives in the sample. In all cases the anticipation of home care is based on a strong sense of gendered family responsibility but not necessarily on personal closeness. The plan to provide personal care varies, however, in the degree of felt constraint: whereas some women see providing care merely as a last resort, others seem more willing to give up their jobs and care for their parents.

Resp: There is no question that I'd look after my parents, that is I would accommodate them here or something. I would never put my parents in an old people's home.

Int: Would you be prepared to give up something for that too? [...]

Resp: I think so. Probably I have to give up less than most because I was already at home a lot before, well, I am now and might be at that time.

(w508, 1 brother, none, mar, housewife, 2 child)

In contrast, the following respondent is divorced and works full-time. Although she feels she has not received parental support during her divorce and refers to the problematic co-residential care arrangement between her mother and grandmother, she anticipates this model of care against her mother's explicit advice. However, if women cannot rely on a male breadwinner, and have children to provide for, home care may not be viable.

If it gets really serious, well, I would sacrifice my job. [...] The problem only starts if somebody is really in need of care, either bedridden or with other afflictions [...] And my mother has said now, because

197

she experiences it every day, she said: 'Goodness me, if this happens to me, don't worry, just put me in a home'. She says 'You ruin your life, really, the strain is immense, don't do that to yourself'. That's what she says now. [...] Well, I'd try it and if there is no other way, well you have to consider putting them in a nursing home.

(w809, 1 brother, sk, cohab, empl, 1 child)

The 'domiciliary care model' and the 'residential care model'

Domiciliary service provision and the accommodation of one's parents in a residential care home are sometimes seen as sequential models and viable alternatives for the majority of those who say that they would decline to provide full-time personal care in the future. Interestingly, more women than men in the German sample support residential care. A substantial minority of men, however, do not articulate any caring model at all. The anticipation of institutional care provision can be based on previous problematic care experiences, as well as on family traditions of residential care for older relatives and an unwillingness to give up one's life plans.

I know of the conflicts that my mother had with her unloved mother-in-law – that they lived through what for years led to terribly stressful situations and ... and awful fights [...] I would think to sustain the normal social environment for as long as possible and justifiable for all sides, with all kind of care services and whatever is possible. Also I think with a bit of commitment, sure. A situation which wouldn't be acceptable is where one has to give up one's own life for the other.

(m054, 1 sister, univ, cohab, empl, 1 child)

This example illustrates the finding that men are differently involved in intergenerational relationships and are able to interpret practical help as fulfilling their filial duties. Whereas the wish to keep their (family) lives separate is a legitimate reason for men to anticipate domiciliary and residential care provision, women are concerned about their ability to continue their working lives, which is a domain seldom questioned by men. Overall, women appear to be more pressured by assumed family expectations and more often defend institutional arrangements as beneficial for the care receiver.

I probably would *not* take my parents. I thought about this very specifically, because my sister had a case, she had to take her mother-in-law into the house, seriously disabled, and that ruined the marriage. [...] Being in need of care means more than cooking, it means that they ring the bell at night, and you have to get up and things like that, right? [...] I would see that they get into a good home. That might sound hard but they have it better there. And I would do everything to keep them in their familiar environment as long as possible with these community workers [...] because as soon as they loose the security within their own four walls, they go into a rapid decline [...] But in a decent nursing home, they have speech therapists, they have carers who can give time and attention to the old people, right? I think you can't do it that way [...]. Basically the person sits in front of the telly all day. It's so isolated, it's a (prison) cell, a family cell, although it is not depicted like that.

(w546c, 4 sisters, sk, mar, empl, 3 child)

The statements, that older people go into a rapid decline when they have to leave their homes and deteriorate when they are cared for within the family, demonstrate once again the impossibility of a satisfactory solution to parental care. The anticipation of service provision for parents has to depict institutional services in a positive light, whilst at the same time excluding the positive effects of a familiar environment. Yet, social service provision is not anticipated out of disinterest or indifference but, for the most part, out of positive concern for the well-being of the parent.

Younger Germans thus anticipate a range of models and draw on multiple, often conflicting, caring experiences. These family experiences can offer the chance to identify with both carers and care-receivers and thus do not provide one 'right' way of dealing with potential parental care needs. Open negotiation is largely absent and respondents both reproduce and transform gendered responsibilities: in comparison with the older generation, younger men prospectively take on more responsibility than their fathers; yet, as this is an expansion of their traditional role, it is considered as a voluntary act that must not jeopardise their own life plans. Women, on the other hand, feel more pressured to uphold traditional care-giving obligations. Whereas some intend to care for their parents at home, others struggle for a more equal distribution of care-giving tasks among siblings and brothers- and sisters-in-law, and more often than men opt for social service provision. Welfare provision thus contributes to an expansion of perceived life choices, particularly for those women who are employed. Their expectations are more complex overall and often include multiple changes of perspectives in the quest for a 'fair' solution.

Care anticipations of second-generation migrants

Only a few of the Turkish research participants had thought in detail about parental care which, for the majority, was not perceived as posing any problems. A stereotypical answer refers to the 'Turkish family culture' in which – in contrast to the German culture – older family members are taken care of in the family and obligations of filial responsibility are still honoured.

Migrant men, particularly, who are traditionally supposed to fulfil this responsibility, proceeded to say that there was no need to talk about or plan for care-giving because either they or their siblings would naturally take care of their parents. Interestingly, the assurance 'I will look after them' is compatible with the anticipation of family care as 'I' often implies the respondent's wife and children.

> Even if my parents were 150 years old, I would look after them, in any case. I, and my wife and my children.
>
> (m26, 27 years, 4 brothers, 2 sisters, univ, mar, unempl, 2 child)

> I'd be ready to do it. If I'm not, the other is there, the other brother or sister. I would like to do what I can, whether here or in Turkey. Care for the people, do everything for them. Well, I would give my last blood for my parents.
>
> (m21, 33 years, 1 sister, 2 brothers, sk, mar, empl, 1 child)

> It's automatic in – in our Turkish society or culture [...] that old people are not – yes, like it often happens here [in Germany], pushed into an old people's home or shoved into it. They will stay in the family, in the extended family. Everybody respects everyone else. And that's the same with my parents.
>
> (m27, 27 years, 2 sisters, 3 brothers, sk, mar, empl, 0 child)

In the last case, however, the interviewee's parents intend to return to Turkey, while the respondent and his brothers and sisters expect to live in Germany. The uncertainty about the parents' prospective country of residence is found to be one of the major difficulties in anticipating specific arrangements. Hence, if filial responsibility is taken seriously, arrangements have to be anticipated from a dual perspective, both for the eventuality that parents will continue to live in the same country as their children, or that they will return to live in Turkey.

> If I was here [and the parents in Turkey], then it probably would be very difficult, that would really bug me. [...] And if I knew the situation was only for a limited time, then I would – yes, I even think, if I knew it would be 1, 2, 3 years I would chuck everything and fly over.
>
> (m13, 35 years, 4 sisters, univ, mar, stud, 0 child)

The respondents' frequent reference to reciprocity is also problematic in the context of migration. First-generation migrants often left children in the care of relatives in Turkey when they came to Germany. Separation is a central theme in the interviews and often described as having led to a permanent split or caused alienation in the relationship with their parents. From the point of view of care received in childhood, there would therefore not necessarily be an obligation to 'repay' one's parents. However, some respondents as adults re-evaluate separations as representing the necessary cost of a better standard of living. Consequently this pervasive theme does not seem to have an overt impact on expectations about future care-giving. There is only one example where a respondent explicitly refers to the absence of parental support to justify her anticipated refusal to provide future parental care, but the felt lack of support is not limited to childhood experiences of 'abandonment'.

> My parents only have one child, that's my brother. When they need care, he'll have to do it himself. When I needed my parents, they weren't there for me. When they need me, I won't be there either. [...] And if I do something, my children won't allow it.
>
> (w20, 35 years, 1 brother, 5 sisters, sk, mar, empl, 2 child)

Traditionally, Turkish women were supposed to care exclusively for their in-laws, but female respondents now feel obliged to provide support for their own parents as well. In the above extract the fact that other relatives have to hinder them, indicates that, following migration, women as daughters become a main source of family support. For second-generation migrant women, filial responsibilities potentially double, because they cannot straight-forwardly decline caring responsibilities for their parents-in-law or for their own parents.

> I would help, certainly. I wouldn't leave my Mum alone, if she was here (in Germany). [...] But you also have to think, if my husband says, for example, his mother is alone, they don't have anybody. I can't really say, 'No, I don't want your mother'. That's impossible. [...] I would take her, I have to. I can't say, 'No, I don't want to'.
>
> (w01, 30 years, 2 sisters, 1 brother, none, mar, empl, 0 child)

Husbands both have the responsibility and authority to take a parent into their household, but they are not the ones who will do the caring work. In the light of second-generation migrant women's increasing commitment as wage earners, family home managers and carers, the following gender neutral state-ment of a migrant man gets a new gendered meaning, which implies the unspoken dual family workload for women.

> Turkish culture says, a person, a married person, has two fathers and two mothers, your own father and father-in-law, Mum and mother-in-law, all four are equal.
>
> (m22, 35 years, 3 brothers, 2 sisters, none, mar, empl, 2 child)

Factors which increase migrant daughters' caring responsibility for their family of origin include their brothers' marriages to German women, who are not considered to be acceptable family care-givers. The high level of willingness and obligation to provide parental care was felt by both men and women, but the uncertainty about the final country of residence and women's increasing family responsibilities create an area of tension in the care-giving expectations of second-generation Turkish migrants.

Models of parental care in the context of migration

Models of parental care expressed by the migrant sample include the 'co-residential care model', the 'domiciliary care model' and the 'residential care model'. In addition, the respondents produce two sets of care models which are specific to the context of migration: First, the 'extended family model' where parents are cared for by relatives in Turkey, and second, the 'financial support model' where money is sent to Turkey to either enable the parents to buy services or to support potential family care-givers.

The 'extended family model' and the 'financial support model'

Both the extended family model and the financial support model are based on the assumption that parents will live in Turkey or spend substantial periods of time there, whereas the respondents themselves will live in Germany. In this situation some migrant men anticipate that relatives in Turkey will take care of their older parents. It appears, however, that their parents' financial ability to buy care is at least as important as their reliance on the extended family.

> And when they're in Turkey, I don't have to worry about my parents at all, they have enough relatives who will look after them. And my parents have no financial problems, they have a lot of houses and real estate and they will get a pension [...] Yes, and if they've money, they have everything.
> (m26, 27 years, 4 brothers, 2 sisters, univ, mar, unempl, 2 child)

But even if members of the first generation have assets and, through long-term financial support, have 'invested' in the family network, daughters tend to view the provision of care by relatives in Turkey with more scepticism.

> My mother wants to return to Turkey, and her brother. She has also brothers, and this is her expectation. Well if this works out – I mean, he never writes letters, he never calls. [...] She does everything for them, and gave up a lot so they were doing better and they don't care at all. Well, she thinks she can live there.
> (w03, 29 years, 2 sisters, 1 brother, sk, single, self-empl, 0 child)

Like their parents, members of the second generation sometimes provide financial support to relatives in Turkey. Yet, only men consider the provision of money as a valid way of fulfilling their filial responsibility. But they do not specify what kind of services parents could obtain in Turkey. Moreover, the financial support model may be questionable if sons are unemployed, like the following research participant.

Resp: Because I'm here and they are there, I support them financially as far as I can. But they don't need it – luckily. But if such a situation arose I'd do everything possible.

Int: Apart from financial support, there can also be the need for personal care?

Resp: Yes, that's true. Yes, I'd hire a carer then or my little brother – I would support my little brother, so he can help.

(m08, 29 years, 1 sister, 1 brother, none, mar, unempl, 2 child)

Defining financial support explicitly as a limited commitment and referring to a family tradition of financial provision is, however, exceptional.

> I often told my parents that they haven't looked after my grandparents either. [...] And then they said, 'Yes, but we didn't have any other option, we sent money'. Okay, then you also get as much money from me as you like. Then they can live on their own.
>
> (m17, 27 years, 1 sister, univ, single, stud, 0 child)

The 'co-residential care model'

The vast majority of both migrant men and women anticipate taking an older parent into their household in Germany. Co-residential care is considered as the counter-model to the parents' institutionalisation, which the respondents reject as inhuman. As there has been no history of intra-familial care experiences, however, the anticipation of co-residential care often remains vague and does not necessarily imply the expectation of full-time personal care. Only a minority of adult daughters reflect on the limits of their capacity to provide personal care. They do, however, only consider 'objective' hindrances, such as specific medical requirements or financial difficulties, and do not question their willingness or consider their own interests.

> My father is very ill [...] and I thought he would die. I always have to plan for the family and then I thought what happens to my mother. Then I immediately thought that I can't take her, because I don't have the money. Then I thought, my brother has to do it, then she lives with him. [...] I would never send my parents to a home, I'd rather take them myself or we would somehow manage amongst

the siblings. [...] that's an obligation for me. I mean apart from the
love, of course, it's an obligation.

> (w30, 32 years, 1 brother, 1 sister, univ, cohab, stud, 0 child)

The 'domiciliary care model' and the 'residential care model'

Given the overall rejection of residential care, which is viewed as a symbol of
neglect, isolation and the abandonment of older people, it is not surprising
that only two younger Turkish migrants consider an old people's home to be
a viable option. However, domiciliary care is comparatively less stigmatised.
Three women in the sample anticipate social service provision as a legitimate
care model – as long as their parents or in-laws live in Germany, where
services can be bought in or are obtainable on the basis of health or care
insurance.

> Yes, if nothing else is possible, I might take her [mother-in-law]
> here. If it's too much, the caring, and she has the money I might find
> somebody to care for her. Here it would be possible, but in Turkey
> it's not like that.
>
> > (w06, 33 years, 1 sister, 2 brothers, none, mar, housewife, 2 child)

The assumption that service provision is relatively unproblematic in Germany, however, contradicts the experience of two women who had cared for
their parents. Their accounts indicate that, if the need arises, migrants can, to
a certain extent, get access to mainstream services. But what becomes obvious
is that these services are by no means adequate to meet the specific needs
of older migrants. It was daughters who, in this situation, stood in both as
financial providers and carers.

> Only now we realise that there is nothing there for migrants in old
> age, for their needs. No social services, no reasonable residential
> homes, where my parents could go to. Maybe they would go, if there
> was anything. Although it would be horrible for me [...] I did
> it [caring] when I was better myself. That is how to put it, all by
> yourself you can't do that much. I had times when both my parents
> were bedridden and we couldn't cope anymore. I lived in N. at the
> time and this moving to and fro and my sister, she had to work,
> somebody had to bring in the money. And I think if there had been
> a Turkish woman to help look after her or help with the household
> that would have been really good. We did try it with a German
> woman but it simply didn't work. Because my mother, for example,
> with her hygiene is terribly fussy.
>
> > (w19, 29 years, 3 sisters, 2 brothers, none, mar, housewife, 2 kids)

On the basis of a cultural repertoire of family care and experiences of migration, second-generation Turkish migrants develop a range of parental care models, which include the participation of the extended family in Turkey. Women's expectations overall are more differentiated than men's and reflect their new role as family managers. In addition, a few can already build on actual care-giving experiences. Their accounts reveal a fundamental dilemma regarding social service provision. On the one hand, second-generation migrant women feel strongly that the older generation has obtained the right to welfare provision in old age and see this as reducing their responsibility. On the other hand, this is counteracted by negative experiences with inadequate domiciliary care and a general rejection, culturally reinforced, of residential care arrangements. As a result, social service provision in its current form does not contribute to an expansion of life choices for second-generation migrants from Turkey.

Building a 'new' generational contract?

The views of younger Germans and of Turkish migrants on parental care in old age, suggest that contrary to fears of a withering of family solidarity, the cohesion between generations remains strong: even where family relationships are problematic, respondents never completely escape filial obligation. Both the Germans and the migrant interviewees produced a variety of possible care models, which reflect different needs and experiences, but also reflect the impact of gender and socio-economic status. Cultural norms, family traditions and social institutions provide resources for the two groups and form a framework within which they will have to reconstitute the generational contract.

For younger Germans, cultural norms often corresponded to an intrafamilial tradition of exclusively female responsibility for the care of older relatives. This legacy of a tacit caring contract is both reproduced and transformed. The development of domiciliary services and residential homes constitute an expansion of possible opportunity structures for anticipating potential care arrangements. For the majority of both German men and women, service provision in its various forms is an important input to their anticipated care models. Although it is not free from ambivalence, institutional support is also thought of as being in the interest of the parents, and includes the expectation of complementary practical and emotional support from the respondents. However, the persistence of women's caring responsibilities is indicated not only by the substantial minority of German women with lower educational levels who, sometimes against their parents advice, envisage providing personal care, but also by the intention of brothers to rely on their sisters' care-giving.

Second-generation migrants from Turkey experienced a divergence between the cultural norm of family care-giving and the actual experience of their parents providing financial support for, rather than hands-on care of, older relatives. The predominance of material support constitutes a new intra-familial tradition after migration. Contrary to our expectations, this absence of a familial caring tradition and the experiences of childhood separation were seen as reflecting the structural necessities of migration, and had no apparent effect on their own anticipation of care-giving. Given that current service provision in Germany is inadequate and ethnically insensitive, and that residential care is strongly rejected by the younger generation, the vast majority of respondents assume that the family will be the central site of care-giving and support for their ageing parents. Thus cultural norms of family care were strongly upheld, even though uncertainty about where their parents would live required that the interviewees had to plan for two eventualities, hands-on care or financial support at a distance. Gender differences meant that while migrant men anticipated upholding their role as providers of practical and financial support, they plan to care *about* but not to necessarily care *for* their parents. For migrant women, on the other hand, care-giving responsibilities can potentially double: whereas they were traditionally responsible only for their parents-in-law, following migration they now expect to care for their own parents as well.

Among both Germans and second-generation migrants, the quality of the relationships between parents and children was far less important in the anticipation processes than cultural, and particularly socio-structural, resources. Government austerity measures and policies, such as the long-term care insurance introduced in 1995, use a language of consumer sovereignty and choice. But by providing care allowances and, more importantly, in the absence of more encompassing welfare provision that considers social, cultural and emotional needs, these new measures are likely to strengthen care-giving responsibilities within the family. On the basis of our findings we can assume that women, although they are the majority of those who explicitly promote social service provision, will continue to be responsible for the organisation of personal care in the German case, and become the 'new' bearers of family responsibilities for migrants.

Under changing social structural conditions, the generational contract has to be built anew. This requires individual agency and is dependent on the regulation and service provision of the welfare state, as the theory of individualisation suggests. Yet, the absence of open communication and concrete planning for the possible care needs of older parents indicates that the publicly invisible side of the generational contract continues to operate through tacit agreements and assignments of responsibilities on the basis of gender, age and ethnicity. It remains a contract that is not openly and politically negotiated.

Notes

1 There is currently a legislative initiative of the new Social Democratic/Green Coalition government to rewrite German citizenship law which would mitigate this situation. It includes the introduction of dual citizenship and German citizenship for children who have at least one parent who was either born in Germany or immigrated before the age of 14.

2 The series of research projects was directed by Helga Krüger at the Special Research Centre 'Status Passages and Risks in the Life Course' at Bremen University, Germany, from 1988 to 1996. The present study was organised in co-operation with the research project 'Status Passage Formation and Intergenerational Legacy' (1994–6).

3 The series of research projects was directed by Lydia Potts at the University of Oldenburg, Germany, from 1993 to 1997. The present study is part of the research project 'Migration and Ageing – Intergenerational Relationships in Migrant Families from Turkey' (1995–7).

4 All quotes have been translated by the authors. The identifier after each quote denotes the research participant's gender (*w* = woman, *m* = man), her identification number and sibling position (a, b, c) if several siblings were interviewed, number and gender of siblings, educational level (*sk* = skilled, *univ* = university degree, *none* = no occupational training), family status (*mar* = married, *cohab* = cohabiting, *single*), current employment status (*empl* = employed, *self-empl* = self-employed, *unempl* = unemployed, *housewife*, *student*) and number of children.

References

Beck, U. and Beck-Gernsheim, E. (1993) 'Nicht Autonomie, sondern Bastelbiographie. Anmerkungen zur Individualisierungsdiskussion am Beispiel des Aufsatzes von Günter Burkart', *Zeitschrift für Soziologie* 22, 3: 178–87.

Born, C., Krüger, H. and Lorenz-Meyer, D. (1996) *Der unentdeckte Wandel. Annäherung an das Verhältnis von Norm und Struktur im weiblichen Lebenslauf*, Berlin: Edition sigma.

Cicirelli, V.G. (1988) 'A measure of filial anxiety regarding anticipated care of elderly parents', *The Gerontologist* 28, 4: 478–82.

Conway-Turner, K. and Karasik, R. (1993) 'Adult daughters' anticipation of caregiving responsibilities', *Journal of Women & Aging* 5, 2: 99–114.

Dietzel-Papakyriakou, M. (1993) *Expertisen zum ersten Altenbericht der Bundesregierung, Band III, Aspekte der Lebensbedingungen ausgewählter Bevölkerungsgruppen*, Berlin: DZA.

Dinkel, B. (1997) 'Die gesellschaftlichen Belastungsdiskurse oder: Können 'wir' uns die Alten finanziell noch leisten?', in E. Olbrich, K. Sames, and A. Schramm (eds) *Kompendium der Gerontologie. Interdisziplinäres Handbuch für Forschung, Klinik und Praxis*, Landsberg/Lech: ecomed.

Hansson, R.O., Nelson, E.R., Carver, M.D., Neesmith, D.H., Dowling, E.M., Fletcher, W.L. and Sühr, P. (1990) 'Adult children with frail elderly parents: when to intervene?', *Family Relations* 39: 153–8.

Hess, B.B. and Waring, J.M. (1983) 'Family relationships of older women: a women's issue', in E.W. Markson (ed.) *Old women, Issues and Prospects*, Lexington, MA: Lexington Books.

Johnson, P., Conrad, C. and Thomson, D. (1989) 'Introduction', in P. Johnson, C. Conrad and D. Thomson (eds) *Workers Versus Pensioners: Intergenerational Justice in an Ageing World*, Manchester: Manchester University Press, pp. 1–16.

Kaufmann, F.X. (1993) 'Generationenbeziehungen und Generationenverhältnisse im Wohlfahrtsstaat', in K. Lüscher and F. Schultheis (eds) *Generationenbeziehungen in postmodernen Gesellschaften: Analysen zum Verhältnis von Individuum, Familie, Staat und Gesellschaft,* Konstanz: Universitätsverlag Konstanz.

Krüger, D. (1995) 'Pflege im Alter: Pflegeerwartungen und Pflegeerfahrungen älterer türkischer Migrantinnen – Ergebnisse einer Pilotstudie', *Zeitschrift für Frauenforschung* 3: 71–86.

Laslett, P. (1992) 'Is there a generational contract?' in P. Laslett and J.S. Fishkin (eds) *Philosophy, Politics, and Society* (sixth series): *Justice Between Age Groups and Generations,* New Haven: Yale University.

Lorenz-Meyer, D. (1996) *The Other Side of the Generation Contract,* LSE Gender Institute Discussion Paper Series, 1, London: London School of Economics.

Mager, H. C. (1997) *Pflegeversicherung in der Bundesrepublik Deutschland,* PflEG-Projekt, Forschungsberichte 9, Frankfurt a.M.: J. W. Goethe Universität.

Nauck, B. (1990) 'Eltern-Kind Beziehungen bei Deutschen, Türken und Migranten', *Zeitschrift für Bevölkerungswissenschaft* 16, 1: 87–120.

Potts, L. and Grotheer, A. (1997) 'Arbeitsmigration als Frauenprojekt? Migrantinnen aus der Türkei zur retrospektiven Evaluation der Migration', in U. Loeber-Pautsch *et al.* (eds) *Quer zu den Disziplinen,* Hannover: Offizin, pp. 36–41.

Schunter-Kleemann, S. (1991) 'Die Familienpolitik der europäischen Gemeinschaft', *WSI Mitteilungen,* 2, 103–14.

Silius, H. (1992) *Contracted Femininity. The Case of Women Lawyers in Finland,* Åbo: Åbo Academy Press.

Sörensen, S. and Zarit, S.H. (1996) 'Preparation for caregiving: a study of multigenerational families', *International Journal of Aging and Human Development* 42, 1: 43–63.

Wilpert, C. (1993) 'Berufskarrieren und Zugehörigkeiten: "Die Töchter der Gastarbeiter" – Europa in Deutschland', in B. Schäfers (ed.) *Lebensverhältnisse und soziale Konflikte im neuen Europa. Verhandlungen des 26. Deutschen Soziologentages in Düsseldorf 1992,* Frankfurt a.M: Campus.

12

CONTINUITY
AND CHANGE

The family and community life of older
people in the 1990s

*Miriam Bernard, Judith Phillips, Chris Phillipson
and Jim Ogg*

Introduction

The post-war period has witnessed considerable changes affecting family
structures and social relationships both within, and between, the generations.
In this chapter we present findings from research which has examined the
impact of these changes on the lives of older people living in three contrasting urban areas of England: Bethnal Green, a deprived, ethnically diverse,
inner-city area of London with a history of transient populations; Wolverhampton, an industrial and multicultural Midlands metropolitan borough,
which has experienced substantial redevelopment and slum clearance; and
Woodford, a relatively affluent, ageing suburb in north-east London. These
three areas provided the locations for a number of classic community studies
undertaken in the 1940s and 1950s: *The Social Medicine of Old Age* (Sheldon
1948), *The Family life of Old People* (Townsend 1957), and *Family and
Class in a London Suburb* (Willmott and Young 1960). The original studies
examined the thesis that, in the context of a developing welfare state, families
were leaving the old to fend for themselves. The reality, however, was found
to be somewhat different as the rich material about the social and family life
of elderly people demonstrated.

This chapter reports on some of the key changes and continuities between
the original (baseline) studies in the 1940s and 1950s, and the Keele research
in the mid-1990s, specifically as it relates to intergenerational contact and
support. First, we provide details of the methodology of the Keele project.
Second, this is followed by a discussion of social networks and social support,
since these issues form the core of our considerations. Third, we focus on the
older people in our study in order to explore who in the network is key in
terms of relationships and provision of support. Finally, using both our

survey data and case study material, we illustrate some of the ways in which intergenerational support and care is exchanged, reciprocated, and managed.

The design of the study

The Keele research was carried out in two main phases: first, a questionnaire survey of 627 older people in the three original urban locations and, second, semi-structured tape-recorded interviews with people over the age of 75 (n = 62); nominated members of the 'younger' generation (n = 19); and Bangladeshi and Punjabi elders in Bethnal Green and Wolverhampton (n = 35).

The size of the achieved samples in the baseline studies was 203 individuals in Bethnal Green, 210 in Woodford (older people only), and 477 in Wolverhampton. The Keele survey aimed for around 200 interviews in each area, achieving 195 in Bethnal Green, 227 in Wolverhampton, and 204 in Woodford. A random sample of people of pensionable age (65+ for men and 60+ for women) was drawn from the age–sex registers of General Practitioners following approval of the project by the respective District Research Ethics Committees. The questionnaire used in the survey was designed to explore general issues of social and family change since the original studies, and the actual work was undertaken by the Social and Community Planning Research (SCPR) organisation in July and August 1995.

Trying to measure social and family change over a 40 year period raises significant issues and problems. The three baseline studies had each used different approaches and rather differently formulated questions, so trying to replicate the original research was not a viable option. Our approach was to draw out some key findings from the baseline studies and explore the extent to which these still seemed characteristic of the family and community lives of older people in the 1990s. Where possible, we retained some of the original questions, albeit in a modified form. We employed a social network approach (discussed below) as one way of trying to understand whether, and how, social relationships and solidarities had been maintained or fragmented in these same three communities over the intervening years.

The second qualitative phase of research sought to examine the issue of change from the standpoint of particular groups of both older and younger people. The primary purpose of these interviews was to provide more in-depth information about the nature of support on which people might draw both from their kin, and from their wider social networks. These discussions were anchored by asking the older respondents to detail the ways in which support was mobilised around a recent real life situation or event. The interviews also explored respondents' relationships with family members, friends and neighbours; what they did on a day-to-day basis; and their perceptions of the future. These interviews were carried out by the Keele team during 1996 and the early part of 1997.

Social networks, social support and the baseline studies

Social networks (and social support) is a central theme of this chapter, there-fore it is important to discuss how these terms were conceptualised and operationalised in both the Keele and the baseline studies. The idea of social networks has a considerable pedigree in the social sciences (Barnes 1954; Frankenburg 1966; Mitchell 1969) and has been extensively applied in recent studies (see, for example, Antonucci and Akiyama 1987; Bowling *et al*. 1991; Kahn and Antonucci 1980; Lang and Cartensen 1994; Knipscheer *et al*. 1995; Wellman 1990; Wenger 1984, 1992, 1995).

A variety of ways and means of exploring the interaction between social networks and social support in the lives of older people has been proposed over the years (see Phillipson *et al*. 1996). However, bearing in mind the thrust of the original studies and our concern with keeping older people at the forefront of the Keele research, we considered that the most appropriate tool for our purposes would be one which emphasised the 'subjective' dimensions of people's networks. Such an approach is important for a number of reasons. First, it makes no a priori assumptions about the nature of the networks in which people are involved: whilst traditional bonds of kinship may be import-ant, respondents can also detail other relationships. Second, it offers a prac-tical and flexible method for exploring, through the medium of people's personal networks, how these interact with communities and localities. Third, it may be used to examine change, charting how relationships develop over time. Finally, it also allows us to investigate how network members respond to one another in terms of providing resources.

The technique chosen for use in the Keele study, was originally designed by Kahn and Antonucci (1980). By means of a visual aid called a 'Personal Network Diagram', the researcher is able to gather information about people who stand in different degrees of 'closeness' to the respondent. Data are collected by presenting the respondent with a diagram of three empty con-centric circles (see example of an older person's network in Figure 12.1). The centre of the diagram contains the word 'YOU'. Respondents are first invited to think about, and name, those individuals they feel 'so close to that it's hard to imagine life without them'. Beginning at twelve o'clock on the diagram, the name of each person mentioned, together with his or her relationship to the respondent, is written down in the inner circle. The middle circle records those people the respondent is 'less close to', but who are 'still very import-ant', whilst the outer circle contains the names of those not already mentioned but who are 'important enough in your life to be included'. A maximum of twenty names (and relationships) can be recorded in this way. Respondents are subsequently asked about a variety of support functions (emotional and practical) that network members provide or receive, and addi-tional questions seek socio-demographic data about the most important people in the diagram. In essence, this model enables us to look both at the

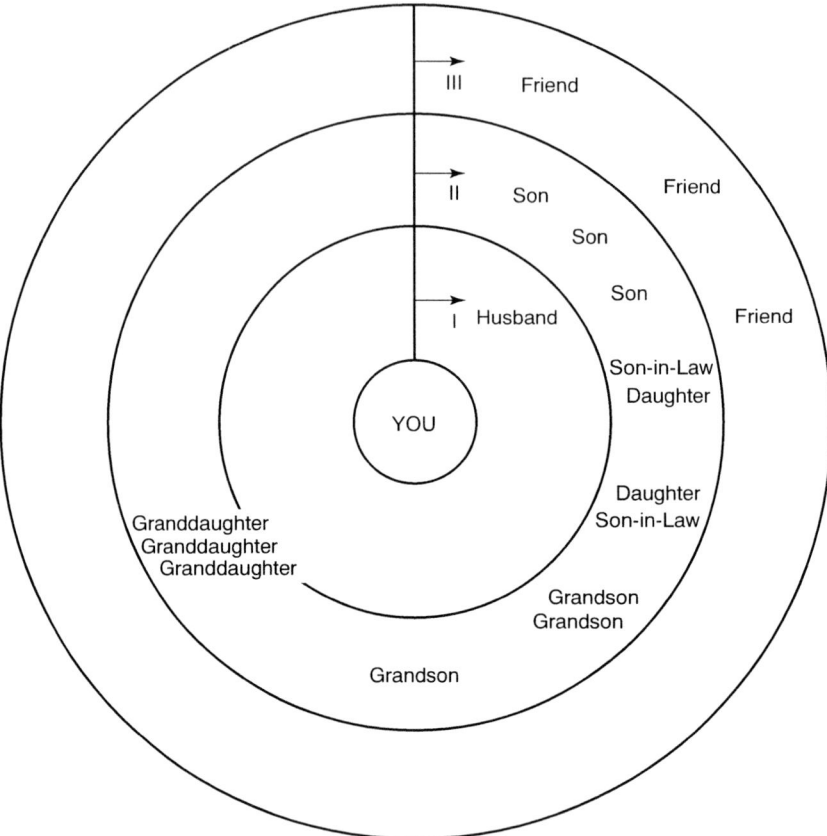

Figure 12.1 Example of an older person's personal network.

'structure' of people's networks and at its 'functions' in terms of the kinds of support which are received, provided and exchanged.

The baseline studies clearly demonstrated the continuing importance of kinship and family life in post-war Britain. Sheldon (1948), for example, describes Wolverhampton society as one in which the old are an essential part of family life. Indeed, old age was most likely to be spent living in the company of at least one other adult, with only 10 per cent of older people living alone at this time. Two-generation households, comprising older people and their unmarried children, were particularly important (29 per cent of older people lived in such households), whilst 13 per cent lived with married children and grandchildren, and 9 per cent just with married children. Non-relatives, in the form of friends and lodgers, were also a feature of the households of older people, with some 15 per cent of Sheldon's respondents living in these situations. Moreover, whilst physical proximity does not necessarily equate with social support, it was evident that in Wolverhampton, the older person – particularly the older woman – was a source of considerable support to both family and community. For instance, Sheldon (1948: 157) argued that the extent of housework undertaken by older women provided 'magnificent testimony to the vital part that the ageing woman plays in the life of the community', whereas the supportive role of older men, although not absent, was less in evidence. Of equal concern was the question of who stepped in to provide help and support to older people when it was needed. In Wolverhampton, Sheldon reported that many daughters had in fact given up work to care for ill or disabled older relatives (mothers in particular).

Townsend (1957) reports on a Bethnal Green community that, despite the devastation suffered during the war, appeared to be remarkably successful in its provision of support to older people. The mother–daughter bond was the most distinct supportive relationship. Indeed, nearly a quarter of Townsend's older respondents lived in two-generation households with their unmarried children, whilst a further 4 per cent lived with married children, and 8 per cent lived in three-generation households with married children and grandchildren. However, in contrast with Wolverhampton, the evidence from Bethnal Green also suggests that older people living alone, or just with a spouse, has been a common experience for much of this century. Over half of Townsend's respondents lived in these circumstances, 25 per cent alone and 29 per cent just with their spouse (compared with 10 per cent and 16 per cent respectively in Wolverhampton): a similar figure to the one reported in the New London Survey of Life and Labour in 1929 (Gordon 1988). Moreover, help and support between the generations was clearly in evidence, with older women helping their adult daughters through, for example, childcare, and daughters in return providing help with other chores such as shopping, cooking, cleaning and washing. But, as Townsend (1957: 46) reported, 'old women surrendered their household duties unwillingly', for to do so would also be to relinquish their status as 'Mum' – a position held in considerable esteem in working-class communities such as Bethnal Green at this time. He further found that 40 per cent of older women provided at least one regular service for relatives living in separate households.

In Woodford, Young and Willmott (1957) observed that whilst geographical and social mobility, mainly of adult children moving from the East End of London to Woodford, loosened traditional ties and obligations, it did not in fact prevent links between the generations. The family still occupied a central role in meeting the care needs of older people, and children continued to feel a sense of duty and obligation towards their older parents. Young and Willmott (1957: 50) expressed this sense of moral obligation in the phrase: 'the old felt they could call on their children, the children that they should respond'.

In sum, the households of older people in the baseline studies were often complex and often multi-generational. Older people in these communities were surrounded by others with whom they had close and supportive relationships, living within what Frankenburg (1966) was later to term 'an environment of kin'. However, in the intervening years, there have been - suggestions that the bonds connecting older people to family members are increasingly fragmented with a distinct move from generations 'living together throughout life' to (sometimes) 'joining when parents grow old' (Willmott and Young 1960: 38). Consequently, we now consider the Keele findings in order to examine the ways in which social networks and social support between the generations may have changed in the decades since the baseline studies.

Living arrangements in the 1990s

Overall, our findings suggest that whilst there have been considerable alterations to the living arrangements of older people, the family still retains its saliency in terms of social ties and social support. We first examine the changes which have happened to the households of older people and, second, discuss the impact this has had on respondents' social networks and the relationships between the generations.

The evidence confirms that the households of older people in the 1990s are substantially different from the early post-war period. Table 12.1 illustrates these trends and makes comparisons with the baseline studies for Bethnal Green and Wolverhampton (comparable data for Woodford is not available).

The major contrast to note is with an old age spent in the company of others, to one experienced either living alone, or with just one other person (usually a spouse). The living arrangements of older people in Woodford represent what may increasingly become the norm, with nearly half of pensioner households comprising a two-person, one-generation household (spouse and partner most commonly). The trend towards solo living is also notable in all three areas, reflecting the growing proportions of widowed older people (in fact 78 per cent of those in the survey who were widowed lived alone).

The proportions of older people living alone or just with a spouse or partner were 83 per cent in Woodford, 78 per cent in Wolverhampton and 72 per cent in Bethnal Green. Alongside this growth has been a decline in 'complex' households, i.e. those consisting of more than one generation. An exception to this is the multi-generational households in inner city Bethnal Green where over a quarter of older people – predominantly drawn from amongst the Bangladeshi families in our survey – live in two-, three- or even four-generational households. Of the twenty-three older respondents in the Bethnal Green sample who originated from Bangladesh, twenty-one had at least one child living at home, and these children were often still at school. Fifteen of

Table 12.1 Household composition in three urban areas, women 60+; men 65+ (column percentages)

Number of Generations	Relatives present	Bethnal Green		Wolverhampton		Woodford
		1954–5	*1995*	*1945*	*1995*	*1995*
One	Lives alone	25	34	10	37	35
	Spouse/partner only	29	38	16	41	48
	Other relatives	4	2	8	1	2
	Other non-relatives	0	1	15	1	1
Two	S/W/D/Sep/Child(ren)	24	14	29	12	10
	Married child(ren)	4	2	9	2	1
	Other relative(s)	3	2	—	0	0
Three	S/W/D/Sep/Child(ren) + G'child(ren)	2	1	—	1	0
	Married Child + G'child(ren)/ G'child(ren) only	8	5	13	5	1
	Other relatives	0	1	—	1	1
Four	S/W/D/Sep/Child(ren) + G'child(ren) + Great G'child(ren)	—	1	—	0	0
n =		100% (203)	100% (195)	100% (477)	100% (228)	100% (204)

Note: 0   means <0.5%
           —   means 'none'
S/W/D/Sep   means Single/Widowed/Divorced/Separated

these respondents (or 65 per cent) also lived in households containing five or more people, and most of those surveyed were in rented (council-owned) accommodation. Some of the characteristics of the Bangladeshi households (and also of some of the Punjabi households in Wolverhampton) are reminiscent of the 'extended family groups' described in the baseline studies. However, it would be misleading to draw conclusions about family support simply from data about living arrangements.

Overall, our findings confirm that adult children (as well as other relatives) tend now to maintain separate households – the key exception to this being a number of the Bangladeshi and Punjabi households. Given this change from the baseline studies, the next issue we discuss concerns the impact this has on respondents' social networks and the relationships between the generations.

Social networks in the 1990s

Our network measure allowed respondents to name a maximum of twenty people. Between them, the 627 respondents named a total of 5,737 network members (mean network size = 9.3 [standard deviation 5.4]), with Bethnal

Green having a slightly lower mean network size (8.3) than Wolverhampton and Woodford (9.6 and 10.0 respectively). Although there was a slight decrease in network size with advancing age, this was not statistically significant. Similarly, whilst women reported larger networks than men (10.02 compared with 8.18; $p < 0.001$), the gender difference was similar in each of the areas. Only seven people out of the 627 interviewed, were unable to name anyone to whom they were 'close'. Few older people, therefore, would appear to be 'isolated' in the sense of lacking close relationships – a finding which held for all three areas and which may be taken as representing at least some degree of continuity with the previous studies.

However, the above findings beg the question about who respondents name in their networks. Table 12.2 divides the 5,735 named people into four categories: immediate family; other relatives; non-kin; and care-related. It is clear that the personal networks of both older women and older men are dominated by kin. The immediate family (spouse, children, grandchildren and siblings), together with a range of other relatives form three-quarters of the named network members. Children dominate this picture, but interestingly too, friends make up nearly a quarter of respondents' networks.

The significance of kin varies according to whether or not children are cited in the network. The majority of respondents (78 per cent) name at least one child in their social network, but 137 (22 per cent) did not. For these older respondents, 39 per cent of named network members are friends, compared with only 20 per cent in the networks of respondents with children. These differences were consistent across the areas, although the importance of friends for childless respondents was most notable in Woodford, where almost half (49 per cent) of the personal networks of such respondents consisted of friends.

Table 12.2 Networks of older men and women: social and family characteristics (Number of respondents = 627; number of named network members = 5,735)

Domain and type	Men		Women	
	n	%	n	%
1 Immediate family	1,129	59	2,148	58
Partner or Spouse	145	(8)	174	(5)
Son/Daughter/-in-Law/Partner	544	(28)	1,012	(27)
Grandson/Granddaughter	269	(14)	552	(15)
Brother/Sister	171	(9)	410	(11)
2 Other relatives	290	15	652	17
3 Non-kin	477	24	973	25
Friends	450	(23)	881	(23)
Neighbours	27	(1)	92	(2)
4 Care-related	25	1	41	1
n (named network members) =	1,921	99%	3,814	101%

A critical factor in support relationships concerns the extent to which those people defined as close and important were living in proximity to our respondents. The baseline studies had demonstrated a clear link between geographical proximity and contact within and between the generations. Today, although 72 per cent of respondents still have their geographically nearest network member living within four miles (higher in Wolverhampton and lower in Bethnal Green), our evidence also suggests that children in particular tend to be more geographically dispersed than in the 1950s. For example, a quarter of Bethnal Green respondents have their nearest network member at a distance of more than 10 miles. In the qualitative phase, only five (or 28 per cent) of the eighteen interviewees who had married and had children, had them still living in Bethnal Green itself. The situations of Mr Barker and Mr Ellis illustrate this point. Mr Barker is aged 76 and lives with his wife in Bethnal Green. They had five children, and have two daughters still living in the area. Mr and Mrs Barker live in a large flat and the lounge is filled with photographs of children and grandchildren. Although they still have children in close proximity, both expressed a sense of grief at the physical separation from their children. Mr Barker said:

> This place was alive when the children were here … I mean, you go into the bedrooms and they are so empty. Oh, they are so empty when they go. It is dreadful. After having rooms full of children and their friends, suddenly it all goes and you think, 'What was it all for: the worrying and the fussing and the cooking and the washing and the cleaning? What was it all for, because now they have all gone?' … And yet, they only moved – Anne only moved just down the road.

Mr Ellis is aged 91 and lives in Wolverhampton. He was widowed thirty years ago and has been living in his present house (rented) for the past fifty years. He has two children:

> Ken, the elder one … he still lives at Codsall where he's lived for twenty years. Gill has just recently moved house but it's only about half a mile from where she was before, and she's come a tiny bit nearer to me. Codsall is about seven miles from here, and where Gillian lived before was Fairgate – about five miles from here – and now it's about four, or something like that. So, she always comes as she has done for ages, to take me up to the Post Office on pension day and do what shopping I need while she is here you see.

Many respondents also spoke of the difficulties of managing and contacting a more scattered family group. Mr Pinner for example, an 81-year-old widower in Bethnal Green explained it in these terms:

> The son in Bracknell rings up every night; Bill in Wales – he rings up once a week, something like that; Jerry – the one over in Ireland – as I say, I can't speak to him until he speaks to me because he is not on the phone. He was on the phone, but his wife kept ringing up home from over there all the time, and he run up a bill of over £400. So, if he wants to make a call, he goes to a call box. Then after a while, I got the number of the call box like, and when the pips go, I say, 'Put the phone down'. And then I ring him back.

Woodford respondents, too, had been affected by the geographical dispersal of children but, for many, this was viewed as a positive family development. Mrs Lewin, for example, had two children: a son living in Colchester and a daughter in Stanstead, Essex. She also had three grandchildren living in different parts of the Midlands and Southern England. When asked about their moving away she commented: 'They should branch out on their own, otherwise you don't get anywhere, do you?' Similarly, Mrs Lindsell, an 81-year-old widow, talked about her daughter who lives in Harlow saying:

> I see my daughter once a fortnight because, as she comes home from Stratford where her firm is, she calls in and has dinner with me once a fortnight. Or, she takes me to a garden centre if I want plants for the front. I don't expect to see them too often. They have got their own lives to lead, haven't they? But I do see her once a fortnight.

In addition, Woodford respondents were themselves more mobile: 65 per cent of the survey respondents owned or had use of a car compared with only 19 per cent of Bethnal Green respondents. In Wolverhampton, by contrast, the chance of having at least one child remaining in the locality was relatively high. In the qualitative phase, thirteen (or 77 per cent) of the seventeen people who had married and had children, still had at least one child living within the town. This illustrates some of the ways in which the social networks of older people in the 1990s vary in their capacity to handle what Fischer (1982) has termed 'the freight of distance', with some older people being better placed than others to cope with the changes to their networks.

Intergenerational support in the 1990s

The Keele research explored different types of support which were both given and received by older people. The findings reveal several important trends: first, it is important to note that, with some exceptions, respondents do not mobilise the whole of their network when seeking support. Instead, only a section of the network is drawn upon – mainly immediate family. Second, as might be expected, there is some variation within the 'immediate family' on who is drawn upon for specific kinds of support and assistance. A third and related issue concerns the ways in which support varies according to the *availability* of children within personal networks. Our findings indicate that this source of support is *especially likely* where children are listed in the network. For those without children, other relatives and friends are more likely to be drawn upon.

To consider these issues in more detail, we examine three kinds of support:

- confiding about things that are important.
- help with household chores if needed.
- talking with someone about one's health.

To begin with married couples: in these instances a spouse is the most likely source of support in time of need. Table 12.3 shows that, for married respondents, spouses clearly play a prominent role in all three survey areas, particularly as confidants and as a source of advice about health matters. Some interesting gender differences are observable with men in each area being more likely to confide in their spouse and to seek health advice from their wife than vice versa. In Woodford and Wolverhampton, over 80 per cent of men say they confide in their wives, while married men in Bethnal Green are somewhat less likely to seek this kind of support, although three-quarters of them do so. Wives by contrast show less tendency to confide in their husbands, particularly in Bethnal Green where just over 50 per cent say they

Table 12.3 Percentage of older men and women who would seek different types of support from their spouse, daughters and sons

	Wolverhampton		Bethnal Green		Woodford	
	Men %	Women %	Men %	Women %	Men %	Women %
Spouse						
Confides	84	68	74	54	86	74
Household chores	46	60	60	56	65	66
Health advice	66	53	67	46	88	66
n (married) =	(50)	(74)	(57)	(48)	(49)	(70)
One or more Daughters						
Confides	71	77	62	67	63	70
Household chores	61	67	54	69	61	61
Health advice	53	64	46	56	45	57
n (1+ daughters) =	(38)	(91)	(37)	(61)	(49)	(69)
One or more Sons						
Confides	72	54	44	48	64	55
Household chores	49	42	48	49	50	42
Health advice	38	35	31	34	39	43
n (1+ sons) =	(53)	(92)	(48)	(67)	(44)	(74)

do this. These findings resonate with other research which suggests that the presence of a partner is especially important for the emotional well-being of older men. They may also reflect the enduring effects of social class noted in the baseline studies, together with the observation of Willmott and Young (1960: 64) about the more companionate conception of marriage held by older people in Woodford. This latter point is also borne out by the fact that in Woodford, both married men and women will call equally on each other for help with household chores if needed.

Turning to the supportive role of sons and daughters, we can see from Table 12.3 that where respondents have children, daughters are more likely to be nominated than sons to provide each of these types of support. The exception to this is confiding relationships in Wolverhampton and Woodford, where older men are just as likely to nominate a son as a daughter. Although the picture is complex, women in all three areas are more likely to turn to their daughter(s) for all types of support, including practical help with household chores. The intergenerational ties with daughters are still substantial for both men and women in Wolverhampton, across all three kinds of support – a finding consistent with Sheldon's (1948) earlier study. In Woodford and in Bethnal Green, whilst these supportive ties are still in evidence, the extent and nature of this support also indicates how expectations of intergenerational support may have begun to alter in response to the kinds of changes in living arrangements noted earlier.

The present-day supportive roles of daughters and sons can be illustrated by reference to some of our qualitative data. Many of our interviews with older women clearly showed an awareness of the ways in which their own daughters were now having to juggle with the different demands placed on their time. Mrs Burden, who lives in Wolverhampton, summarises her daughter's commitments in the following way:

> My daughter rings me up every other night to see if I'm alright, you see. But of course, she can't do everything. She's got two teenage boys, a husband who is quite busy – an estate agent, dashing around all hours. She works hard for her church: she's a local preacher in the Methodist Church, and also she's teaching full-time. So really, she hasn't got very much time to … .

Likewise, Mrs Thompson, who lives near her daughter in a sheltered housing scheme in Woodford, describes their relationship in the following words:

> When I first came here I could walk to my daughter's house. I don't go out at all now, only by car. I can't walk in the street – I'm too shaky, too wobbly … But, my daughter comes in and she phones me. We communicate with each other every morning at 9.30am … I mean, my daughter is very good to me but she does live her own life,

you know. I mean, she is interested in flower arranging. She used to be helping at school. She wasn't a school teacher, but she used to help with some of the backward children, you know that couldn't read ... She didn't get paid for it, it was voluntary work you know ... She is the kind that does things.

Other respondents talked about the different kinds of support and relationships they have with their different children. Mrs Franklin who lives on her own in Bethnal Green, has three sons and two daughters, all of whom live outside the area. She is reliant on them visiting, particularly as she is now restricted to a wheelchair and, when asked about whether some of her children are more important to her than others, she replies:

Well, John is the best. Yeah, he has got his own little business and has been a good kid to me. I don't want for nothing from him ... he has done all this in here ... this carpet down here; me bedroom – that's his trade. He sees me alright, oh yeah ... he phones me up every night that boy. And sometimes, I phone my Eileen and it's, 'Oh Mum, I can't talk now, I'm too tired and I want to get to bed'. That's all I get out of her. I don't worry now. She comes up every week but it's getting that she don't come up so much. I don't worry.

Finally, it is also important to observe that there are vulnerable groups of older people in each of the three areas, in the sense of those who have no one to turn to for help and support. This seems rather more characteristic of respondents in Bethnal Green where older (white) people have been more affected both by the decline of co-residence with adult children and by more geographically dispersed family networks.

Reciprocation of support

The Keele study found clear evidence of older people continuing to be active in reciprocal exchanges across their network. However, as we would expect, this tends to be more common for certain support activities than for others. In particular, older people appear to have a very important role as confidants, with a majority of respondents active in this sphere. There are, though, some differences between the three areas with respondents in Bethnal Green being more likely to report that nobody confides in them (around one in four). The data about those giving health advice to others shows a similar pattern. Moreover, much of this supportive activity is located within the immediate family, although other members of the network are also beneficiaries.

When we turn to more direct or instrumental forms of help, the picture changes somewhat. Predictably, we find higher proportions unable to identify people whom they would be able to help in respect of household chores, transport and finance. There are also some noticeable area differences, particularly relating to financial help. For example, over 40 per cent of Bethnal Green respondents were unable to cite anybody to whom they could give financial assistance. Conversely, 64 per cent of respondents in Woodford indicated someone in their immediate family (usually a child) to whom they would give financial help (compared with 44 per cent in Bethnal Green and 56 per cent in Wolverhampton). Similarly, with respect to transport needs, 91 per cent of those in Bethnal Green listed nobody they could help, compared with 73 per cent in Wolverhampton, and 64 per cent in Woodford. These findings are a reflection of the 'higher' levels of car ownership and greater affluence of older respondents in Woodford noted earlier.

Overall, the Keele data confirm that help given, like help received, is focused around the immediate family, and children in particular. In this sense, the data is conforming to a basic rule of reciprocity: the immediate family is the source to which older people are most likely to routinely go for help; likewise, the immediate family is the group who most benefit from the advice and support of older people themselves. Our qualitative interviews reinforced these findings, and we illustrate the reciprocal nature of intergenerational support with reference to (separate) interviews conducted with Mr Smith and his son Paul:

Mr Smith is aged 78, and lives on a large public housing estate in Wolverhampton. He is very independent and physically fit, although he suffers from angina and recently underwent a heart operation. He owns his own home and has lived there for forty-six years. He worked locally until the age of 64 when he was made redundant from his job as a manager in a shoe manufacturing company. Mr Smith has been married for fifty-five years, but has lived alone since 1990 when his wife was admitted to a nearby nursing home. Vera, his wife, appears in the inner circle of his network diagram, along with his son Paul and his daughter June. He also has five grandchildren – mainly teenagers still at school. They all live locally in Wolverhampton. The family is something that he describes as extremely important and he comments that they are 'Little islands of solidity and value in amongst chaos.'

Mr Smith chose to describe the situation with his wife as an example of how he and his family managed, and continue to manage, issues around care and support for each other. His wife suffers from multi-infarct dementia and experienced several small strokes while living at home. The gradual onset of his wife's dementia was extremely difficult for Mr Smith and, in the interview, he comments on the uncertainties and difficulties he faced at that time:

> I didn't turn to anyone. I was self-sufficient in that I could look after things like that and make her hot drinks and cook her food that would not upset her stomach as I thought in those days. It's not just the crossroads, it's a buffer stop and then you pick up the pieces.

Initially, he describes the process of *'containing'* the illness, and how his attempts to support his wife at home succeeded until he himself was forced to enter hospital for an arterial bypass operation. It was at this juncture that he had to call on support from the family. Crossing this boundary, and accepting help from his children, came only after a crisis situation. He recalls:

> I didn't call for support; Paul and June knew that Vera wasn't quite the same as she had been and I didn't go into details, I didn't bother them. So when I had to go into hospital myself I talked it over with this chap. They [his children] then had to look after Vera as best they could, which was pretty awkward. I think June settled to have her weekend full time and Paul looked after her during the day – the best he could. It was then that I found out what was really going on. I then had lots of support, I was inundated with a wealth of visitors and do-gooders ... whoever. I got meals on wheels, knocking at the door, cleaning – knocking and doing all the work for me. That was when I came out of hospital.

Mr Smith's son also talks about the difficulties of supporting his father though his mother's illness, and says that he would have intervened at an earlier stage in the process if he had not respected his father's wish to remain self-reliant and independent. Although others may recognise the vulnerability of the situation, respecting autonomy of older parents can be, in his own words, 'very difficult.'

At the time of interview, Mr Smith's daily routine was structured around visiting his wife. He wakes at 6.30 a.m. and tries to sleep again but normally he lies awake and starts thinking about Vera: 'Vera is the first thought always.' He gets up about 7.30 a.m. makes a cup of tea, opens the mail, and does household tasks before going to visit his wife: 'I always go to see that she gets the main meal of the day and this is obviously demanding but this is a demand that I am more than happy to comply with.'

Mr Smith is enabled to cope with the physical separation from his wife because of the support he receives from his children and from his son in particular. Proximity is an important consideration here. Paul lives nearby and this proximity facilitates frequent and flexible contact, as well as reciprocation of support. He sees his father every night or at least once a day for anything up to two or three hours, particularly when his father is in a very low state. They also phone each other. In terms of the support offered to Mr Smith by his son, Paul judges this to be at the right level and appropriate for his situation. At the same time though, he worries that his father has cut off extended family and friends, and this may make him increasingly vulnerable.

Such support, however, is not-one way and Mr Smith provides a great deal of support to his children and grandchildren. He reciprocates his son's emotional help by offering a listening ear to any problems which Paul might have, and often puts a different perspective on the problem: 'Particularly if the kids are sending me up the wall, I can come down here and talk it over with Dad and calm myself down. That, you know, is quite a major thing – emotional support.' He also provides practical assistance in the form of 'baby-sitting'. Indeed, during the interview, Mr Smith was looking after his daughter June's child while she was at work, because she had tonsillitis and was unable to go to school. He baby-sits regularly for both Paul and June and, if any of the children are ill like this, he will willingly look after them. He has also helped out in financial emergencies, particularly in relation to his son buying his first house.

Mr Smith feels that the support he gets from his son and daughter is related to the support he has given them in the past:

> Obviously when you are rearing your children, if you are a decent parent – and I'm not particularly sure I was, but I couldn't have been too bad – you do your best for them. And as they grow up they grow up to look after themselves – you support them – I still support them when Vera's down. But it's mutual, reciprocal support, it's not all one way.
>
> When my legs go then maybe I'll need some more help.

Both father and son have thought about the future, and Mr Smith is clear that he does not wish to 'be a burden' on the family, and wants to retain his autonomy. He would turn to the local authority rather than go to his family:

> I would throw myself willingly and happily on the local authority however efficient or inefficient they might be, and have that dreadful cleaning lady coming again, and I'd have to suffer it all again, I suppose. And a bath lady coming to bath me – God forbid – I just can't visualise it and yet it could happen. I'd have to find myself a bit of a nurse, I suppose. If June would have me, or Paul for that matter, that would be an even worse alternative really, to say 'You have to move in with us Dad.' I'd sooner much be around with the local authority and the bath lady and the dinner lady and the cleaner.

Paul, meanwhile, sees himself spending longer periods of time with his father as he gets older. He feels this will need to be planned more and more because of other competing commitments, but says, 'We would work it out on a rota if he wasn't able to help with his own shopping and cleaning, and just get on with it.' However, when it comes to more serious illness or long-term disability, he would in fact consider the possibility of moving his own family to his father's house:

> The family would come down mostly for their meals, and then go back home and do their own thing as such, and get some sort of

balance in, so that we can keep the family together. I think Dad would resist, but he would probably accept us coming down here.

Mr Smith's situation clearly demonstrates the ties which still exist between parents and children, and how intergenerational support is negotiated, managed and reciprocated over time. However, the ways in which these relationships are conducted in the 1990s also highlights how important it is to maintain a sense of independence and autonomy in old age.

Conclusion

This analysis of the Keele findings leads us to conclude that there are both continuities and change in the family and community life of older people in the three areas in the 1990s, compared with the 1940s and 1950s. First, there are some notable differences between the earlier studies and the Keele research. In the mid-1990s, Wolverhampton best approximates the picture of local extended families painted in the baseline studies, whereas in Bethnal Green, whilst dense, locally-based networks are still flourishing – at least among the Bangladeshi families we interviewed – the lives of our white elderly respondents are characterised by typically having only one child close by, with others dispersed around Essex and beyond. Woodford also represents this more dispersed extended family network, where regular contact (weekly or more) is maintained, crucially through the motor car and the telephone. In other words, despite the continuing saliency of relationships with children, this is conducted through the medium of a variety of family forms in which geographical proximity is no longer the most important factor.

Second, there are important continuities with the baseline studies. Kinship remains central in terms of the social ties of our respondents. When asked to name who is important to them, most older people identify kin as being the main group with whom reciprocal relations are maintained, and children are key. Indeed, our findings suggest that those who are significant to older people are either their own age (their partner, friends and siblings especially), or the next generation down (mainly children). Fewer than one in five of those interviewed placed themselves within a network which stretched beyond two generations. These findings confirm other network studies by Wenger (1984; 1992), and Wellman and Wortley (1989), in highlighting the prominent role of kin in supportive ties. Indeed, while older people today still have a range of relationships to draw upon, the reality is that relatively few provide real help in relation to the kinds of household chores, transport, financial help and other services we explored. In this context, we suggest that whilst the bonds of kinship remain of major consequence in urban areas in the 1990s, supportive relationships are perhaps more focused than in the past, with children (and in some instances, friends) the centre of attention.

Third, another important finding concerns the vital role older people play within the helping network and the reciprocal nature of these intergenerational ties. Older people continue to see themselves as playing a supportive role to family and friends, notably in areas such as confiding and giving advice on health. We suggest that ties across the generations, and the management of support, are therefore much more clearly located within a framework of equality than they were in the earlier studies. Children (and particularly daughters) have created a measure of space between themselves and their elderly parents. Very few now live in the same household or same street and, even if they live nearby, they have their own families and their own working lives to contend with. There is also evidence that, even if daughters are still crucial in respect of supportive relationships, sons too act in caring roles of various kinds.

In conclusion, the Keele findings clearly demonstrate that intergenerational support is crucial to the present-day family and community life of older people. Older people are not being abandoned wholesale by their families, neither are they falling victim to extensive conflict between the generations. Rather the family – and particularly the immediate family in respect of spouses, daughters and sons – still provides the bedrock of support for older people. However, our research emphasises that there is considerable selectivity in the way in which support is negotiated, handled, managed and reciprocated. In reality, there are likely to be relatively few people actually involved in support and care, as opposed to the policy image of extensive networks of family, friends and neighbours. This indicates an urgent need to refocus the debate on what the support and care of older people really means and what, exactly, the form and limits of family and community involvement might be in the future.

Acknowledgment

The work on which this chapter is based was supported by a grant from the Economic and Social Research Council, reference number L315253021.

References

Antonucci, T. and Akiyama, H. (1987) 'Social networks in adult life: a preliminary examination of the convoy model', *Journal of Gerontology* 4: 519–27.

Barnes, J.A. (1954) 'Class and committees in a Norwegian island parish', *Human Relations* 7: 39–58.

Bowling, A., Farquhar, M. and Browne, P. (1991) 'Life satisfaction and associations with social network and support variables in three samples of elderly people', *International Journal of Geriatric Psychiatry* 6: 549–66.

Fischer, C.S. (1982) *To Dwell Amongst Friends,* Chicago: University of Chicago Press.

Frankenburg, R. (1966) *Communities in Britain*, Harmondsworth: Penguin Books.

Gordon, C. (1988) *The Myth of Family Care? The Elderly in the Early 1930s*, London: The Welfare State Programme, London School of Economics.

Kahn, R. and Antonucci, T. (1980) 'Convoys over the life course: attachment, roles and social support', in P.B. Baltes and O. Brim (eds) *Life-Span Development and Behaviour*, vol. 3, New York: Academic Press.

Knipscheer, K., de Jong Gierveld, J., van Tilburg, T.G. and Dykstra, P.A. (eds) (1995) *Living Arrangements and Social Networks of Older Adults*, Amsterdam: VU University Press.

Lang, F. and Cartensen, L. (1994) 'Close emotional relationships in later life: further support for proactive aging in the social domain', *Psychology and Aging* 9: 315–24.

Mitchell, J.C. (ed.) (1969) *Social Networks in Urban Communities*, Manchester: Manchester University Press.

Phillipson, C., Bernard, M., Phillips, J. and Ogg, J (1996) *Social Networks and Social Support in Old Age*, Keele University: Centre for Social Gerontology, Working Paper No 4.

Sheldon, S. (1948) *The Social Medicine of Old Age*, Oxford: Oxford University Press.

Townsend, P. (1957) *The Family Life of Old People*, London: Routledge and Kegan Paul.

Wellman, B. (1990) 'The place of kinfolk in personal community settings', in B. Wellman (ed.) *Families in Community Settings: Interdisciplinary Settings*, New York: Haworth Press.

Wellman, B. and Wortley, S. (1989) 'Brothers' keepers: situating kinship relations in broader networks of social support', *Sociological Perspectives* 32: 273–306.

Wenger, G.C. (1984) *The Supportive Network*, London: George Allen and Unwin.

——(1992) *Help in Old Age*, Liverpool: Liverpool University Press.

——(1995) 'A comparison of urban with rural networks in North Wales', *Ageing and Society* 15 (1): 59–82.

Willmott, P. and Young, M. (1960) *Family and Class in a London Suburb*, London: Routledge and Kegan Paul.

Young, M. and Willmott, P. (1957) *Family and Kinship in East London*, London: Routledge and Kegan Paul.

INDEX